D0333724

THE
TRAMPLED
WIFE

And the vitriol madness flushes up in the ruffian's head
Till the filthy by-lane rings to the yell of the trampled wife . . .
                          Alfred, Lord Tennyson, *Maud*, I. x

          When lovely woman stoops to folly
          And finds too late that men betray,
          What charm can soothe her melancholy,
          What art can wash her guilt away?
                          Samuel Goldsmith, *The Vicar of Wakefield*

THE
TRAMPLED
WIFE

THE *SCANDALOUS* LIFE OF
MARY ELEANOR BOWES

DEREK PARKER

SUTTON PUBLISHING

First published in the United Kingdom in 2006 by
Sutton Publishing Limited · Phoenix Mill
Thrupp · Stroud · Gloucestershire · GL5 2BU

British Library Cataloguing in Publication Data
A catalogue record for this book is available from the British Library.

ISBN 0-7509-3955-9

Typeset in 10.5/13.5pt Sabon.
Typesetting and origination by
Sutton Publishing Limited.
Printed and bound in England by
J.H. Haynes & Co. Ltd, Sparkford.

For
Jacqueline Korn,
friend and agent

Contents

Preface

This is the story of a woman whose misfortunes sprang partly from her own lack of judgement, but mainly from the social conventions of her time. Extremely rich, Mary Eleanor Bowes, later Countess of Strathmore – a direct ancestor of Queen Elizabeth II – had the misfortune to be brought up to believe that she could pursue her own interests, and even preserve and manage her own fortune. Though she quickly learned that neither of these suppositions was acceptable to her contemporaries, she was not prepared to be bullied into submission, either by a brutal husband or a disapproving society.

The trial of Andrew Robinson Stoney Bowes for the abduction of his wife and the ensuing divorce proceedings were among the most sensational events of eighteenth-century social life. Bowes, an impoverished Irish army lieutenant, had by a mixture of charm and bravado contrived to win the heart of the recently widowed Countess, one of the richest women in England. When having married her he found that she had safeguarded her money, he set about violently persuading her to annul the deed by which she had done so. She, in turn, discovered that he was a wife-beater and serial adulterer. After suffering his violence and promiscuity for some time, she sued for divorce – whereupon he and a group of bravos seized her and carried her off to the North Country where she was threatened with rape and dragged about the bleak countryside for weeks in sub-zero temperatures.

The following trial and divorce case were extensively reported in the newspapers of the time, and eagerly read. What is surprising to us is that the Countess was treated as badly by the press and town tattlers of both sexes as by her husband. The press could be bought – Bowes, indeed, purchased an interest in a newspaper specifically to libel her. But why should the public, even those of her own sex, take so violently against so persecuted a woman? Jealousy of her riches was no doubt one explanation for this but, more potently, she was seen as not knowing her place as a wife.

Her loving father did her a great disservice by teaching her the classics rather than the conventional pieties of the time. As she herself put it, he 'was continually talking of, and endeavouring to inculcate into me, sentiments of generosity, gratitude, fortitude and duty to himself; and an insatiable thirst for all kinds of knowledge. But I never heard him once say, to the best of my recollection, that chastity, patience and forgiveness of injuries were virtues.'[1] Her mother remained in the background, and she received no schooling in the normal attributes of a well-to-do eighteenth-century wife and mother: the production of and care for children and the polite social accomplishments – needlework, the setting of a good table, consideration of the needs of one's husband, and for her own entertainment perhaps an interest in drawing or music, provided she was not too accomplished at either. Serious proficiency in any field other than housekeeping was discouraged in a wife – and, indeed, in women in general. If a woman knew anything about anything, she was advised to hide it (as Lady Mary Wortley Montagu put it) 'with as much solicitude as she would hide crookedness or lameness'.[2]

Mary Eleanor was not inclined to hide her native wit; though she enjoyed flirting and dancing at Almack's, she was genuinely curious about botany, and pursued her enthusiasm intelligently. She was interested too in literature, and sought out other women who shared her taste. This did not endear her to her contemporaries – perhaps particularly to women, for very few of them shared her view that she, or any of her sex, had the right to a life outside the sphere in which most people thought they should be confined. (Even Hannah Moore, in her *Essays Addressed to Young Ladies* published in 1777, found the whole idea of women's rights ludicrous: 'The world will next have – grave descants on the rights of youth – the rights of children – the rights of babies!'[3])

Clearly disappointed by the Earl of Strathmore's lack of interest in her except as a breeder of children, of which she had given him three, and having put up for some time with every kind of neglect, she was inclined to seek pleasure elsewhere. At the time of his death she was pregnant by a lover and, with remarkable equanimity, gave up her plans to marry him when the charming Irish lieutenant, Andrew Robinson Stoney, appeared on the scene. None of this behaviour endeared her to society, and even the violence she suffered at Bowes's hands attracted little sympathy, either from the public or from the judges in the various courts through which she passed, who were always ready with a snide comment, particularly on what was considered her outrageous inclination to believe she had a right to keep at least one hand on her fortune. Significantly, among her few sympathisers were the colliers who worked in the pits from which most of her family's fortune had come. It was they who marched on the house in which Bowes imprisoned her, threatening to tear it down if she was not released. And although everyone sneered at her genuine friendship (which indeed may have been more) with one of her footmen, he – George Walker – is one of the few sympathetic characters in the story.

Even in the middle of the twentieth century, the author of the most recent biography[4] of the Countess could not shake off the conviction that she had brought her misfortunes upon herself. In a sense, of course, she did – but she was not the first woman, and will certainly not be the last, to lose her heart to the wrong man. What made her different was that she was not, in the end, prepared to put up with his violence, greed and sexual shenanigans. We can perhaps now eschew the tone of slightly shocked disapproval with which she was treated by her biographer in 1957. Nor need we censor her autobiographical *Confessions*, or leave unpublished some parts of the evidence in her divorce case which were considered too racy to be reported.

One of the subjects on which her last biographer was reticent was the nature of the Countess's relationship with Walker. Eighteenth-century women were often remarkably easy and familiar in their dealings with their male servants, and footmen in particular routinely had as free access to their mistress's private rooms as did their personal maids. Across the Channel, Voltaire's mistress, Emilie du Châtelet, dismayed her footman by commanding him to attend on her while she was bathing – and went on to demand yet more of him. While there is no evidence that Walker was anything more than a devoted servant, it was certainly generally believed that he was, and it may have been so. Mary Eleanor was a warm-blooded woman, and may well have taken comfort and support where she found them.

She was not especially intelligent or politically aware – she had no ambition to use her experience as an argument in support of the rights of women. But we can respect her tenacity: the time in which she lived was unkind to women, of whatever station – an intelligent woman was regarded by most men as eccentric and even 'silly', and marital violence was common and taken for granted. Her struggle for intellectual and physical independence – a struggle not only with her husband, not only with men in general, but with the press and public opinion – was remarkable for its time. After putting up with violence and degradation, she at last rebelled; and when the violence was renewed was steadfast in resisting it. She deserved the final quiet decade of her life, reconciled to her son and living at peace with her dogs and her devoted housekeeper.

Acknowledgements

I am grateful to a number of people and institutions whose help has been invaluable. These include the staff of the Fisher Library, University of Sydney, of The National Archives at Kew, and of the British Library; Edith Ho, State Library of New South Wales; Durham University Library; Tristram Issen of the Bank of England; Malcolm Beasley, Botany Librarian, Natural History Museum; Trisha Darley, State Library of South Australia; Ruth Kenny, National Portrait Gallery, London; Richard Higgins, Durham University Library; Suzanne Morris, National Library of Australia; Tony Walton, Property and Project Manager, National Trust, Gibside; National Trust; David Adams, General Manager, Glamis Castle; Sue Simpson, National Library of Australia; Fiona Douglas, Durham County Library; Mike Marcus and Gareth Barker, British Library; Dr Linda Harris; Cathy Day; Brian Tompsett; the Rt Hon. Simon Bowes Lyon; and to Mr and Mrs Martin Bronkhorst for their kind hospitality. I am as usual grateful for the attention and goodwill of my editors at Sutton, Jaqueline Mitchell and Clare Jackson.

My wife Julia has once again read the manuscript, made many suggestions and corrected some errors.

ONE

Innocence and Imprudence

My father's whole care and attention was bestowed on the
improvement of my knowledge, in whatever I showed a genius for.
Mary Eleanor Bowes, *Confessions*

The wedding was a fine show. Mary Eleanor Bowes, married on the day of her eighteenth birthday – 24 February 1767 – was one of the great heiresses of England. When her father died in 1760, she inherited an estate valued at £600,000 – an estate which in today's terms would be worth £43¼ million.[1] Two large properties, Streatlam Castle and Gibside, brought her an annual income of at least £20,000 a year (£1½ million) on which she would have been paying well over £6,000 a year in tax – a rate of 6s 5d in the pound was exacted. On the death of her mother she would inherit a handsome third estate, St Paul's, Waldenbury. This placed her towards the top of the list of the wealthiest families in the country. She was not a particularly handsome young woman, but her riches and her high spirits lent her a decided glamour. The groom, suave and handsome, was John, 9th Earl of Strathmore – 'the beautiful Lord Strathmore', who brought to the church his title and his good looks, but no wealth to compare to his bride's.

The crowd that gathered outside St George's, Hanover Square, was not disappointed by the display. Mary Eleanor and her mother arrived at the church in a handsome new dark green landau, Strathmore in his own more splendid carriage. The bride's wedding dress was spectacular – her diamond stomacher, together with the other diamonds which decorated her dress, glittered in the cold winter sun.

It seemed a fairy-tale wedding, and as the couple drove off in the landau, leaving Mrs Bowes to follow, muffled against the cold, in a post-chaise with a postboy in a bright yellow jacket sitting astride one of the two horses, the words 'happy ever after' must have occurred to at least some of the less wealthy and fortunate lookers-on. What they did not know was that within the past few weeks, and certainly before she walked up the aisle, Mary Eleanor had realised that she was marrying the wrong man.

Alan the Black, Earl of Richmond and Captain of the Tower of Bowes, who commanded 500 archers in the service of William the Conqueror, is sometimes claimed as the earliest traceable ancestor of the Bowes family. Two centuries later, Sir Adam Bowes was certainly a member of the family. A lawyer and Chief Justice of the Court of Common Pleas, he married Alice Trayne in 1310, and thereby acquired Streatlam Manor, 3 miles from Barnard Castle in County Durham, which is still in the family. Thereafter the Boweses steadily grew in stature and influence. Sir William (1389–1460), shattered by the death of his young wife after less than a year of marriage, went off to the French wars and became chamberlain to the Duke of Bedford, younger brother of Henry V. Knighted on the battlefield of Verneuil, he came home after seventeen years impressed by the magnificent châteaux of France, and set about rebuilding Streatlam.

Sir Robert (1495–1554) became Master of the Rolls; Sir Ralph fought at Flodden Field in 1509. Sir George (1527–80) and his brother Sir Robert (?1535–97) were diligent in the service of Queen Elizabeth I. In 1557 Sir Robert was appointed ambassador to Scotland – an extremely sensitive post, but one to which he brought such tactful diplomacy that in the following year he more or less singlehandedly prevented civil war. Even after his recall to England he continued to be Treasurer of Berwick, and often returned to Scotland on special missions. His work for Queen Elizabeth brought him no great rewards; she neither paid him for his services nor reimbursed him for what he spent.

His brother was even more distinguished. By the time he was twenty-two, George Bowes was in command of cavalry at the Scottish wars, had become Marshal of Berwick and was knighted there in 1560. For the next few years he concentrated on running his castle and estate at Streatlam, but in 1568 was appointed to escort the captive Mary Queen of Scots from Carlisle to Bolton Castle, a duty he discharged with such consideration that she came to regard him as a friend. In the following year, when the northern earls threatened the throne, he did his greatest service for Elizabeth. Living as he did in an area of the country most disaffected from the Queen, he gave all his energy to arguing on her behalf, becoming as a result intensely unpopular. Indeed, one neighbour, Lord Hundson, wrote that 'the country is in great hatred of Sir George Bowes so as he dare scant remain there'.[2] He was eventually forced to leave Streatlam for the safer Barnard Castle, of which he was steward (it was then a crown property). There he and his brother Robert were joined by a group of neighbours loyal to the Queen. The castle was besieged by the rebel earls; after eleven days Sir George capitulated, and was allowed to march away with some four hundred men. When the rebellion petered out, as provost of the army he was appointed to administer punishment to the ringleaders, and organised their execution. Like his brother, he looked vainly for repayment of the considerable fortune he had spent on the Queen's behalf. Though he was, her Secretary of State Lord Burghley assured her, 'the surest pillar the queen's majesty had in these parts',[3] by 1596 George was complaining that his estate was 'broken' by the expenses of his embassy, which he had borne himself; all he got for his considerable pains was a grant of some relatively valueless land. And when he agreed to serve, following his brother, as Marshal of Berwick, it was the same story – he was almost ruined by the expense.

The family might have perished in penury but for Sir William, who in 1691 married Elizabeth Blakiston, the great-granddaughter of William and Jane Blakiston, and the heiress of Gibside, a mansion standing above the River Derwent near Gateshead. She bore her husband ten children, of whom eight survived, and when he died comparatively young it was she who cared for the estate until her son William came of age.

The family's money came not from land but from iron and, more importantly, from 'black diamonds' – coal. The previous two generations of Blakistons had opened a number of pits in County Durham, and William Blakiston Bowes (1696–1721) opened more. It was a shrewd move. For centuries, wood had been the major fuel for homes, but by the middle of the eighteenth century, sixty-five of the great forests of medieval England had been razed,[4] and imported timber was so expensive that there was a new, enormous demand for coal. The mining process was dangerous, but the shallow shafts needed little in the way of expensive propping, and though methane and carbonic-acid gas choked the miners, labour was cheap and plentiful.

William was not an especially attractive character, and devoted not to Gibside but to Streatlam. Returning from the Grand Tour he, like his ancestor Sir William, two and a half centuries earlier, began to rebuild the castle on the model of the châteaux he had seen and admired in France. Before completing the work, however, he died unexpectedly in 1721, his death followed within twelve months by that of his brother Thomas, which left their twenty-one-year-old youngest brother, George Bowes, the sole heir. On the face of it, his accession might have been a disaster: ostensibly a handsome rogue, he was a cavalry regiment captain who put himself about among the ladies and was no stranger at the gambling tables. Some anonymous scribbler described him in doggerel:

> He's about six foot in Height,
> Would he walk but upright . . .
> His complexion is good . . .
> His Mouth & Nose small . . .
> His Eyes grey as a cat
> Hansom legs, *Autre Chose*,
> And his name is George Bowes.[5]

This at least confirms the pronunciation of the family name – rhyming with 'nose' rather than 'boughs'.

George Bowes's daughter was to write of him that he 'would never give his mind in the least to study' and was passionate, 'uncommon handsome and a great rake'.[6] Perhaps surprisingly, he quickly settled down and made himself agreeable to his neighbours in the country as a fox-hunting squire[7] with a few tenuous metropolitan interests – in 1725 he became Whig[8] Member of Parliament for Berwick, though he rarely attended the House of Commons and made only one speech there. He proved a shrewd businessman with a keen eye for profit, and considerably enhanced the family fortune – partly by undercutting the price set for coal by his competitors. His brother William had constructed a remarkable road from his pits towards the River Tyne in order to speed the transport of coal: 'it is a work of such importance & crosses so many Mountains and Vales which are all levelled, that I can compare it to nothing more properly than to the Via Appia.'[9] This certainly speeded the coal on its way, as did the Causey Arch which George Bowes built in 1725 to carry his coal to the banks of the Tyne itself, whence it was loaded into colliers for London. He also organised a price-fixing cartel which kept the price of coal up, becoming the major figure in the industry in the north (known, aptly enough, as 'the Tsar').

In 1724 he married the beautiful and intelligent fourteen-year-old Eleanor Verney, granddaughter of Lord Willoughby de Broke of Compton Verney in Warwickshire. He clearly adored her – as did everyone who knew her – but sadly she died within the year. He remained a widower for over twenty years, then in 1746 married Mary Gilbert, the daughter of a family whose home was at St Paul's Walden in Hertfordshire, a handsome house 5 miles south of Hitchin.[10]

The gardens at St Paul's Walden had been created by George Bowes's father-in-law, Edward Gilbert (1720–60), and Bowes spent much time and money developing them. He came there at a time when English garden design was going through an interesting phase, influenced particularly by contemporary poets such as Pope, who were themselves influenced by the gardens of imperial Rome as described by Virgil and Ovid. The Romans' taste in gardens, Pope remarked, was for 'the amiable simplicity of unadorned nature', and taking the hint Bowes (who probably also knew Robert Castell's *The Villas of the Ancients*, the best-known textbook of the time on Roman gardens) concentrated on beautifying what was already there, emphasising the smooth luxuriousness of the English lawn – the beautiful one in front of the house, for instance, guarded by a pair of marble wrestlers. There was to be no more geometry, with straight symmetrical paths, clipped hedges and carefully sculpted trees. In *The Spectator*, the influential essayist Joseph Addison had argued violently against the 'cones, globes and pyramids' people made of their trees,[11] and the best modern authorities recommended shady, meandering walks through natural countryside (or an approximation to it); and instead of ugly fences, streams and ha-has to keep livestock in their place.

Bowes proved an excellent follower of the new fashion, though he also ran avenues through the woods, built a decorative octagonal summer-house, and either constructed or enhanced a handsome set of broad stairs at the head of which still stands the Discobolos known popularly as 'the running footman'. His daughter, one of whose chief interests was botany, was to continue her father's work in the gardens at St Paul's, planning shrubberies, flowerbeds and lawns, and planting flowers and shrubs.

George Bowes did not care for Streatlam, which his elder brother had intended to make his home and on the rebuilding of which he had spent a considerable amount of money. George preferred Gibside, and soon after he inherited decided to make his home there rather than either at Streatlam or St Paul's. Gibside, now ruined, had been built almost a century and a half earlier by William Blakiston; Bowes extended it, but more importantly between 1729 and his death redesigned the gardens along much the same lines as those at St Paul's. He has been credited with the whole design, but it appears that he also consulted a prominent garden designer of the period, Stephen Switzer, for there is a record of a payment of £10 to Switzer for producing a plan, which sadly has disappeared.

When Bowes fell fatally ill, he at last instructed the architect James Paine to prepare plans for the chapel which he had always intended to build in memory of his first wife, and in which he wanted to be buried. A charming Palladian building in a commanding position at the end of the Long Walk, it was not completed until 1816 – over forty-five years after Bowes's death; his body was at last moved into the vault there from a temporary resting-place in a nearby church.

Against the odds, the unpromising ne'er-do-well army officer failed to become a simple, thick-headed country squire. As he matured, he grew keenly interested in the arts. He learned to play the harpsichord and collected furniture and pictures (he paid 1,500 guineas for a Rubens, and commissioned a portrait of himself from Enoch Seeman, the fashionable rival of Hogarth). He acquired a good library, the contents of which reflected his interest in the most modern developments in architecture – he bought copies of William Kent's *Designs of Inigo Jones* (1727), Isaac Ware's edition of the sixteenth-century Italian architect Palladio, and James Gibbs's *Book of Architecture* (1728).

If in his youth he had been uninterested in study, this was certainly not true of his later years. He also, at last, took a keen if chiefly theoretical interest in local and national politics. He was made mayor, several times, of Hartlepool and Durham, and though as an MP he was not particularly active, he kept abreast of contemporary affairs. For the first time in history this was not difficult even for someone who spent most of his time in the country. By 1714 eleven weekly newspapers were available (by the end of the century, there would be fifty-three), and to their squabbling hectic voices were added the more literary and intellectual tones of the magazines – the *Grub Street Journal*, the *Gentleman's Magazine*, the *Edinburgh Review*.

Bowes was well established at Gibside by the time his only child, Mary Eleanor, was born there on 24 February 1749. She was happy in her fortune, and fortunate in her parents. In the mid-eighteenth century most female children of wealthy families, while no doubt loved by both parents, were nurtured almost entirely by their mothers, who looked forward to teaching them the arts of housekeeping and capturing a husband. Bowes was a somewhat elderly father, and as is often the case in those circumstances was particularly devoted to his daughter. After the first few years of her childhood her mother retired into the background while he looked to her education.

Children in the eighteenth century were treated as small adults, if sometimes rather disorderly ones. This, in the case of boys, showed itself in the advanced lessons they had to learn, especially in Latin and the reading of the classics. George Bowes set a somewhat similar standard for his daughter, whom he expected to become 'as accomplished at thirteen as his favourite first wife was at that age, in every kind of learning'.[12] He was determined she should have a good education, and her mother 'did not interfere' with this.

It was by no means the case with most young women that they were given – or even allowed to have – a decent education: Jonathan Swift complained of the lack of education of 'the daughters of great and rich families, left entirely to their mothers, or boarding-schools, or put into the hands of English or French governesses, and generally the worst that can be gotten for money'.[13] Lady Mary Wortley Montagu (later to become Mary Eleanor's friend) was forced to study surreptitiously: 'My sex,' wrote Lady Mary, 'is usually forbid studies [of the classics and of languages], and folly is reckoned so much our proper sphere we are sooner pardoned any excess of that, than the least pretensions to reading or good sense. . . . There is hardly a creature in the world more liable to universal ridicule than a learned woman.'[14] She believed – in all seriousness – that men kept women ignorant in order to make it easier to seduce them, while Sarah Fife Egerton thought men simply fearful of an educated woman:

> They fear we should excel their sluggish parts
> Should we attempt the sciences and arts.[15]

Mary Eleanor did not have to struggle for an education. 'At four years old,' she wrote, 'I could read uncommonly well, and was kept tight to it, made to get many things off by heart. . . . My father's whole care and attention was bestowed on the improvement of my knowledge, in whatever I showed a genius for.'[16] Indeed, he encouraged in her 'an insatiable thirst for all kinds of knowledge'. But there were some disadvantages in her father's somewhat bizarre view of what it would be advantageous for a young girl to know and, being intelligent, she would have profited more from a better-directed education. As it was, hers was somewhat lop-sided – comprised almost entirely of classical literature. Finding she had a natural talent for languages, her father read with her Ariosto and Tasso, Fontaine and Pascal. He also persuaded her to learn chunks of Milton and much of Ovid's *Metamorphoses* by heart – no doubt his friends were impressed when he encouraged her to stand up and recite them.

He also told her about the religions of the Greeks and Romans, about Judaism and classical Islam. 'My mind was so puzzled with such a variety of religions,' she later wrote, 'that except the firm belief of a God, I knew not which of all the modes of worship to adopt from real conviction, as to the weak judgement of a child all appeared equally supported by tradition.'[17] In her *Confessions*, a short autobiography which she wrote at the demand of her second husband, she complained bitterly that George Bowes had given her no firm grasp of morality. 'I am convinced,' she said, 'that the want of a proper sense of religion has been the original cause of all my errors.'[18] Her father's stories of 'the mythology of every Heathen nation that ever existed', and praise of 'the patriotic virtues and shining merits of the ancient philosophers and heroes'[19] were of little help in explaining how vice and virtue could co-exist in the world as comfortably as, she observed, it did.

His daughter was allowed to read whatever books and papers were lying around in George Bowes's library, and even random reading in the magazines and newspapers of the time suggested to an intelligent girl that social, economic and political morality – though she would not necessarily have known those terms – were at a nadir. Gambling, encouraged by the courts of George I and II, was a favourite recreation of rich and poor, drinking was even more popular, great fortunes were made from smuggling and slavery, while little could be accomplished, politically or in trade, without recourse to bribery. It was all very confusing – Mary Eleanor was perhaps fortunate that her father did not read Voltaire to her, which would have confused her even more.

Her education ran entirely counter to every early eighteenth-century idea of how to bring up a daughter. The great majority took the view expressed by Mrs Malaprop: 'I would by no means wish a daughter of mine to be a progeny of learning; I don't think so much learning becomes a young woman; for instance, I would never let her meddle with Greek, or Hebrew, or algebra, or simony, or fluxions, or paradoxes, or such inflammatory branches of learning.'[20] Without going that far, there is no doubt that George Bowes's over-ambitious education of his daughter sometimes confused her. Her first biographer, Jessé Foot – who actually knew her – suggests that as a child Mary Eleanor's mind 'was never left at liberty to be attentive to her most favoured delights, but was always solicited to embrace new objects, as if that mind was designed to comprehend the knowledge of all languages, and all the products of every country, in the four quarters of the globe'.[21]

There were lighter moments, however. When she was twelve, Mary Eleanor was given her own little garden by the Green Close not far from the house. Fenced off to protect it from the ravages of rabbits, it was no doubt planted with the popular jasmine and honeysuckle, sweet peas and mignonette, and perhaps had apricot and peach trees trained against the walls (regularly doused against aphids with a mixture made from tobacco stalks and wood soot).

Mary Eleanor was by this time already interested in plants, and in 1772 was to build a handsome 'Green House', well planned, with Tuscan columns, tall windows looking out to the south-east and smaller ones facing north-west, whence colder winds blew. There was one large room, and smaller ones at the rear of the building, which could be kept warm for the more exotic plants she collected to add to the more common auriculas, camellias and magnolias.[22] The gardens at Gibside still exist, now cared for by the National Trust, and it is possible to enjoy them as Mary Eleanor enjoyed them during her childhood and teenage years. She may well have picnicked in the Banqueting House which overlooks much of the estate (though that would have been an elaborate affair, for there is a kitchen and pantry besides the main room, once handsome with an elaborate plaster fan-vaulted ceiling). Then there was the more inspiriting pleasure to be had at the now vanished Bath House, its interior decorated in stucco by an Italian workman; it offered a cold plunge pool as well as fireplaces at which to warm oneself afterwards.

George Bowes not only looked after his daughter's education but, in her words, was determined 'to acquire me a great stock of health, hardening and strengthening my constitution by every possible means'.[23] The precautions he took included inoculating Mary Eleanor, when she was two, against smallpox. This was a brave step, for though inoculation had been practised for at least thirty years (since the smallpox epidemic of 1721, after which Princess Caroline had had two of her daughters inoculated) it was still a long way from popular acceptance; indeed, as late as 1772 the Revd Edward Massey was to be heard fulminating against 'the dangerous and sinful practice of inoculation'.[24]

Mary Eleanor's constitution was not weak, but she did suffer throughout her life from what she described as 'hysteric fits', which were at first mild, but became more severe after the birth of her children, when she suffered 'incredibly, both in health and looks, being exceedingly reduced and weakened'.[25] These fits were almost certainly epileptic: they were often prompted by tension; she said that she felt their approach; and she was sometimes able to stop them developing by plunging her hands in cold water. She also found camomile tea helpful. All this is suggestive of epilepsy.[26] There is, however, no suggestion that she actually lost consciousness or had to be physically restrained, and apart from worrying her and clearly making her feel very unwell, the fits do not seem to have interfered with her life – unlike the 'obstructions' (presumably severe constipation) and unduly heavy menstrual bleeding from which she suffered from time to time.

Her childhood was happy, if somewhat bewildering, and ran smoothly until her father's death in 1760, when she was twelve. A year later his widow took a house in London,[27] and from then on she and her daughter lived for part of the time there, and for the remainder at Gibside, with occasional visits to St Paul's Walden, which had come to Mrs Bowes upon the death of her parents. She was devastated by her husband's death, and was (Mary Eleanor says) 'incapable of attending either to my education or morals' – not that she had previously attempted this, or shown any interest in either. She had never been a figure on the social scene, and now retired completely from public view. Whether in town or country, she only rarely went out, and left her daughter to her own devices under the sketchy care of the child's unmarried aunt, Jane Bowes. Mary Eleanor came to believe that much of the pain of her later life might have been avoided had she had the support and advice of a sensible mother; Mrs Bowes may or may not have been sensible, but certainly there was little real communication between them: 'I never durst open my heart to her', the daughter complained.[28]

Miss Bowes was neither a good chaperone nor a good influence, as Mary Eleanor later herself realised. She had once been a celebrated beauty, but was silly and vain, over-interested in the social whirl, and inordinately proud of having in her charge a young woman not only reasonably pretty but also possessed of more intelligence than most girls of her age and position, and of one of the greatest fortunes in England. It is surprising that the heiress managed to escape predatory suitors for as long as she did, especially since at fourteen she was already an attractive and inveterate flirt.

She had doubtless learned the facts of life – probably from Miss Bowes rather than from her mother, with whom any kind of conversation was difficult. She also knew more than the bare facts: no one who lived in the London of the time could possible be unaware of their implications. The immorality of the city was notorious, even in eighteenth-century Europe. There was an enormous number of prostitutes (estimates vary wildly between ten and twenty thousand) openly advertising themselves at the windows of Exeter Street and the Strand, at public dances, city gardens, concerts and theatres – and she must have learned from someone how they earned their living, for married women talked openly about sex, and younger girls listened. Mary Eleanor was used to reading, and there was a thriving trade in pornographic novels, to which Miss Bowes was not averse. English pornographers were beginning to compete seriously with their French counterparts, and Cleland's *Memoirs of a Woman of Pleasure* (better known as *Fanny Hill*, and first published in the year of Mary Eleanor's birth) was in clandestine circulation, together with such works as Thomas Stretser's *A New Description of Merryland* and such scatological offerings as Sir John Harington's *The Benefit of Farting*. Pornographic periodicals such as the *Rangers' Magazine* lay openly about, and the columns of *Town and Country* and other magazines purveyed gossip which made it clear to any bright girl with a questioning mind that passionate relationships between the sexes were not necessarily restricted to the marriage bed.

Mary Eleanor was no fool. By the time she reached puberty she knew perfectly well what went on between a man and a woman, and the indications were that men and women found the activity pleasurable. However, we can almost certainly take her at her word that while she was 'imprudent', she was 'most innocent both in thought and deed, in my flirtations'.[29] The earliest of these had taken place when she was thirteen and met, at a 'children's ball' given by the Duchess of Northumberland, fifteen-year-old Campbell Scott, the brother of the Duke of Buccleuch. They got on well: 'he liked my conversation,' she says, 'and as he was smart and clever, I liked his.'[30] But while they may well have enjoyed, at first, discussing the myths of Greece and Rome (like her father, the teachers at Eton College, where Campbell was a student, encouraged such interests), such classical diversions did not detain the two young people for long. After her cousin, Frank Liddell – a schoolfellow of Campbell's – told her that Campbell was in love with her, and then informed Campbell that she found him attractive, the pair had no difficulty in convincing themselves that they were to be 'lovers'. But flirtation was as far as things went – or so we must presume, although she later described the 'affair' as 'a great imprudence'.[31] Another young Etonian drawn to her was Charles James Fox, the same age as she. He grew up to be one of the most handsome and attractive men of his day, Foreign Secretary, a notable statesman and 1st Lord Holland. But he was already, as a schoolboy, addicted to drinking and whoring, and she rejected his advances – in any case she preferred Campbell Scott. Fox became very jealous of his schoolfellow, and put it about that the flirtation with Mary Eleanor was something more than innocent.

Campbell was not deterred by the gossip. He told Mary Eleanor that he liked her company better than that of any other girl, and she in return professed her 'tender esteem' for him.[32] When he went into the army and was ordered to Germany, he begged her to exchange rings. She gave him a ring set with a blue stone – one her father had given her; she took the precaution of getting her aunt to give her a similar one, so that its absence would not be noticed. The little affair was clearly not going anywhere; but in any event within a year Campbell was dead of the smallpox, 'in the natural way' as Mary Eleanor phlegmatically put it.

TWO

The Beautiful Strathmore

Though grieved and provoked, I put on a cheering countenance, and danced frequently at Almack's with various people who followed me, though they had not then declared themselves.

Mary Eleanor Bowes, *Confessions*

While Mrs Bowes, who after the death of her husband spent the rest of her life mourning him, did not particularly care where she spent her time and made no distinction between life in London and life in the country, Mary Eleanor, now in her teens, was irresistibly drawn by the glamour of the city.

She found the new social life she was able to lead and the flirtations she could enjoy too agreeable to wish to spend much time with her newly appointed governess, a Mrs Parish. We know nothing of Mrs Parish's origins – presumably she was a widow – but she was to play a considerable part in her pupil's life, as were her brother and sister, a Mr and Miss Planta. She may have been appointed by Mary Eleanor's mother with the idea that she should give her daughter a rather more conventional education than her father had given her – the kind of education calculated to instruct a young woman in how 'to devote her time, her talents, and her fortune, to the improvement of public morals, and in increase of public happiness'[1] – for at the time of her father's death she was sorely deficient in the usual accomplishments of an eighteenth-century young girl: dancing, etiquette, posture, sewing and knitting, drawing, and supervising servants. Indeed, her attitude to the latter would have been considered severely wanting by her contemporaries, had they observed her giggling and gossiping with them, to say nothing of using them as go-betweens.

Mrs Bowes may also have hoped that Mrs Parish would take a stronger line than Miss Bowes where the danger of predatory males was concerned. Alas, the new governess was not especially successful in either capacity. Mary Eleanor was already wilful. She confesses that as a young teenager she amused herself with 'alternate study and diversions, such as public places, &c'.[2] There is no reason to suppose that she did not devote some time to study – she was already interested in botany, for instance; but there is no doubt that the diversions available in the city were equally if not more attractive.

The young woman loved gossip – to the extent that she would even listen happily to the prattling of her footman – and she was soon giving others something to gossip about. When society began to talk about her – and she knew perfectly well that people must pay attention to a young woman as wealthy as she – Mary Eleanor was pleased rather than offended. 'I was always extremely silly,' she said later, 'in not minding reports – on the contrary, rather encouraged them, partly that I might laugh at other people's absurdities, and partly because I left it to time and reason to show that they were false, and thought a variety of reports would puzzle people, so that they would look upon every one relating to me as equally false, and even not credit the truth.'[3]

Miss Bowes did not feel it necessary to keep her charge on too tight a rein: she was indeed 'so indulgent a chaperone that I must say, if I had not been more prudent than most girls, I might have been less so'.[4]

However, Mary Eleanor knew her value as an heiress, and was not ready to fall into the arms of the first man who proposed. The moment an object of her flirtations got too serious and decided that he knew her well enough to make an offer for her (and her enormous fortune) she retreated, smiling, from the situation, and told him to apply to her mother. This had two advantages: first, it made it easy for her to refuse him and, second, it made it possible for her to boast about her conquest without fear of the young man declaring that he had never made the offer.

Young men came, flirted, and went – she received offers, she says, from 'a great many men of rank', and refused them all. One man did, however, monopolise her attention for over a year. He was described as 'a young Venetian Marquis'. How she came across him we do not know – he seems to have been in London mainly in order to learn idiomatic English; we know nothing of his antecedents or even his age, but for some months he was seen with her everywhere. He was, she declared, her *cicisbeo* – the Italian term for the acknowledged platonic gallant or *cavalier servente* of a married woman, though in this case of a young unmarried one. There might have been talk – no doubt there was, for though both the noun and the position were acknowledged in England, the uncharitable often disputed the platonic nature of the relationship – and indeed when the married woman concerned was much married, elderly and plain, the uncharitable were often accurate in their suspicions. In this case the young and reasonably attractive Mary Eleanor almost certainly kept the Marquess at arm's length – and got away with the situation without causing scandal, partly because Mrs Bowes and her late husband were known to have had a partiality for Italy and Italians, and the widow went out of her way to entertain the Marquess in her house. Her daughter meanwhile had the advantage of improving her Italian, and the Marquess that of learning colloquial English. Eventually he left the country to continue his education in Paris and then in St Petersburg. He sent Mary Eleanor two spaniel puppies from Paris and one or two letters, but that was all.

Not all her time was spent in frivolity, or studying with Mrs Parish. Her intelligence and bookishness were noticed, and although she was only fourteen, she was taken up by the Bluestockings – an informal club of intelligent, well-educated women whose members scorned the usual female accomplishments and took turns to host evening parties where literature, music and the drama were discussed, and where there was an emphasis on what women had contributed to culture in the past, and what they might accomplish in the future.

By the 1760s the celebrated 'Queen of the Blues', Mrs Elizabeth Montagu, had already been admired for some years for her learning and wit. The extremely wealthy friend of Dr Johnson, she was at the centre of the Bluestockings. It is a tribute to Mary Eleanor's intelligence that she was taken up by this highly intellectual woman almost thirty years her senior, who 'was pleased to honour me with her friendship, approbation and correspondence'.[5]

It is not surprising that she was impressed by Mrs Montagu: most people were, and had been from her childhood. At eight years old she was already highly literate – but no cold, cerebral highbrow. 'Handsome, fat and merry',[6] her nickname was 'Fidget'. At twenty-two, in 1742, she had married Edward Montagu, a grandson of the 1st Earl of Sandwich, a seriously wealthy man (owning coal mines in Northumberland and property inherited from a brother), and from 1750 on she made her husband's London house in Hill Street, Mayfair, a Mecca for the intelligentsia of the age – 'I never invite idiots to my house'[7] she told the actor David Garrick – and indeed many members of the aristocracy were disqualified by their dim-wittedness.

The popularity of Mrs Montagu's 'conversation parties' was a reaction to the male view that women should confine themselves to three activities: the running of a household, the bearing and care of children, and obedience to their husbands. Married life, for intelligent women, was for the most part intensely frustrating – even when the husband was, unusually, sympathetic. Women were not allowed to be magistrates or MPs and could not become doctors or members of the clergy, while custom encouraged them to be quiet and uncomplaining about their lot. The women who attended her gatherings[8] were prepared to flout the general opinion of the times, to be assertive and vocal, to follow their creative instincts well outside the production of miniature replicas of their husbands. There was an interest too in social matters, and many of the women associated with the circle played a part in helping those less fortunate than themselves. They also took a keen interest in political affairs, attacking forced marriage and slavery.

Much fun was made of the Bluestockings by the conventional men of the time – and most of the men of the time were highly conventional. Horace Walpole, for instance, wrote scathingly in a letter to his friend Richard West: 'You have not been witness to the rhapsody of mystic nonsense which they debate incessantly . . . only figure the coalition of prudery, debauchery, sentiment, history, Greek, Latin, French, Italian, and metaphysics; all, except the second, understood by halves, or not at all.'[9]

The group liked to encourage young people, and Mrs Montagu 'took up' Mary Eleanor, the young heiress, as later she was to take up the young Fanny Burney. We don't know to whom she was introduced among the members of the group, but it is unlikely that she did not at least set eyes on, for instance, the magisterial Mrs Delaney, who corresponded with Swift and was on easy terms with Alexander Pope and Horace Walpole, or on such impressive older women as Mrs Hester Chapone and Mrs Elizabeth Carter, who regularly contributed to Dr Johnson's magazine *The Rambler*, and Miss Sarah Fielding, author of the highly successful novel *The Adventures of David Simple*. No doubt it was in the company of these intelligent, supportive women that Mary Eleanor first began to think that she might perhaps become a writer.

The gatherings of the Blues were not restricted to women: like-minded males were also included, provided they shared the general antagonism to card-playing, the social round, and to the view that the only education women needed was in such frivolous pastimes as needlework. Some men, indeed, began openly to support the intelligent and creative women of the circle – such men John Duncombe, and George Ballard, the author of *Memoirs of Several Ladies of Great Britain Who Have Been Celebrated for their Writings or Skill in Learned Languages, Arts and Sciences*.

But Mary Eleanor was not made of such rare stuff as Mrs Chapone or Mrs Carter. She toyed with writing – and was to continue to do so for some time; but she was also interested in the social life, and in her appearance. The latter interest was shared by Mrs Montagu herself, known for the splendour of her diamonds, which were as brilliant as her conversation, and for the luxury in which she enjoyed living (Montagu House, which she built in the 1780s, was to contain rooms whose magnificence was unequalled – 'the room of cupidons', its walls painted with roses and jessamine among which little cupids gambolled, and 'the feather room', hung with the feathers of every kind of bird, in designs by herself).

By 1765 Mary Eleanor was sixteen. It was high time, everyone agreed, that she was married, or at the very least had an acknowledged suitor, and a proposal was indeed made – by the Bowes's neighbour in the north, John, 9th Earl of Strathmore. The seat of the earls of Strathmore was Glamis Castle, just north of Dundee, which had been the family home since it had been given to an ancestor in 1372 by Robert II of Scotland. Only a few miles separated Glamis from Gibside, and Mary Eleanor did not need to be formally introduced to Strathmore. She was well aware of his existence, and would certainly have made his acquaintance as a child, though as he was twelve years older than she, they would scarcely have been intimate. Did she ever think of him as a possible husband? It is not unlikely – few eligible young women would have failed to do so, for he was, after all, considered by everyone to be extraordinarily handsome, apart from also being an earl. His beauty – he was known as 'the Beautiful Strathmore' – was, she conceded, 'very great'. Moreover, she had a dream in which she married him, and while she admitted she was foolish to pay much attention to a dream, it clearly had its effect.

She was not perhaps surprised to receive his proposal of marriage, though she may have been surprised by the manner in which it was made – not in the course of a personal interview, but in the form of a letter sent via another neighbour in County Durham, a Mrs Baker; this lady came down to London to stay with Mrs Bowes bringing with her the letter in which Strathmore made his offer. She handed it to Mary Eleanor when her mother was out; the girl read the first two or three lines, realised that it was a love-letter, and immediately handed it back saying that she was not interested in letters delivered in such an under-hand manner, whoever they came from. . . .

Mary Eleanor was then interrupted by Mrs Baker, who told her the name of her admirer. This made all the difference. She sent a message to Strathmore inviting him to make his application to Mrs Bowes, but said nothing to her mother until they had returned to Gibside. It seems that there had previously been some talk about Strathmore as a possible suitor, and that for some reason Mrs Bowes had been against the idea. Mary Eleanor thought she should not give her mother time to work up her indignation against the Earl before he actually came to her with his request for her hand.

Strathmore now lost no time. He rode over to Gibside, asked for an interview with Mrs Bowes, and put his case. Mrs Bowes received him coldly, merely telling him she would pass on his proposal to her daughter, that they were shortly leaving for London, and that if he cared to call on them there he would have his answer. She did not tell Mary Eleanor that the Earl had called, though her daughter was in the house at the time. It was two days before she mentioned Strathmore's declaration, and then seemed to take it for granted that the offer would be refused. When Mary Eleanor asked what her mother had against him, she said that there were three objections: 'disorder in the family; a mother and many brothers and sisters whom perhaps I should find troublesome; and lastly (the chief with her) his being a Scotchman'.[10]

The incident makes Mrs Bowes seem unsympathetic and there was certainly little love lost between mother and daughter; yet there are indications that she was far from cold or insensitive: she was described by Jessé Foot as 'a truly good and charitable woman, indeed her charity was indiscreet. As St Paul's Walden lies out of the common road, the beggars which flocked there infested the parish [yet] she gave food, clothes and lodging to all who came.'[11]

A mother's dislike of the family of a potential son-in-law is not uncommon, but as it happened Mrs Bowes was right about the Earl's relatives – there would indeed be trouble with them. Neither was her prejudice against the Scots surprising; it was shared by many otherwise civilised Englishmen of the time, Dr Johnson being a famous example, with his notorious pronouncement that 'the noblest prospect which a Scotchman ever sees is the high road that leads him to England!'[12] and his continual sneers at Boswell's home country. Mary Eleanor did not share either prejudice: indeed, she was particularly partial to Scotsmen – and Irishmen, for that matter; unfortunately, as it turned out. Celtic constitutions seemed more promisingly passionate than those of the cooler English fops. As to the 'disorder in the family', we can only assume that Mrs Bowes was complaining about some alleged mental or emotional imbalance, for which there was no foundation – the story was the result of spiteful gossip.

Mary Eleanor told her mother that of course she would not marry Strathmore if Mrs Bowes was completely set against it; but if she did not marry him, she would not marry anyone. Though Mrs Bowes had an ally in Mrs Parish, who also (for no known reason – perhaps simply to curry favour with her employer) advised against the match, there was little the mother could do other than give way. They would leave for London immediately, she said, and Strathmore could be given his answer.

Matters did not go forward as swiftly or easily as that, for Strathmore had to postpone his visit to London because of the death of an uncle, which left business which had to be settled first. Mrs Bowes was aware of this, but did not go out of her way to send him any reply to his proposal – or indeed to explain his absence to her daughter. Because of his preoccupation with his uncle's estate or through plain indifference (and the latter is not impossible; he was never a considerate man, except through lethargy), he failed to write even the simplest note to the young woman to whom he hoped to become engaged. One wonders whether he was having second thoughts: Mary Eleanor, though financially a desirable property, may not have appealed to Strathmore in any other way – she was not especially beautiful, and her reputation for intelligence was not a recommendation. Men did not like intelligence in a wife – indeed, Lady Mary Wortley Montagu went so far as to advise women to conceal any sign of it.[13]

After a week or so had passed, Mary Eleanor was perhaps understandably put out by her suitor's silence. Characteristically, she did not languish in her room at home as a Jane Austen heroine would have done, looking out of the window for the post. 'Though grieved and provoked,' she wrote, 'I put on a cheering countenance, and danced frequently at Almack's with various people who followed me, though they had not then declared themselves.'[14]

Almack's rooms had just opened their doors in Pall Mall, and the Great Room – measuring 100 feet long by 40 feet wide – was *the* place to be seen for anyone who was anyone in the London of 1765. For a subscription of 10 guineas one could sup there every night during the twelve weeks of the London season. But membership was not easily obtained, and the ability to afford the subscription did not necessarily ensure acceptance: the Lady Patronesses – initially, Lady Pembroke and Lady Molyneaux – carefully scrutinised the applications. They were resolute in excluding anyone of questionable morals – though one must suspect that they also turned down some applicants simply because for one reason or another they were not in favour. Captain Rees Howell Gronow, whose memoirs are among the most amusing of the period, tells us that 'very often persons whose rank and fortunes entitled them to *entrée* anywhere else were excluded by the *cliquism* of the lady patronesses, for the female government of Almack's was a pure despotism, and subject to all the caprices of despotic rule'.[15] Among the unfortunates refused admission during the first year were the Duchesses of Bedford, Grafton and Marlborough, Lady Holderness, Lady Rochford and Lord March. Even when one had been accepted, there were perils – during the first week the great Duke of Wellington was turned away because he arrived seven minutes late and – worse, much worse – was wearing trousers rather than knee breeches, the required dress for gentlemen.

In the gambling rooms of Almack's one could play at hazard, faro, basset, roly poly, and other dice or card games. The players were confirmed gamblers though ladies and gentlemen rather than the merchants, tradesmen and clerks, the puffs, flashers, squibs, dunners and flash captains who congregated in the forty or more less reputable gaming houses of the city. The gamblers at Almack's wore leather bands about their wrists to protect their lace cuffs as they handled the dice or the cards, and wide-brimmed hats to keep the bright lights out of their eyes. Sometimes they wore masks to hide from other gamblers any expression which might give away the value of the cards they held as they asked 'What will you lay?', tempting their adversaries to higher and more hazardous speculations.

Mary Eleanor was not interested in the gaming rooms, however, but in other less risky but no less amusing diversions. Almack's, Gronow says, was 'a matrimonial bazaar where mothers met to carry on affairs of state', and many a promising introduction was made in the stuffy supper room, where guttering candles illuminated tables spread with 'tepid lemonade, weak tea, tasteless orgeat,[16] stale cakes and thin slices of bread and butter – the only refreshment allowed'. Attentive beaux and would-be beaux grew warmer and more pressing in the ballroom.

It was in the supper room, perhaps on an occasion when Mary Eleanor felt more than usually flirtatious (she herself confesses to 'girlishness, mischievousness and vanity')[17] that trouble erupted one evening between Lord Mount Stuart and a Mr Chaloner, both of whom wished to sit next to her. Voices were raised, attitudes were struck, and the whole room was soon in an uproar. Embarrassingly, Mount Stuart's sister, Miss Windsor, was sitting next to the cause of the commotion. She begged her friend to intervene in favour of her brother, who had become hysterical; bread-and-butter went one way, cakes another. But Mary Eleanor was enjoying herself too much to attempt to pacify the two young men; a challenge was issued, and the potential duellists strode out of Almack's in a passion. One or other must have backed down, however, for there the confrontation ended.

The heiress's mischievousness did not. She positively encouraged Mount Stuart's mother, Lady Bute, to believe that she would accept him if he offered. Mount Stuart was delighted, and encouraged his mother to call on Mrs Bowes to put the question. The latter was bewildered – she had never heard anything of the young man from her daughter. Lady Bute went home mortified, and Lord Mount Stuart went to bed for a week ('downright girlishness', Mary Eleanor commented).

Eventually, Lord Strathmore came round to making enquiries, and was told that he had been accepted. There was no pleasant interval of agreeable courtship, however – the two young people going about together, showing themselves at Almack's and the opera, calling on the fiancée's friends so that she could introduce her husband-to-be. Instead there were eighteen months of haggling about the marriage settlement, with the two families arguing over the financial conditions of the marriage. Presumably the couple did meet from time to time, but though Strathmore would certainly have been concerned with the progress of the financial discussions, and presumably Mary Eleanor was not entirely uninterested, the actual negotiations were conducted by their lawyers. The alliance between so distinguished a family and so wealthy an heiress must be most carefully contrived.

Though in 1753 Lord Chancellor Hardwicke brought in a radical Marriage Act which made it possible for the state to interfere in the right of British citizens to marry, this had done nothing to change women's situation within marriage. It was still the case that their legal status ran parallel to their social status: apart from their husbands they were non-persons with no legal identity, much as were lunatics, idiots and outlaws. In common law they had no civil rights; they could not own property, make wills, testify in courts or obtain a divorce. Nor had they any legal redress against marital violence or rape. Their children, like their own bodies, were the property of their husbands. Later, Mary Eleanor was to realise just how difficult it was for a woman to get free of a husband while retaining property which was her own.

Her father had devised some conditions with which any successful suitor for his daughter's hand must comply, and Strathmore was not particularly happy about them – particularly about the one which stipulated that any man who married Miss Bowes must pay for the wealth she would bring him by adopting her maiden name as his surname. Strathmore and his lawyers argued, wriggled, cajoled – but to no avail, and eventually, after exploring every possible escape route, the Earl reluctantly agreed, and also confirmed that any children of the marriage would use the name of Bowes (as they did).

It was settled that the marriage should take place on Mary Eleanor's eighteenth birthday, 24 February 1767. The moment the date was fixed

– and certainly by the time she walked up the aisle of St George's, Hanover Square – the bride was convinced that she had made the wrong choice. Disappointment was almost inevitable, for her expectations of marriage were unrealistic. It is unlikely that she ever discussed the matter with her father – she had been too young for him to have brought it up. But she certainly knew of his devotion to his first wife – others would have told her, if he did not – and his relationship with her mother, while we know almost nothing about it, seems to have been at least untroubled, while Mrs Bowes's mourning at his death was genuine enough to suggest that theirs was a loving marriage. Moreover, the growing child's own relationship with her father had been close and loving – he had encouraged her to stretch her intellect, and while teaching her to read had read *with* her rather than simply making her learn by rote. She had not been taught to consider herself as in any way inferior because she was female, and when she began to think about marrying, she looked forward to a relationship like the one she had had with her father.

Doubt may have crept in when Strathmore declined to court her as she expected to be courted. Handsome and elegant though he was, the Earl shared none of her tastes and was unwilling to consult them. Their characters were different – hers passionate and volatile, his cool and deliberate. His idea of entertainment was to spend an evening sitting with a friend over a bottle of claret. He had perhaps heard of Almack's, but it would no more have occurred to him to suggest a visit there to show the world his own and his fiancée's happiness, than to dance with her, had he ever done so. He was also quite as chauvinist as any other man of his period, and seems not to have shown the slightest interest in her more serious pursuits – botany, for instance, or literature. Both, he thought, were irreconcilable with her future position as his wife and the mother of his children. Mary Eleanor learned this much about him during their engagement: 'our tempers, dispositions and turns [were] different – [I] wished to retract . . . but my pride and sometimes my weakness would not let me.'[18]

The wedding provided the town with a fine subject for gossip and enjoyment: no one could complain at the display in Hanover Square, both before the ceremony and after it, when the bride and groom, now Earl and Countess of Strathmore, magnificent in their wedding clothes, climbed into their landau and set off for St Paul's Walden. Mrs Bowes had been most generous in her presents to her daughter and son-in-law, not only dressing her daughter for the occasion at enormous expense, but giving the couple three handsome carriages, and all the linen, furniture and jewellery which had been left at Gibside by her late husband, with the exception only of what was entailed and must remain in the house. She also turned over to her daughter the lease of her house at 40 Grosvenor Square, which became their London home.

Mrs Bowes had invited a number of guests to share in the festivities she had devised in celebration of the wedding, and incidentally the first few days of her daughter's honeymoon. There was of course a wedding feast, with favours given to the guests, and so on, after which the Count and Countess of Strathmore remained at St Paul's for a fortnight with Mrs Bowes and her other guests. It is not impossible that Mary Eleanor was relieved rather than agitated to discover that the first days of her marriage were to be lived in public, as it were.[19] The prospect of being, at last, alone with her husband literally made her sick. When, after a fortnight, they set out on the uncomfortable and prolonged six-day journey to Gibside over winter roads which were in some stretches almost impassable because of mud and pot-holes, she immediately fell ill – and not only because of the irregular movements of the coach. In her *Confessions*, she says that a number of her mother's guests suffered from stomach ailments due, she thought, to her mother's port wine. But she was almost certainly disingenuous in suggesting that this was the reason for her own nausea and extreme diarrhoea. Almost certainly, we can assume that the illness was psychosomatic – it was to recur throughout her life at times of stress.

Mary Eleanor tells us little about her married life with the Earl. We can infer that for some time – six years at least – she was faithful to him. She certainly did her duty by him, bearing him five children: Maria Jane, born in 1768 (the church bells rang out at Gibside to mark the occasion), John (1769), Anna Maria (1770), George (1771) and Thomas (1773). Strathmore did not consider it necessary for his wife to enjoy a life away from his side. He put a stop, for example, to her intimacy with the Bluestockings, obliging her to break off her friendship with Mrs Montagu 'in a very rude and abrupt manner . . . telling me she was a wild, light, silly woman of bad character, and not fit for my acquaintance. Sadly against my inclination, I was forced to comply, and give her up, with many others.'[20]

Strathmore took some notice of public opinion. In 1770, for instance, he organised a celebration at Gibside for Mary Eleanor's twenty-first birthday – an ox was roasted whole and barrels of beer were supplied for several hundred workers on the estate and selected colliers. Tenants' wives were invited to tea-parties, and the house was thrown open to visitors and a 'publick table' kept – boiled beef, plum pudding and more ale. There was dancing until four in the morning. We can safely assume, however, that a gathering of rustics, together with a few country squires, dancing to the music of a fiddle and a drum, was not the kind of entertainment that Mary Eleanor considered either satisfying, or her due. But she was by now used to an unexciting and undemanding life. She took some interest in household matters, for instance in reconstructing the east wing at Gibside, building a new dairy, bakehouse and laundry and improving the servants' quarters. But housekeeping and bearing and caring for her children were simply not enough for her lively mind. Her children, indeed, interested her little – though she was fond of her daughters, she does not seem to have paid them much attention until they were in their teens, while she conceived a positive dislike for her eldest son, John, and was for many years at best indifferent and at worst positively antagonistic towards him. Pathetically, it seems that she may have believed that the years during which she was almost permanently pregnant contributed to her husband's neglect of her: she wondered whether 'having children, made a man like his wife less'.[21]

Forced to make her own amusements, she turned to two in particular: writing, and botany. Her father's concern for the design and maintenance of the gardens at Gibside, and his furthering of her early pleasure in gardening and plants, had nurtured the latter interest and Mrs Parish also played a part in its development. Her brother, Joseph Planta, worked as an assistant librarian at the British Museum. A Fellow of the Royal Society and later keeper of manuscripts there, he and his sister Eliza, a teacher (among her pupils were the children of George III) in turn introduced Mary Eleanor to their friend Daniel Charles Solander, another employee of the British Museum. Solander had been a pupil of the great Swedish botanist Carl von Linné, better known as Linnæus, who had built up an enormous and elaborate means of classifying plants. In 1768 Solander had accompanied Sir Joseph Banks on Cook's voyage in the *Endeavour* in quest of *Terra Australis Incognita* (during which Banks almost died in the snows of Tierra del Fuego).

The *Endeavour* expedition resulted in the discovery of an extraordinary number of new species of exotic plants. Banks brought back more than 30,000 new plants and animals and discovered 2,400 new species (he named Botany Bay for the plethora of new species he found there), prompting the *London Chronicle* to announce that Banks and Solander had made 'more curious discoveries in the way of astronomy and natural history than . . . have been presented to the learned world for these fifty years past'.[22] The two men – whose achievements overshadowed those of Cook himself, at least in the public mind – were commanded to Richmond, where they enthralled King George III with their descriptions of the new world they had seen. The King proposed that the living plants they had brought back should be transplanted to the Royal Gardens at Kew. By the end of August the newspapers were reporting that 'Dr Solander and Mr Banks . . . have the honour of frequently waiting on His Majesty at Richmond, who examines their collection of drawings of plants and views of different places.'

Fifteen hundred drawings and paintings had been executed during the voyage by the brilliant young British artist Sydney Parkinson, who tragically died before the expedition returned to England, and the King admired the almost violently red blooms of the tropical hibiscus (*Hibiscus rosa-sinenses*) which Parkinson had seen garlanding the necks of Polynesian girls, the so-called paperbark tea tree (*Melaleuca quinquenenervis*) with whose bark the Australian aborigines stuffed their children's pillows, and the bulbs of the ant plant (*Myrmecodia beccarii*) in which ant colonies made their homes.

What fascinated the King must fascinate the country, and the British public was captivated by the idea that the world had so many new and strange plants to offer. Mary Eleanor was naturally flattered by the great botanist's interest in her, and took his advice when she bought Stanley House in Chelsea, and in its gardens built conservatories and extensive hot-houses in which she nurtured exotic plants some of which were collected for her by William Paterson, a botanist with an extensive knowledge of what he called 'the Hottentot Country'.

It was Solander who introduced four more people to the botanical salon – Mary Eleanor was happy to entertain, generously, Captain James Mario Matra, who had also sailed with Cook in the *Endeavour*, and his brother, who seems to have had some kind of career as a British Consul in North Africa.[23] Then there was another botanist, only known to us as Mr Magra, and Eliza Planta's fiancé, the Revd Henry Stephens. All were enthusiastic hangers-on of the Countess – Jessé Foot dubs them the votaries of a 'Temple of Folly in Grosvenor Square'.

Mary Eleanor's interest in botany was serious, with Foot describing her as 'the most intelligent female botanist of the age'. So was her other interest, writing. No doubt this arose from her connection with the Bluestockings, many – even most – of whom were ready with their pens. Some women she may have met actually wrote for money, most notably Sarah Robinson Scott (1723–95) and Elizabeth Carter (1717–60). But they had other means, and it was not until the late eighteenth century that such women as Mary Wollstonecraft (1759–97) and Catherine Sawbridge Macaulay Graham (1731–91) actually turned to writing as a profession. Mary Eleanor obviously had no need to do so, and probably began to write simply to show her peers among the Bluestockings that she could, as well as for whatever satisfaction the activity gave her as a pastime. The text of her single play, *The Siege of Jerusalem*,[24] unfortunately shows that, as a writer, she was a very good botanist. Apart from the fact that it is much too short, its author shows no talent whatsoever for dramatic writing. This is not to say that the text is completely uninteresting; but the piece was never produced, though it was published – at her own expense – in 1769.

THREE

'Love within Bounds'

I consented to accept the love of a man whom I could always keep within bounds.

Mary Eleanor Bowes, *Confessions*

There are very few failed marriages in which the faults are all on one side. Doubtless Mary Eleanor had her shortcomings. Impatience was certainly among them. But her first husband, though there is no evidence that he ever treated her badly in the way of violence, certainly did not go out of his way to make her life pleasant. He recognised her faults, but made no effort to discover her virtues.

Lord Strathmore was not, as Jessé Foot points out, 'exactly calculated to make a learned woman a pleasing husband'.[1] He showed not the faintest interest in her writing, made his view of the Bluestockings very clear, and forced her to break off her attendance at their meetings. He was suspicious of her interest in botany, thinking it somewhat indelicate. Linnaeus' division of plants into 'phanerogams' (those with visible reproductive organs) and 'cryptograms' (those, like mosses and ferns, with none) could be, and was, considered by some to be suggestive and at worst even prurient. Strathmore, completely devoid of enthusiasm for anything except drinking and sport, seems to have been one of them. In any case, his wife's interest was, he thought, mere folly and extravagance. She must give up her glass-houses at Chelsea and sell the house there. She obstinately refused to do so. Nor was he any more sympathetic to her more homely likes and dislikes. She had, for instance, a passion for cats, but disliking them he forbade them the house. Again, she ignored his instruction, and upset him by multiplying the number she kept.[2]

Strathmore was a fine one to talk of extravagance: he himself, a few years into their marriage, owed £30,000 – more than £1½ million in today's terms – mostly in gambling debts. He spent a great deal on maintaining an unnecessarily large stable of horses, but more dangerously subscribed eagerly to the common mania for gambling.

Mania is the word. Betting not only took place at the loo tables, at hazard (a dice game) or EO (a sort of roulette); one could bet on the results of tennis matches or horse racing, on who could drink the most or who would die first. Men bet on the most extraordinary events. Lord Rockingham bet Lord Orford £500 on the result of a race from Norwich to London between five turkeys and five geese. A member of Almack's bet that he could jump from the window into the first barouche that passed, and kiss the occupant. Another member wagered that a man could live under water, drowned one man in trying to prove his point, and then, undeterred, submerged a second. Bets were often ridiculously one-sided: two men bet on the result of a cricket match – one lost £72,000 – the other had bet only half-a-crown's worth of wine.[3] When a man dropped down dead at the door of White's club, bets were immediately laid on whether he was really dead or not, and when a surgeon was about to bleed him there were complaints that that would affect the fairness of the wager.

The sums of money won and lost are almost unbelievable, as is the coolness with which losses were accepted. Charles James Fox, the young man who would have wished to flirt with Mary Eleanor when they were children, lost £140,000 in three years – £10 million, more or less, in modern currency. After one enormous throw which failed, he calmly sat down at a table and began to read Herodotus. Horace Walpole reported that one player, Sir George Bland, lost his whole fortune at hazard in one evening and that at Almack's young men frequently lost between £10,000 and £15,000 at a single game; Lord Stavordale, still under twenty-one years old, lost £11,000 one evening – then recovered it by one hand at hazard, remarking 'Now, if I had been playing *deep*, I might have won millions.'[4]

The Countess was not interested in gambling (some women were, though they rarely appeared at the tables); nor was she the kind of woman who could content herself with the role of mother and housekeeper – to think of herself as one of her husband's less important possessions – much less to disappear from view under his shadow, as most men expected of a wife ('In marriage, husband and wife are one person, and that person is the husband', as Sir William Blackstone put it[5]). She was not, during the first ten years of her marriage, notorious for entertaining lovers, as many fashionable women were. But it is not perhaps surprising that after the birth of her youngest child in 1768 she did not go out of her way to rebuff those who found her attractive. Many did so:

She possessed a very pleasing enbonpoint; her breast was un-commonly fine; her stature rather under the middle class; her hair brown; her eyes light, small, and she was near-sighted; her face was round; her neck and shoulders graceful; her lower jaw rather under-hanging, and which, whenever she was agitated, was moved very uncommonly, as if convulsively, from side to side; her fingers were small, and her hands were exceedingly delicate. . . .[6]

She was also extremely fashionable in her dress, though her appearance was sometimes extreme – the Hon. Mrs Osborne described her dresses as 'the wonder of the town';[7] it sounds as though she made the most of the hoop petticoats which were now popular, often so wide that it made it necessary for the wearer to enter a room sideways – Joseph Addison claimed that one woman invited to his house 'endeavour'd Twice or Thrice to come in, but could not do it by reason of her Petticoat, which was too large for the Entrance of my House, though I had ordered both the Folding-Doors to be thrown open . . .'.[8] Mary Eleanor also wore her hair à la mode in the 'tower', thoroughly greased with lard and powdered each day (fleas and lice found these edifices excellent lodging, and when they were demolished were caught in droves). Mrs Osborne said that her head was 'a yard high and filled, or rather covered with feathers to an enormous size'.

She did not dress for the benefit of her husband. They were not only incompatible, but had no opportunity to rub along together on the basis of daily proximity, which might have shown them how to tolerate each other. The Earl was absent from home for most of their married life. This was not entirely his own fault: the onset of tuberculosis was treated, on his doctor's advice, by his taking the waters at Bath. But long separations can have done little for the stability of the marriage and it seems to be the case that having impregnated his wife Strathmore left her severely alone during the term of her pregnancies. He made no attempt to stay in the same house, even when his health would have permitted it. Nor was he a passionate man, and there was little chance that their sexual relationship was any warmer than their social one. This was another fatal flaw, for Mary Eleanor was a hot-blooded young woman, who now began to tolerate and even welcome admirers, with varying degrees of warmth.

The first of these of whom we know is Robert Graham, of Fintry, a pretty village not far from Culcreuch Castle at the head of Strathendrick, the valley of Endrick Water as it flows down from the Fintry Hills. Graham, the eldest of three brothers, was Strathmore's gamekeeper at Glamis, and Mary Eleanor obviously knew his family well. In 1773 she responded rather more warmly than was wise to his obvious interest, and began a mild flirtation with him. As soon as this seemed likely to lead into dangerous territory, she backed away, and he, in a temper, went off and without his parents' consent married a local girl (whom, once married, he violently abused).[9]

His place as a suitor was taken by his younger brother James. All three brothers had a penchant for Mary Eleanor – the middle one, David (in her view the most handsome) found her just as attractive as did his siblings; their sister told Mary Eleanor that when he spoke of her 'his eyes used to dart fire, and sparkle like diamonds'.[10] But James was the one she favoured. She speaks in her *Confessions* of his being 'extraordinary', of his having 'shining talents'. He was still in his teens, bright, intelligent and more than usually handsome. He was also 'much too forward for his years';[11] but she does not seem to have minded this too much, and was clearly flattered by his attentions. These were obviously more than merely polite; he tried time after time to secure an invitation to Glamis Castle when she was staying there.

Mary Eleanor was clearly on very friendly terms with the Graham family – indeed, occasionally she even stayed with Mrs Graham, the boys' mother, at her cottage. It was perhaps a pleasure to get away from Glamis and its cold and restrained atmosphere. One cannot know what Strathmore thought of this, or of the friendship between the countess and the gamekeeper's family, but he did not object when in turn Mrs Graham and her daughter were from time to time invited to Glamis. James Graham persistently angled for just such an invitation, and even asked his mother to take him with her, uninvited, when she visited the castle. Perhaps instinctively suspecting his motives, she declined – so he made his own opportunity: he and some friends put up at a cottage near the castle at a time when his sister was staying at Glamis and, when she walked the 3 miles to the cottage to visit him, insisted on accompanying her back to the castle as her protector against the droves of wild cattle which roamed over the local roads (or so he said; happily she was of a nervous disposition).

Having reached the gate he entered the castle uninvited, and introduced himself to Mary Eleanor and to Strathmore, who for once was with her. Deploying all his bright charm, he managed to impress the Earl, who invited him to stay – which he did, for a fortnight, taking the opportunity to court the Countess with every stratagem he could devise.

Mary Eleanor was at first flattered, then interested, and finally captivated. While she claims only to have seen James in the presence of his sister, she hints in her *Confessions* that their relationship became more intimate,[12] admitting 'a violent passion' for James, and professing that in her opinion no heart could be proof against him. Though it is always facile to read between the lines of any 'confession', the tone of her references to James is suggestive, and their relationship may have gone further than she admits – she speaks of a 'more than affectionate friendship'[13] and indeed of 'headlong passion'.[14] He drew her portrait – an excellent likeness, it seems – before he had to go off to London to join his regiment, taking with him a lock of Mary Eleanor's hair which (she says) he had persuaded his sister to acquire, but which she may well have given him herself. She wanted to send him some money, though never actually got round to doing so. There was a correspondence of sorts, helped by his sister, who passed on his letters, written in a very simple code which would have deceived no one had they been intercepted. These were destroyed as soon as they were read – she was so nervous that she went so far as to burn one, mix the ashes with water, and drink it (an act which suggests a degree of self-dramatisation). She seems to have written to him only once, but sent verbal messages via his sister and with the help of one of the Gibside footmen, William Stamp – the first time she used a servant to help in a romantic intrigue; but not the last.

Miss Graham, for one reason or another, pretended friendship to Mary Eleanor while simultaneously hinting to anyone who suspected the affair that her brother was the innocent object of a lascivious woman. She seems to have managed to persuade Mrs Parish – the Countess's sometime governess, who remained with her as a sort of paid companion – that all the running was being made by the Countess, and that James was the blameless and unresponsive victim of her attentions. Miss Graham may have intercepted and kept some of her brother's letters. Mary Eleanor certainly thought so. She eventually wrote a letter which was so rude about her and her brother (he could go and hang himself, she said[15]) that the relationship was broken off. When she was in London and he tried to call on her, Mary Eleanor at first sent James away. She did meet him, but only once more: considerably later, just before he went off with his regiment to Minorca. The meeting was an uncomfortable one, for by then each had reason to suspect the other of lack of feeling – he possibly because she had promised him money and sent none – she because of the missing letters. At all events, he was cool and unaffectionate; so much so that, she says, it almost broke her heart.

It is perfectly possible that in one way or another Strathmore's family knew of these flirtations – Mrs Parish was a tattler. From the first they – the Earl's brother Thomas and his sisters – had taken the firm view that the Earl had married beneath him, and treated Mary Eleanor if not with disdain at least without affection or regard. Thomas Lyon was particularly contemptuous, and Lady Susan and Lady Anne, both married to Durham husbands, were no more friendly. Mary Eleanor 'put up with the disagreeable behaviour of the rest of the family, and concealed it as much as possible from the world, till he [Lyon] publicly, and causelessly, as many can witness, insulted me in the public rooms at Edinburgh, where I was with him and Mrs Lyon, who was just married, all the race-week without Lord Strathmore; during which time, he behaved in such a manner, as scandalized the whole town of Edinburgh; who, at that time, hated him as much as they liked and pitied me. I complained mildly to Lord Strathmore about his brother; but it was an unfortunate and most prejudiced rule with him, that Mr Lyon could not err; so I got no other redress than his saying, that though he was hasty, he had a good heart, and never meant to offend.'[16]

We can have no idea what Lyon did or said to cause such offence. They had got off on the wrong foot from the time of her marriage, and there had already been an angry dispute when he had refused to advance a small sum of money which she believed her husband had asked him to pay her. In this case the argument may have been about something fairly innocuous, but something which brought all Mary Eleanor's feelings about her marriage and her husband's family to a head. But it is at least possible that her brother-in-law complained of an intrigue – far more serious than the flirtation with the Graham brothers – with a man of whom nothing is known except that he became her lover. His name was George Gray.

Gray was a man who, according to the Countess's first biographer, was 'a gentleman from India, who had served under Lord Clive in no very high capacity, but had made a fortune, and purchased land in Scotland'.[17] He seems to have been an attractive but languid and lackadaisical man in his forties, who came along just at the right psychological moment, when Mary Eleanor felt particularly neglected by her husband and had just been abandoned by her lover.

Gray seems to have met the Countess sometime in 1774. From their first encounter, he paid her, she says, 'constant attention' and in the spring of 1775, while Strathmore was – inevitably – taking the waters in the West Country, he made a more serious move: 'Just as I was going to Paul's Walden for two months,' she writes, 'Mr Gray ventured to give me some verses, which expressed in a delicate, though rather too tender a manner for mere friendship, his regard for me, and his great concern for my leaving London.'[18]

She claims to have behaved, at first, perfectly properly, but is somewhat disingenuous: having 'a high opinion of the goodness of his heart and disposition' and being 'unwilling to lose his friendship', she did not immediately break off any correspondence with Gray, but on the contrary regularly exchanged letters with him, which was not something an entirely respectable married woman of the time would have done with a man who had shown signs of paying her undue attention. Eventually, he made his intentions clearer in an 'enigma' or 'charade' – an acrostic or some other literary verse or puzzle – which was often used when a man wished to give a woman the opportunity either to make it clear (by angrily denouncing it as improper) that his attentions to her were unwelcome – or the excuse to make it clear (by pretending not to understand it) that they were welcome.[19]

Mary Eleanor chose the latter course. She clearly found Gray attractive, and was ready for an affair, but one which would not involve her emotionally. She was still half in love with James Graham (whose last call on her took place after she had met Gray), and she told her new lover that her heart 'had long been in possession of another, from whom I had determined to withdraw it'. But she consented, she writes, 'to accept the love of a man whom I could always keep within bounds'. She welcomed him to her house, and 'one unfortunate evening when I was off my guard' took him into her bed.[20] Thereafter, he frequently returned – often while Mrs Parish was visiting her brother at the British Museum – and Mary Eleanor engaged the help of her footman, George Walker, in arranging to meet Gray elsewhere. We can be sure that at least at this point the familiarity between the Countess and the footman extended only to this kind of thing, but the confidence she placed in him was almost unbounded and (she admitted) 'imprudent' – she not only entrusted him with messages to and from Gray, but left him to organise visits to the theatre, dinner parties, and to give orders about the house – orders which in a more normal establishment would have been given by a housekeeper. She also instructed him to report to her on the behaviour and movements of her botanical friends, whom she soon suspected of knowing the truth about her relationship with Gray. The tension of the situation made her slightly paranoid; she suspected that one of them – or perhaps Mrs Parish – might be in touch with or even in the employ of the Lyons relatives. It was as well to keep an eye on them. Her relationship with Mrs Parish was by now extremely sour, partly because the woman still seemed to think she should have some authority over her mistress, and partly because she had simply come to dislike and mistrust her – the Countess accused her among other things of being ill-tempered and unpleasant to the children.

Walker always accompanied Mary Eleanor on her assignations with Gray, presumably to keep a watch for any acquaintance of the Earl or Countess who might see the lovers together, and their letters to each other were always addressed under cover to him. He became a trusted agent both of the Countess and in some way of Eliza Stephens. How he served the latter, we cannot know – but she clearly felt she owed him something, for she gave him a locket with a lock of her hair in it, in which she had entwined a little of Mary Eleanor's ('an odd present', the latter called it – quite rightly, we may think). The Countess herself gave him a watch and some 'horse furniture' – bridles, saddles, and so forth – which he sold for £20.[21]

The Countess's close association with her footman may seem unusual to us, but was not remarkable in the eighteenth century and earlier – Restoration plays are full of footmen who are the close confidants of their masters or mistresses, often taking an eager and ingenious hand in conceiving and carrying out plans for seductions or financial scams. They were peculiarly useless people – known popularly as 'fart-catchers' for their duty of walking decoratively behind their employers – and since they had no particular duties other than serving at table, cleaning the silver and running errands, they were of all domestic servants those with the most leisure to spare for gossip (an occupation of which Mary Eleanor was particularly fond) and intrigue.

For her part, the Countess seems to have been perfectly honest with Gray, telling him that her marriage was extremely unhappy, that she had been let down by a former lover, and that she had made a vow never again to give her heart to a man. In other words, their affair was to be carnal, only carnal, and possibly brief. Strathmore was more or less seriously ill – his tuberculosis was resisting the curative effects of the waters at Bath; but even if he were to die, she said, there could be no question of marriage – while if he lived they must break off the affair. In the meantime they enjoyed a tactful but full-blooded liaison. There seems to have been a narrow escape when Strathmore suddenly returned to London while Gray was at the house, and only George Walker's quick warning avoided discovery. Gray went off to Bath while Strathmore was at home, promising not to write to Mary Eleanor until she sent a message summoning him back to London.

After a few weeks, Gray could not resist slipping up to town and sending his mistress a note asking permission to see her just for an hour or two. She agreed to meet him, 'accidentally', at a coffee house, but in fact they met very early one morning in St James's Park. This was not an unusual place for an assignation. Charles II had opened the park to

the public, and by the middle of the eighteenth century it had become
the fashionable place to be seen – at least during weekdays; at the
weekends (according to an anonymous writer[22]) it became the haunt of
the hoi polloi – 'well-dressed Gentlewomen and ladies of quality [were]
drove out of the park . . . by Milliners, Mantua-makers . . . Stay-
makers, Sempstresses . . . and butchers' daughters'.

The day on which Mary Eleanor had her assignation was wet, her
shoes and the bottom of her voluminous petticoats got soaked, and on
the way home she slipped on some ice and cut herself. She caught a
fever – whereupon Strathmore hurriedly retreated to the West Country.
Gray, on the contrary, sent a written message to Mary Eleanor every
morning and sat with her every evening while she was ill – and she was
very ill, literally blind with pain in her head. She also suffered from
chilblains, treated no doubt with the universal panacea, a poultice of
mashed turnip.

If Mrs Parish had not been aware of the relationship before, she
certainly was now. Even if the couple avoided direct confrontation with
her, the gossip about town was growing almost daily – George, the
footman, returned to the house again and again with news of more
scandalous (and mostly ridiculous) anecdotes which were circulating.
'We used to laugh at them,' the Countess said.

We can assume that the Earl now knew what was going on though
how and when he first learned of his wife's affair with Gray, we can
only guess. In mid-February 1776, he let it be known that he was
leaving for Lisbon, in an attempt to alleviate his tuberculosis and
prolong his life. It was a last effort: the conventional cures such as
snails or live woodlice boiled in milk, and the elaborate potions of the
doctors (some contained as many as fifteen different ingredients, added
to hot ale) had done no good. He and his wife parted without any
obvious regret on either side. He died at sea, on 7 March.

FOUR

None but Him

Precautions were taken; but an instant's neglect always destroyed them all; indeed, sometimes, even when I thought an accident scarce possible.

Mary Eleanor Bowes

The relationship between the Countess of Strathmore and George Gray was, once it was consummated, an extremely passionate one. With Strathmore on the way to Lisbon, they contrived to meet almost every day – sometimes in St James's Park, sometimes in St Paul's Cathedral or Westminster Abbey; and on days when they could not do so, they exchanged notes at the hands of the footman George Walker. On alternate evenings Gray came surreptitiously to the Countess at eleven o'clock and stayed until four or five in the morning, when he left before the household was roused. They were together only on alternate nights, Mary Eleanor said, because after six hours with Gray she needed a full night's sleep – and also 'that by the intervention of one night, we might meet the next with more pleasure, and have the less chance of being tired of each other'.[1]

Gray seems to have captivated her by sheer animal magnetism. We know so little about him that one can only conjecture; but it is apparently the case that after years of neglect by her husband Mary Eleanor found herself thoroughly beguiled by simple wanton pleasure. We hear nothing of her discussing literature or art with Gray, or of their spending time together at the Royal Academy, at concerts or the theatre. There would have been no reason, certainly after Strathmore's departure, why he should not have played the part of *cicisbeo*, as the young Italian Count had done years before. There might have been some gossip, but it would have been harmless gossip. As it was, although her husband was out of the way, and Mary Eleanor was careless of what society thought of her, the couple was careful not to be discovered. When the Countess found that in order to meet her lover at the agreed time she must leave the opera or the dinner table so early that people were curious, if not

suspicious, she kept her social engagements to evenings when she did
not expect him.

It is nevertheless surprising that the affair did not become public
knowledge. It was almost impossible in the eighteenth century to have an
adulterous affair in your own home; the servants would inevitably know
all about it as soon as it began. They were, after all, ubiquitous: they put
warming-pans in the bed, helped their master or mistress undress at
bedtime, and came into the bedroom first thing in the morning to light
the fire. If an adulterous couple did not lock the bedroom door – and
many bedroom doors simply had no lock – they could easily be caught in
the act when a servant came in about his or her usual business. And if
they did lock the door, or tell the servants not to disturb them unless they
were sent for, these were in themselves suspicious acts.

Servants took the very keenest interest in what went on in their
masters' and mistresses' bedrooms – not necessarily as useful evidence
for blackmail, but just for the fun of it. Jonathan Swift, in his
Directions to Servants, advised a chambermaid to 'Get your favourite
footman to help you in making your lady's bed; and, if you serve a
young couple, the footman and you as you are turning up the
bedclothes, will make the prettiest observations in the world, which,
whispered about, will be very entertaining to the whole family and get
among the neighbourhood.'[2] It was easy to collect material for gossip:
people were extremely careless about what they said or did in front of
their servants. One did not speak to a servant unless one wanted
something, and unless one had a particular need for their services. It
was all too easy for a maid or a manservant simply to become invisible
– to cease to exist as sets of eyes and ears.

In this case, the servants were on the side of the adulterous couple.
There was no doubt plenty of enjoyable gossip below stairs, but though
Mary Eleanor was at the mercy of her maid and her other servants
there is no implication at any time of their threatening to blackmail her.
This suggests what was the truth – that they liked and sympathised with
her. Usually, servants became extremely worried when they discovered
their mistress having an affair under the nose of their master, but in this
case Strathmore as husband was much more often absent than present,
and they certainly knew of his coldness towards his wife – of the fact
that after the conception of the children she had been completely
neglected in the way of any comforting human contact. Moreover, the
Countess was not betraying the Earl with one of his friends – most
servants took an extremely severe view of that. Strathmore, if he had
ever met Gray, certainly did not in any sense know him.

The timing of the lovers' trysts was not the only matter about which Mary Eleanor and Gray were careful. Condoms were easily obtained, usually made of sheep's intestines softened with oil and tied on with a ribbon – Boswell called them 'armour' and Casanova 'English overcoats'. A Mrs Philips supplied them readily to anyone who applied to her – 'ambassadors, foreigners, gentlemen, and captains of ships going abroad'.[3] But although Gray used them ('precautions were taken', as the Countess says), the mutual passion of the couple defeated them more than once 'even when I thought an accident scarce possible'.[4] Mary Eleanor thrice found herself pregnant. She persuaded Gray to acquire a quack medicine to bring on a miscarriage (they had to be careful: abortion was a criminal offence). The potion, which tasted of copper and sounds as though it consisted of some chemical mixture, worked on two occasions; on the third, she relied on swallowing quantities of pepper washed down with brandy; this apparently had the desired effect.

The Countess did not hear of her husband's death until early April 1776. While no doubt he hoped that the milder climate of Portugal might prolong his life, Strathmore must have known that he had not much longer to live. Doctors were still muddling their way towards a cure for tuberculosis, and no intelligent man once assured that he had the disease really expected to recover from it. Just before his death the Earl wrote his wife a letter composed (Jessé Foot says) 'of admonition and forgiveness'.[5]

Admonition outweighs forgiveness, though Strathmore begins by saying that he pardons his wife all her 'liberties and follies (however fatal they may have been to me)', suggesting that 'they were not produce of your own mind, but the suggestions of some vile interested monster'.[6] Who was the monster? Though the Earl may have known of Mary Eleanor's affair with Gray, he would surely have named him had he thought her lover was the sole instigator of her 'liberties and follies'. He may have been thinking of one of the botanical circle, or perhaps one of the Bluestockings. In any case, the follies he referred to were more likely the innocent amusements which had so irritated him – her writing, for instance: he accuses her, entirely unjustly, of an 'extreme rage for literary fame'. He also accuses her – with greater justice – of gossiping: 'I would wish you to avoid all appearance of malice, and entreat you not to be tempted to say an ill-natured thing for the sake of sporting a *bon mot*.' Surely a venial sin, if one of which she was probably guilty. Gossip was virtually an industry in eighteenth-century London – led by that inveterate prattler Horace Walpole.

More seriously, Strathmore begged his widow (for he already thought of her as that) to lay aside the prejudices she had against his family, and above all – and with much greater reason – 'to give up your foolish partiality for your daughters, and that most unnatural prejudice you have against your eldest innocent son. All children should rank equally in a parent's mind, at least until they have forfeited that regard which was due to them from their birth; favour is commonly more hurtful to the child than the contrary, but either without reason is an infallible mark of the badness of the parent's heart.'

Finally, he points out with perfect justification that she is absolutely hopeless where the management of money is concerned, begging her to appoint a trustworthy agent who would advance her a fixed sum each quarter or half-year, as income; this would be fairer to the children, and safer where the running of the estate was concerned. It was a suggestion she would have done well to follow.

The Earl certainly believed he was being honest when he wrote that 'no one ever studied with more attention to promote the happiness of another than I have constantly done to promote yours'. But the statement only underlines the fact that he had absolutely no understanding of his wife's nature. He may well have believed that her attempts at writing were vain, but there is no evidence that she 'raged' for literary fame; it seems more likely that he was simply jealous of her attachment to a group of literary and artistic women for which he and most of his friends had nothing but contempt. He had done his best to destroy her interest in botany, perhaps for the same reason – women had no right to be interested in such things. The suggestion that she was in any way responsible for his death betrays just that incipient hysteria which was one of the effects of tuberculosis (later it was to show itself in the letters of the dying Keats).

Any idea that he had been more than commonly attentive to her is simply ludicrous. If she neglected him – and certainly she could have shown more sympathy with his illness – it was because no real love had ever existed between them. He had treated her with coldness and contempt, and if she made no effort to seduce him into a loving relationship, it was because their natures were irreconcilable.

We do not know how she took the letter. Though their relationship had for years been unloving, we can guess that it hurt and depressed her; it must certainly have confirmed what she had known since before her wedding day – that she had been extremely unwise ever to marry the man. Well, now she was free of him – and free to marry Gray, if that is what she wanted to do. We can assume that it was what *he* wanted her to do. It has always been supposed, certainly by Jessé Foot, and by the Countess's only subsequent biographer, Ralph Arnold, that he was after her money; and while he was certainly an ardent lover, it was no doubt common knowledge that Strathmore was seriously ill and unlikely to recover – so no one can refute the claim that he had her money in mind. But whatever his motives, she was besotted with him – and there was an additional reason why she should think of marriage. In December 1776 she once more found herself pregnant by her lover. This time, she decided to keep the child.

It was probably just after Strathmore's death that Mary Eleanor had arranged to meet Gray at St Paul's Cathedral and there promised to 'marry none but him',[7] accepting from him a ring which she placed on her finger. Now they began to make plans for a wedding in early April 1777, four months before her baby was due. She wanted to keep the situation secret until the very last minute, perhaps even to be married abroad. Privately, she planned to spend three or four years out of the country, travelling in France, Italy, Hungary and perhaps Spain and Portugal, though she did not tell Gray this.

Meanwhile, there was trouble with Mrs Parish, who had been making herself unpleasant for some time. It seems likely that she learned of the affair with Gray almost as soon as it started, and disapproved of it. We cannot know why: she may have been a thoroughly moral character (though her subsequent actions suggest otherwise). She may simply have been inherently ill-natured. Now, after Strathmore's death, she perhaps saw her way to a fortune, and made obscure threats which threw the widow into such fear that she handed over no less a sum than £2,000 – the equivalent of over £140,000 – to her former governess.

In her *Confessions* the Countess writes that the money was a present, 'as [Mrs Parish] had lived with, and partly educated me so many years. . . . This, I thought, would be sufficient to make her easy in circumstances.' But it cannot have been only that, for she also claims that Mrs Parish's conduct had been 'the most vile, ungrateful, and pernicious, that ever was heard of'.[8] Moreover, the lengths to which she went to raise the money indicate something much more dangerous to her than Mrs Parish threatening to tell Mrs Bowes or Strathmore's family about the affair with Gray. Though her income was probably about £20,000 a year (a £¼ million in modern terms), Mary Eleanor had at that moment little ready cash – her husband's recent death had put her financial affairs in temporary disarray. She tried to persuade several friends and acquaintances to lend her the money, and in desperation even sent the footman, George, to a number of Jewish money-lenders – but their terms were so steep that she was forced to reject them. How she eventually raised the sum is obscure.

Why the hysteria? It would have been embarrassing had her husband's family learned of the affair with Gray – even of her pregnancy – but no more than embarrassing. Fortunately neither came up to London on a regular basis, and town gossip was infrequently spread to the country; so far the news had apparently not reached them. There would certainly have been some mortification had Mrs Parish gone about the town confirming and elaborating on the affair – but Mary Eleanor was not especially sensitive to public opinion, and the moral tone of the age was not such that she need have feared ostracism. It is possible that Mrs Parish knew about the abortions, and threatened to denounce the Countess; but she would have had no proof, and the threat does not seem likely to have provoked such anxiety. The episode remains a mystery. However, Mary Eleanor did decide that it was time to tell her mother about Gray, and in the summer went down to St Paul's Waldenbury expressly to do so.

While she was away, Mrs Parish took her generous present and left the house in Grosvenor Square – only to be replaced by her sister, Eliza Planta. Eliza's little circle of confidants had by now become the Countess's closest friends, and the Revd Henry Stephens a particular one. A widower, he was known to Dr Solander and Joseph Planta, and was an admirer of Eliza Planta. When he was introduced to Mary Eleanor she decided that he would make a good tutor for the children. Her admiration for him seems not to have diminished when he almost immediately asked her for help in paying various debts which amounted to over £7,000. 'I told him,' she said with the usual mixture of folly and generosity, 'that if he made Mrs Stephens a good husband, and behaved in the manner I had no doubt he would, I would take care he should have no trouble from his debts.'[9] And she did. Stephens introduced her to his brother George, who took to her, and took some liberties *with* her – he certainly kissed her from time to time with his arm about her waist, and called her his 'wife'. But she was in general free with her kisses – on one occasion a Mr Lee was showing her some plants at a garden in Hammersmith, and said he would give her one she particularly admired if she would allow him 'the honour to salute a Countess'. She took the plant home for her collection.

Stephens's change of fortune – his acquisition of the Countess as a patron – persuaded him to make a formal offer for Eliza's hand. Mrs Parish and Joseph Planta disapproved. Henry Stephens had no money and was in debt; no match for any young woman. Eliza confided their difficulties to Mary Eleanor, and the opportunity of irritating Mrs Parish may have played its part in persuading her to give the engaged couple the money to elope, and marry in Scotland in or about August 1776.[10] This created considerable ill-feeling, reported to her by the footman George, and thoroughly enjoyed, at a safe distance, by the Countess.

We are not told how her mother reacted to the announcement of Mary Eleanor's engagement to Gray. But by the time she had revealed it, she was already thinking of reneging on her promise, for by then she had met Lieutenant Andrew Robinson Stoney.

FIVE

An Innocent Frolic

*Upon Thursday next, at one o'clock, I shall be in the garden at St
Paul's Walden. There is a leaden statue, or there was formerly, and
near that spot . . . I shall wait.*

Andrew Robinson Stoney, Jessé Foot, *Lives*

In 1776 Andrew Robinson Stoney, a lieutenant of the 30th Regiment
of Foot stationed at Newcastle-upon-Tyne, scraped acquaintance with
a Miss Hannah Newton, daughter of William Newton of Burnopfield,
County Durham, some 14 miles southwest of Newcastle. Like the Bowes
family William Newton had made his money in the coal trade. Miss
Newton was locally believed to have £20,000 in her own right,[1] and
possessed a house and estate which her father had bought for her twenty
years earlier at Cold Pike Hill – an address often referred to popularly as
Coal Pig Hill – near Lanchester about 7 miles south of Burnopfield.

Jessé Foot reports one of Stoney's two sisters as saying that he was
born in 1745, which would have made him twenty when as a younger
son he was listed as an Ensign in the 4th (King's Own) Regiment of
Foot.[2] The cost of his commission was no more than the cost of
apprenticing your son to some respectable trade or other – though as
far as the ensign himself was concerned, there was little prospect of him
making his fortune. He would receive in pay no more than £100 a year,
while it would cost him certainly half of that sum to live even modestly.
Four years later Stoney was still an ensign, though in 1770 we find him
promoted lieutenant in the same regiment. Six years later, he was still a
lieutenant, now attached to the 30th Regiment of Foot, and on half-pay
(though he always liked, in later life, to be described as 'Captain'
Stoney, there is no evidence that he ever reached that rank). The
position of the regiment at that time is uncertain: it has been claimed
that it was disbanded in 1763.[3] This does not appear to have been the
case, though it was not uncommon for regiments to be disbanded, then
reformed later when some colonial war broke out.[4]

Foot says that the family was 'in possession of wealth, respectability
and honourable connexion', but that he 'would not wish to stain their

fair fame by the insertion of their names in this disgraceful relation of one so closely allowed by blood, but so estranged by nature'. The novelist William Makepeace Thackeray perhaps gives us some more clues about the status of Stoney's family. He was told Stoney's story by his friend John Bowes, the Countess's grandson, with whom he stayed at Streatlam in the summer of 1841 – only thirty-one years after Stoney's death. Thackeray immediately saw its fictional possibilities, and the result was his first substantial novel, *Barry Lyndon*, whose eponymous hero is clearly based on Stoney.[5]

It would be as silly as it would be mistaken to assume that the family history Thackeray gives to his hero is necessarily a close approximation of Stoney's, but it does reflect what we know of the latter's claims: that his family was one of Ireland's noblest, that his father was trained as a lawyer, practised in Dublin, kept race-horses and hunted with the Kildare and Wicklow hunts. We also know that even if his family was noble and possibly wealthy, Stoney had no personal fortune, so like many younger sons he went into the army with the help of a relative who was a general officer.

Stoney was not much of a catch, but Hannah Newton may have been one of those girls who – like Lydia Bennet in *Pride and Prejudice* – was easily captivated by a man in uniform. Young men who had nothing to do with the services often dressed in quasi-military attire simply to attract the girls, and officers and men alike were considered romantic and energetic lovers. Stoney was certainly that, and appears to have had no difficulty in charming Miss Newton with his ready smile, his soft Irish accent, sandy hair, bright dark eyes and reasonably tall, attractive figure clad in regimentals. He also clearly had strong animal magnetism – sometimes characteristic of men who are not particularly handsome: Jessé Foot reports that 'there was something uncommon in the connexion of his nose with his upper lip; he never could talk without the nose which was long and curved downwards, being also moved ridiculously with the upper lip. This I have often laughed heartily at . . .'.[6] The two portraits we have of him tend to confirm Foot's opinion.[7] He also suggests that Stoney lisped, and clearly showed a lack of education. He admits, however, that he had 'a ready wit', and there is no doubt that he was able to make himself agreeable to the ladies. He made himself sufficiently agreeable to Hannah to persuade her to accept his proposal of marriage.

Hannah was good-natured, dumpy and plain, and Stoney did not in the least care for her. It was soon common knowledge in the neighbourhood that he treated her badly. As an amateur but knowing poet put it,

Possess'd of her person, her portion and purse,
He kick'd her, he beat her, he stripped her, nay, worse; –
A further relation, I now must forbear,
To recount all his tricks, would offend the chaste ear.[8]

One of Hannah's friends told Foot that on one occasion Stoney shut his wife in a small closet for three days, either naked or dressed in a flimsy chemise, feeding her only on one egg a day; and it was commonly believed that at least once he threw her bodily down a flight of stairs. Perhaps unsurprisingly, she bore him no live children (though at least one was born dead) and herself did not live long. She had been wise enough before her marriage to put £5,000 in trust for any children they might have had – but there were none, and just before she died early in 1775 she altered her will – perhaps under pressure? – leaving Stoney her entire estate.

The widower, now a reasonably wealthy man, took himself off to London (though he was also often seen at Bath and other watering-places). He began to appear at the coffee houses of the town. Most men used these as convenient places to meet sympathetic friends – it was often easier to find a man at his favourite coffee-house than at his home. Stoney was most often to be found at the Cocoa-Tree, at the corner of Pall Mall, much frequented by Tory and Jacobite politicians. He was also regularly to be seen at cock-fights and race-courses, gaming and gambling clubs. He specially loved the latter, and supported them enthusiastically. He was as profligate a gambler as Strathmore, if not more so, and found London in particular a great place for disposing of his late wife's fortune in that way. He lost money incautiously and without regret, and it seems soon to have been generally accepted that, having once successfully married for money, he was on the lookout for another rich victim. In the words of our poet:

By gaming and lewdness so much he had wasted,
His purse and his credit being almost exhausted,
His wants became great, and his stock being small,
Without a recruit he surely must fall.
His fortune once more he determined to try,
On no less than a Countess he fixed his eye.[9]

Stoney did his research. He soon knew of her pregnancy, and that her marriage was likely to take place within the next month or so. It would have seemed to most men that despite the appeal of her riches, it would be vain to hope to capture the pregnant fiancée of another man. Stoney was made of sterner stuff. He soon uncovered a number of facts which seemed to him to offer the possibility of success.

First, there were the relatives of the late Earl. Their distress at Strathmore's death was equalled by their fury that his rich wife, whom none of them liked, was now in possession not only of her title but of the property he had brought to the marriage. They were no less horrified to discover that at the time of her husband's death, she was already pregnant by a lover, and planning a second marriage. How he could use their repugnance, and the Countess's equal dislike of them, to his own advantage may not immediately have occurred to Stoney, but there were obviously possibilities.

Then, there was the group of botanists and others who gravitated around her. It did not take him long to discover that Mrs Parish and her brother Joseph Planta had no love for the Countess. That might be useful in some way, while a little conversation with Mr and Mrs Stephens made it clear that the fact that they remained more or less faithful to her (doubtless because she was a ready and generous source of income) might also be used to his advantage. He certainly immediately saw that the Revd Stephens was sufficiently malleable to be of use to him.

It was probably Mrs Parish who revealed to Stoney the fact that Mary Eleanor was superstitious. She had had her fortune read by gypsies at St Paul's Waldenbury, and had sought out other fortune-tellers since. Mrs Parish herself had accompanied her to a 'conjurer' on Ludgate Hill and to a second in Crown Court; Mr Stephens and others had gone with her when she visited Crown Court a second time.

It was a superstitious age, and there were plenty of 'conjurers' about – the term embraced all sorts of fortune-tellers, from fraudulent astrologers and mediums to palmists, psychics, numerologists and card readers. Now, Eliza Stephens told her of yet another 'conjurer' it might be interesting to visit – she proposed an expedition to Pear Street,[10] where a much-vaunted interpreter of the future was holding court. Mary Eleanor was easily persuaded, and after breakfasting with Matra, Eliza and her husband, and another man called Pennick (of whom we know nothing), she walked, attended by the ubiquitous footman George, through the dirty, wet streets to the Old Bailey, meeting Magra (by appointment?) on the way. There, Mary Eleanor writes,

we met a little boy, who came up to us and asked if we wanted the gentleman who so many people came after, and that he would conduct us to him. We said yes, and he carried us through blind alleys to Pear-street: Mrs Stephens told me afterwards it was not the man she had been to before.

It was between 11 and 12, as near as I can recollect, when we got to Pear-street, and there were such a number of people in the room we waited in, to whom the Conjurer was first engaged, and they took so long a time to have their fortunes told, that it was almost 6 o'clock before they began with us.[11]

It was not a pleasant wait, in a dirty, ice-cold room furnished only with two or three broken chairs and an old wooden trunk. They managed to find a couple of logs of green wood and light a fire in the grate, which gave out a great deal of smoke and very little heat. Mr Pennick and Mary Eleanor attempted to amuse the party by making up verses, which they wrote on the wall:

> Thro' Dirty-street we bent our way
> To have our fortunes told today . . .

but no one was particularly diverted. They talked to the other waiting clients; one woman told the Countess her life story, impressing on her how much more satisfactory it would have been had she taken notice of the conjurer's advice – she now consulted him two or three times a year. Mary Eleanor gave her the impression that she herself was a grocer's widow with ten children – but such nonsense did not amuse her for long. By the time they were summoned to the man of visions, they were irritated enough to have been very short with him had he not come up to expectations – apart from anything else, they had eaten nothing since breakfast. What they got from the conjurer may have been inanity, but appears to have impressed them for 'Capt. Magra and self were weak enough to go down twice to the cellar or room below stairs'. Magra was particularly persuaded of the man's accuracy – or so he said.

When they got home the party sat up until well after midnight. Eliza played the piano and sang, and they all talked and and joked about what the conjurer had said. The Countess does not tell us what this was, but we might suspect that it was something in favour of 'Captain' Stoney, and that the visit had probably been organised on his behalf ('conjurers' were often employed to lead their clients in the way in which other clients wished them to go). She says in her *Confessions* that a while before the consultation she had spent an evening during which George Stephens had talked about nothing but the Irish adventurer, and it may well be that Stoney, having ingratiated himself with Stephens and perhaps others, was beginning his campaign by bribing the 'conjurer' – perhaps through Stephens – to mention a lover waiting in the wings; maybe even a handsome, Irish lover.

Stoney's next move was to persuade Mary Eleanor that Gray – whom she was still planning to marry – had been in communication with the late Earl's family and made himself acceptable to them. He drafted, and got someone to copy, a letter addressed to himself and apparently written by an unknown woman living in Durham (it bore the Durham post-mark). Stoney had been courting her, the letter inferred, but the writer now believed him to be in love with the Countess of Strathmore. Much space was given over to vituperation, and then at the end the writer confessed that she was relieved to hear that the Countess was to marry Mr Gray, and would then be received into the bosom of the Strathmore family, leaving Stoney free for the writer. The letter was unlikely in the extreme, and it is a mystery how Mary Eleanor came to believe any part of it. Perhaps she did not, but by this time Stoney had managed to get himself introduced to her, and was beginning to exert his powerful natural charm, which seems to have been irresistible when he chose to exercise it.

Becoming acquainted with the Countess was not difficult. Stoney was apparently respectable, and though he was known as a gambler, that was no bar to his being received in polite society – had it been so it would have been impossible for a lady to receive half the aristocracy of the country. He moved in the best circles, was seen in the best places and, once they had met, he could deploy his Irish charm. His motives were quite clear – they were financial. But he also wanted to *be* somebody. In *Barry Lyndon* Thackeray has his hero ask himself, 'Why should I not win her, and, with her, the means of making in the world that figure which my genius and inclination desired? I felt I was equal in blood and breeding to any Lyndon in Christendom, and determined to bend this haughty lady. When I determine, I look upon the thing as done.'[12]

At first Mary Eleanor was suspicious of Stoney's intentions, but though she had heard stories of his cruelty to his late wife, she was persuaded to dismiss them as malicious tattle. The advocacy of the Stephenses and perhaps the words of the conjurer had their effect. Soon, she had invited the Irishman to her house and, once his foot was inside the door, he had no difficulty in making himself a regular visitor. By the time the Countess went down to St Paul's Waldenbury in December to visit her mother – who still believed that within a few weeks her daughter would be married to Gray – they were on more

than friendly terms, and she was already flirting with him. He wrote her
a letter – clearly in reply to one from her. 'Woman's a riddle,' he begins;
'I never felt the proverb more than upon the honour of receiving your
ladyship's letter.' He begins by praising Eliza, harping on the perfection
of her marriage, then turns to marriage in general.

> A free choice is happiness; and bliss is the off-spring of the mind. Those
> only possess joy who think they have it; and it signifies little whether
> we are happy by the forms our connections[13] would prescribe to us or
> not. I believe it will not be denied, that many are miserable, under the
> opinion of the world, of their being very much the contrary. You tell
> me, that your good mother (Heaven bless her) is well employed for an
> old lady; but by the soul of Angelica[14] you vow (and I know she was
> dear to you) that her pursuits do not at this time engage your attention.
> Now by the living sick Jacintha,[15] by every thing I have to hope, I
> swear, that I am highly interested in your present thoughts; and were I
> Proteus,[16] I would instantly transform myself, to be happy that I was
> stroked and caress'd, like them, by you; and, discovering the secret of
> your mind, I might experience what I hope Eliza will never be a
> stranger to, or be placed beyond the reach of further hope. I am all
> impatience to see your Ladyship; I really cannot wait till Saturday; I
> must have five minutes chat with you before that time. You will think
> me whimsical; but upon Thursday next, at one o'clock, I shall be in the
> garden at St Paul's Walden. There is a leaden statue, or there was
> formerly, and near that spot (for it lives in my remembrance) I shall
> wait; and can I presume that you will condescend to know the place?
> Eliza shall be our excuse for this innocent frolic; and the civilities shall
> never be erased from the remembrance of your faithful, &c.[17]

Obviously the couple were on more familiar terms than might have
been expected – here is Stoney prompting Mary Eleanor to think of
herself as stroking him as she might stroke a beloved and familiar cat.
It is just the kind of sensual, teasing image which appealed to her.
The letter – and of course he may have written others – is much more
to her taste than anything which might have been written to her
by Strathmore, even when he was courting her – or indeed by the
passionate but plain-speaking and rather dull Mr Gray, of whom, from
now on, we hear virtually nothing. Mary Eleanor was delighted by her
new lover, and Stoney knew his victim well. As Thackeray puts it in
Barry Lyndon, 'No-one piqued herself more upon her principles, or
allowed love to be made to her more profusely.'[18]

How did Stoney know anything about the garden at St Paul's Waldenbury? Perhaps he had gone down there to reconnoitre – it was a private house, but it was often possible to gain entry on the pretext of wishing to see a house and garden – in *Pride and Prejudice*, Mr and Mrs Gardiner and Elizabeth Bennet visited Pemberley, Mr Darcy's house, while he was absent.[19] Stoney clearly *did* know the house, to the extent of suggesting a precise meeting-place. And was there a tryst in the garden? If so, it must have been more like a scene from a Russian novel than a French romance, for it was almost Christmas 1776, and a remarkably cold winter; but the thought of the Countess in heavy furs and her lover perhaps in a romantic black cloak is not unattractive, and we can forgive Mary Eleanor, who had had little enough romance in her life, for finding it charming. Perhaps the meeting was continued indoors. In her *Confessions* she admits to sleeping with Stoney before their marriage,[20] and it would not perhaps have been surprising had the event taken place after such an assignation, even with her mother in the house.

To drive home the feeling that he was a far better proposition than Gray as a prospective husband (and the Countess had had enough both of cool respect in a marriage and of sexual passion without wit or charm, so the fascinating Irishman had an advantage from the start) Stoney shortly afterwards produced another forged letter from the lady in Durham, and this time had it directed to Mary Eleanor herself. To arouse her jealousy, the writer started by attacking Stoney himself:

The sacrifice I have made to this abominable man – the disobedience I have incurred from the most indulgent parents – and the sport of my friends, to whom I have imparted my confidential prospects, drive me to despair. Besides, I love him; and without him, though I am apprised of his faithless nature, yet I am determined, at the risk of my fortune, my character, my future comfort of life, and all that is dear to love and passion, to throw myself into his arms. And must you, who possess all the wealth of the North, think that you have the right of thus defrauding an honest heart, too fatally wounded and devoted, because, not from your personal charms or intrinsic worth as one of our unhappy sex, you thus lay claim to my prize, but merely because you possess more acres, and that you are a Countess. I will not, I cannot sit silently down in submission to this usurpation; I will haunt you night and day 'till I have procured a restoration of that peace of mind, so long torn, distracted and broken down with wrongs, and entirely by you, by this foul and dear seducer.

Why don't you abide by your first love as I do? Why should Mr Gray be abandoned by you for the sake of a man who stands before you a perjured lover? Why am I to be the sacrifice to your almighty influence, and thus plunged into despair and oblivion, for no end but to gratify the wantonness of your caprice? And that you, Madam, may have the pride and exultation of despoiling and erecting upon my despair your felicity? . . .

Then he attempted further to alienate Mary Eleanor from Gray by suggesting once more that the latter had formed an alliance with the Strathmore family:

Cultivate Mr Gray's affections, because your late Lord's friends and relations will accept of him as your husband, but not of Captain S——. It is impossible that Mr Gray should keep these secrets from you. Mr Gray has had the address (which my simple and easy fool never could obtain) of first establishing his pretensions to you, upon the confidence and zeal of your late Lord's relations and friends. . . . It is with their warm approbation that he has wisely made his way to your heart. Plunge not, therefore, an artless, hopeless, desponding and forsaken maiden as I am into destruction and utter ruin, but restore some ray of comfort to the unfortunate

S.[21]

Nothing could have been calculated to irritate Mary Eleanor more than the suggestion that Gray was hand-in-glove with the Strathmore family. By now, it may well have been true. It is very likely that Gray had been in touch with Strathmore's brother, Thomas Lyon, and his sister Lady Anne Simpson – and we know that he had visited Mrs Bowes. It was beginning to look to the Countess as though her fiancé was being rather too careful about the minutiae of the marriage arrangements. She did not want another carefully arranged liaison. She wanted a passionate lover, and if Gray's passion was now to be subject to the consideration of pounds, shillings and marriage arrangements, the time had certainly come for a change.

SIX

The Injured Bridegroom

I married him from motives of gratitude and compassion . . .
without reflection, and without the advice and knowledge of any
of my friends.
Mary Eleanor Bowes, *Proceedings in the Court of Chancery*,
19 June 1788

Although by the beginning of 1777 Stoney had seduced the
Countess, and she was beginning to prefer the prospect of a
liaison with him to marriage with George Gray, there was still some
way to go. Stoney was not going to propose marriage to her until he
was very much more strongly convinced that she would accept him. To
this end, he now decided to make use of the press.

Attacks on Lady Strathmore began to appear regularly in the
newspapers, and particularly in the *Morning Post*, a paper which had been
founded in 1773 by the Revd Sir Henry Bate. Bate was a curious figure – a
true member of the quite substantial line of eighteenth-century eccentric
English parsons. In his time he was an editor, courtier, magistrate and
duellist. Born in Chelmsford in 1726, he had inherited the nearby rectory
of North Fambridge from his father, but was ill content to live on the
small income the living provided, and decided to enter the literary world.
He began contributing squibs and short essays to the existing newspapers,
and then on 2 November 1773 published, as editor and part-sponsor, the
first edition of the *Morning Post*. When, four years later, Stoney began to
send the newspaper articles attacking the Countess of Strathmore, Bate
was quite happy to publish them – then, as now, gossip about aristocratic
or well-known individuals was staple fodder for the columns of the press.

It is the general view of everyone who has considered Stoney and his
career that he was the author not only of the letters attacking Mary
Eleanor, but also author or at least instigator of others defending her.
Some years later, a prosecutor in one of the court cases involving Stoney
and his wife accused him of just that, and he did not deny it. He had
invented the fiction of an alleged mistress in Dudley; now he added
miscellaneous fictional contributions to the *Morning Post*.

Signed 'Hamlet' (the allusion to the faithless Queen Gertrude of the play was lost on no one) a letter published on 3 January spoke of 'a character, whose leading features are a proper object for the scorn and derision of the public', and went on to suggest that 'It would have been better for the house of S——, had the noble dame procured only the slight satirical ill will of any of the family, that would have just kept a few gossips awake at a tea-table, and have slept at the first *sans prendre*.'

The writer goes on to remember the late Lord Strathmore as 'a handsome, virtuous youth, who brought her honour, and sought her happiness; who knew her, when her fondness for him was fulsome to excess; who knew her, when sickness laid his heavy hand upon him, and can bear witness to her cold indifference to the letters that passed between them, where all was ceremony, and where there was not enough of prudence in her to supply the want'.

But, he concludes, she was now spending her time parading herself in the Mall in the company of 'the hymenial throng', when her time would be better spent 'perusing the letters she received from her fond and doting noble lord . . . or in visiting her eldest son, whom she has forsaken'.[1]

Two days later, 'Monitus' replied, in a long letter whose circumlocutions are extreme, but which is passionate in its defence of the Countess, concerned by 'a long chain of falsehoods propagated daily, with no other interest than to cause a general conflagration, and forcibly to wrest her from the good opinion of those that were neither acquainted with her benevolent, nor misguided translations; but who are now led to give credit to gossip-hatched aspersions of those draining wasps, who long extracted the substance of this flower, which they had found to be pure, as well as it was rich!'

The anonymous contributor goes on to summarise the blameless life of a rich, virtuous, innocent girl, 'untutored in those arts and deceptions so familiar to courts', 'the darling and hope of a fond parent', who had married a husband who had cause to be proud of her: 'Happy must that man have been, when blessed with a woman whose purity of mind led her to those acts of true benevolence and charity, which thousands of the poor can testify.'[2] Those who suggested that there was coolness between husband and wife were liars, to which her 'agonizing and heart-felt sorrow' at the death of her husband had testified.

Curiously, Jessé Foot claims to have been shown a manuscript of the first of these letters – shown it, he claims, by a friend, a Mr Peter Nichol, a former acquaintance of the Countess, who had ceased to call on her because he disapproved of the goings-on in Grosvenor Square. But Foot makes no comment on it – whether it was in Stoney's writing or that of Joseph Planta, who has been suggested as helping the suitor in his campaign.[3] A few more letters found their way into the newspaper, and Lady Strathmore found herself the focus of perhaps more public attention than even she, who enjoyed attention, relished. She seems to have ridden the storm, however, with considerable equanimity, and collected newspaper cuttings both of attack and defence with equal enthusiasm, pasting them into a scrapbook.

It is a little difficult to understand just what Stoney thought he had to gain by arranging the publication of these letters, if indeed he did so – unless he let her know in some way that he was 'Monitus'. Even so, the exchange was surely not one likely to give him any real advantage over Gray. The whole episode is a curious one.

Though Mary Eleanor was by now Stoney's lover, she does not appear to have broken off her engagement to Gray, who may well have had no idea of his rival's existence, or at least of his connection with the Countess. When she asked him to intervene with the editor of the *Morning Post* and persuade him to bring the correspondence about her to an end, Gray demurred. The mere threat of a duel, she suggested, might do the trick. It was not uncommon, in the early days of newspapers, for journalists and editors to be 'called out' – a duel was cheaper than a libel suit, and speedily resolved a situation. But for whatever reason, Gray declined to pursue the matter. This did not improve their relationship, and Mary Eleanor declared to Eliza Planta that the man who challenged the Revd Sir Henry Bate would have her heart and hand. Eliza was not slow to pass the word to Stoney, who immediately issued a challenge via her botanical friend James Matra. Bates, 'The Fighting Parson', as he was called – he had already fought several duels – refused to make any apology. A pugilist as well as a swordsman, he was also an excellent shot and perfectly capable of defending himself. Stoney sent him a note informing him that he intended 'to give you every provocation till I can bring you to a proper sense of your conduct'.[4] The choice was between swords and pistols. The duellists appeared to have decided on both.

On 13 January 1777 at about six in the evening a Mr J. Hull, sitting reading in a room of the Adelphi Tavern in the Strand, heard two pistol shots in the room below, closely followed by the unmistakable sound of swords clashing. He ran downstairs, and helped by two waiters burst into the room from which the noise had come. The room was in darkness – the candles were all out – but by the light from the door Hull could see that Stoney was still wielding his sword. He bravely intervened between Stoney and Sir Henry, who seemed to be hurt.

'I prevailed upon Captain Stoney to yield me up his sword,' he recalled later, 'and as he at that time seemed to be very weak, I apprehended he was hurt, and upon my examining him I found he was much wounded; I think there were three wounds on his right breast, and one upon his sword arm.'[5]

Hull sent for a surgeon, an acquaintance – Dr Jessé Foot.[6] The latter takes up the story. In a room at the Adelphi he found Sir Henry Bate, whom he knew, and another man whom he did not, but who introduced himself as Captain Stoney.

> Bowes was sitting on a chair with his collar unbuttoned, throwing himself back, and was assisted by smelling bottles, and wine and water.[7] He looked very pale, and I thought ready to faint. He attracted my attention most; and after speaking to his opponent, and enquiring from himself the nature of his wound, he recommended me to look to Bowes, as his own was not of this serious importance. This gallant conduct sent me to Bowes; and upon examination I saw the wound on his right breast, from whence the blood was then trickling; upon a closer inspection, I saw two wounds on the substance of the right breast, about four inches distance from each other, in an oblique line with each other . . . there was another wound, but not so important.[8]

Bate had been wounded painfully but not dangerously, in the right thigh.

Much mystery surrounds this affair. It came to be generally believed that the duel had been contrived by Bowes as part of his plan to win the Countess's hand. Some years later there were attempts by witnesses in a trial in May 1788 to suggest that the duel had never taken place.[9] Many of the statements made in that trial are at variance with Foot's report. Thomas Mahon, who was Bowes's valet in 1777, stated that he had been sent to Wagden's, the gunsmith in the Haymarket, to buy pistols, and that he had seen Bowes – or Stoney, as he still was at that time – sitting in Osborne's Hotel with Parson Bate, William Davies, Dr John Scott, and a Captain Donnellan, who was despatched to the Haymarket to fetch Mr Matrow, who was to be Stoney's second. Can this have been a mis-hearing and misprint for Matra, the Countess's friend? If so, it would appear that Stoney had infiltrated the Countess's circle of 'friends' more thoroughly than has previously been thought.

When Matrow or Matra returned, Mahon told the court, he found Stoney fainted away, and Dr Scott bleeding him. He saw no blood anywhere but that which the doctor had drawn from Stoney's arm, and thought Stoney had fainted as a result of being bled. When Dr Hawkins attended Stoney later, at his rooms in St James's Street, he simply took his pulse and went away. Mahon saw two or three small holes in Stoney's waistcoat, but no holes in his shirt, and certainly no sign of blood on it. He was sure of this, because it was actually his, the valet's, shirt, which his master had put on by mistake. Bate, as far as he could tell, was not wounded, and though his breeches were torn at the thigh, again there was no sign of blood.

If we are to believe this, it sounds conclusive; the judge before whom the evidence was given certainly thought so. Yet in his book, published thirty-three years later and after Bowes's death, Foot angrily asserts the truth of his account, and a Dr Scott and he were signatories of a statement published in the *Gazetteer* describing the wounds suffered by the combatants, and stating that they had 'every reason to believe that the *rencontre* must have determined fatally, had not the interposition of the gentleman who broke into the room put an end to it'.[10]

Bate was so experienced a duellist, and Stoney so inexperienced in anything of the sort, that it would be surprising had the Irishman proposed a duel in the first place. He was not known for his courage or swordsmanship. That said, it is startling that he was only slightly wounded, and that he had managed to wound the parson at all. And what of Foot finding the two duelling with swords in a darkened room? How had the candles been extinguished? Possibly on purpose, to explain why the more experienced duellist had not run his opponent through? There were rumours at the time that Bate had accepted a bribe of £200 to accept the challenge but not to pursue it to the extent of inflicting serious injury. That may have been the case – the newspaper was in some financial difficulty, and the Fighting Parson, while jealous of his honour, may not have been averse to making a tidy sum by a little subterfuge.

Stoney must have been aware of the likely effect upon Lady Strathmore of the news of the duel – and he made sure that it was widely spread. His pursuit of her is a curious mixture of clumsiness and cleverness. The exchange of letters in the *Morning Post* may have done his cause little good, but a woman who found that she had been the subject of a duel in which a lover had been wounded in an encounter with a well-known, dangerous opponent might well be impressed – and she was. She hastened to call on Stoney to enquire after his health – but Gray was even quicker, appearing early on the morning after the duel to shake his rival warmly by the hand and thank him for his defence of the lady. Mary Eleanor was even warmer in her thanks than her fiancé.

She begged from Stoney the sword which had wounded her enemy, took it home and hung it over her bed.

Three days after the duel, on the evening of 16 January, she came to see him again. He seemed, unaccountably, to have lost ground since her last visit, and was visibly weak, his voice low; when he moved, he winced as though in considerable pain. He endeavoured bravely to keep the truth from her, but at last admitted that he believed he was on his death-bed, and could not expect to live more than another twenty-four hours. Was it possible she might consider. . . . If she would only marry him, he would die happy.

What woman could have resisted? Of course she would marry him! She may have done more than promise, for when the faithful George Walker was sent to Stoney the following morning to enquire after his progress, the invalid sent his compliments to the lady with the message that 'the plaster she had given him last night had quite cured him'.[11]

Marry him she did, 'from motives of gratitude and compassion . . . without reflection, and without the advice and knowledge of any of her friends'.[12] Four days after the duel, Stoney was carried on a stretcher from his lodgings in St James's Street to the altar of St James's Piccadilly, where the Revd Edward Gardiner married him to the Countess of Strathmore. And so

> to the altar of Hymen they went
> Which deed she has often had cause to repent.[13]

The groom was supported by Walker, and twice almost fainted during the ceremony. After it, he professed that his injuries would not allow him to consummate the marriage, and while Mary Eleanor returned to the house in Grosvenor Square, he went back to his rooms, no doubt pleased with himself.

He would have been less content had he known of a meeting which the Countess had had with her solicitor eight days before the ceremony.

SEVEN

The Way to Wealth

Having taken such precautions on my children's account . . . with a man who I knew I could trust, I ought not to be less cautious with one whom I could not be so strongly assured of.

Mary Eleanor Bowes, *Confessions*

Andrew Robinson Stoney was now, perforce – but proudly – Andrew Robinson Stoney Bowes, for as a condition of the marriage he, like the Earl before him, took his wife's maiden name as his own surname. Mary Eleanor of course retained her title – she was still the Countess, Lady Strathmore. News of the marriage was put about enthusiastically by the gossips of the town, and not only friends but would-be mendicants walked or rode through the brisk cold mornings to Stoney Bowes's St James's Street rooms to leave their cards, pay their respects, and perhaps obliquely congratulate him on his acquisition of enormous wealth.

Bowes celebrated his marriage by giving a formal reception at his rooms, lying dressed in full uniform on a chaise longue and bearing the pain of his injuries with admirable fortitude. No fewer than three generals were among those invited to the party – Generals Robinson and Armstrong, both distant relatives, and a General Lambton, related by marriage to the bride's former husband. In his jubilation the groom nevertheless set time aside to write to his wife's mother, down at St Paul's Waldenbury, assuring her that any uneasiness she might feel at the news of her daughter's sudden marriage would be unwarranted. He had, alas, found it impossible to call upon her and obtain her approval of the wedding (nothing would have contributed more to his present happiness, he said), but he absolutely promised to dedicate the rest of his life to the honour and interest of her daughter and her family. 'My grateful heart,' he concluded, 'will make me her faithful companion, and with unremitting attention I will consult her peace of mind, and the advantage of the children.' He saw before him 'the pleasing prospect of domestic happiness', would be 'happy to regulate [his] conduct so as to merit [her] approbation', and begged permission to subscribe himself her affectionate, humble servant.[1]

His letter was only a surprise to Mrs Bowes in the degree of its impertinence, for she had already received news of the wedding from Eliza Stephens, whom the Countess sent down to St Paul's for that purpose. Mrs Bowes did not live long enough to realise just how much Stoney Bowes was forsworn. She died in January 1781; most people said, with hindsight, of a broken heart. Meanwhile, his wounds healed, Bowes moved into Grosvenor Square with the happy bride, and began to enjoy himself with his wife's money, giving splendid receptions, dinners and evening parties to which he invited the fashionable world – or that section of it that had not already set him down as an adventurer, and decided to have nothing to do with him. He kept 'a fine table', Jessé Foot tells us, his guests served not with the relatively simple, frugal fare of the middle classes, but with the monstrous meals of the wealthy – course after rich course, with the best cuts of meat and the finest sea food – crab, crayfish, turbot, turtle and salmon followed by venison and pigeon, ham and sweetbreads, duck, pheasant, hare, snipe and turkey, accompanied by asparagus, bottled peas, broccoli, salad and root vegetables and followed by elaborate sweet dishes such as 'transparent pudding covered with a silver web' (of spun sugar), syllabubs, blancmange and cheesecakes, truffles and tarts – all washed down with the best claret and burgundy, champagne, sack, port and brandy.

The Countess's botanical club was disbanded: we hear no more of Messrs Magra and Matra, of Captain Matra and Mr Solander. The Revd Stephens and his wife, however, continued for the time being to live in the house in Grosvenor Square, looking after the Strathmore children. Mr Stephens had strongly advised the Countess against marrying 'Captain' Stoney. Mary Eleanor later told Bowes that she thought this proved Stephens to be an honest clergyman – and perhaps he grudgingly agreed, though he was not pleased to hear that his wife had given Mrs Stephens £1,000 on the day before her wedding and a bond for an annuity of £300 a year – on top of having discharged his debts. The clergyman claimed that the money was in compensation for the chance of preferment he had given up when he entered the Countess's household – he could, he said, have been a minor canon and a chaplain to another, wealthier family.[2] Bowes felt that too much of his money – or money which would have been his a few hours later – had been given away to a mere acquaintance.

He was right: it was a very large sum to give to a friend or a servant (the Stephenses were more or less both). There is no evidence that on this occasion the gift was made under threat. The Countess had no financial nous, enjoyed having money, could not imagine *not* having money, and had so much of it that £1,000 seemed neither here nor there. She was the very opposite of a miser. But now that her money was to all intents and purposes her husband's (or so he thought), Bowes took a sullen view of her generosity. He was even less sanguine a few months later, when, according to George Walker, £12,000 – about £865,000 in 21st-century terms – was handed over to George Gray, to keep him quiet.

Gray had, not unnaturally, been furious when he heard of the wedding. Despite the fact that London society was rife with rumour, he claimed to have heard nothing of Mary Eleanor's marriage plans until they were accomplished, when he immediately threatened to sue her for breach of promise of marriage. He may not have been wholly serious. Very few men took that course, and the male plaintiffs who did so were usually adventurers who had courted or seduced women for their fortunes, and had been disappointed. When, rarely, a man did attempt to take such legal action he made himself a public laughing-stock, and even if he won his case was usually awarded only symbolic damages of 1s. Gray already found himself playing the clown's part in a masquerade, and saw no good reason to exacerbate the situation by making a public display of his foolishness. But he made it clear that he intended in one way or another to be a nuisance, and the Countess decided (with or without her husband's approval) to pay him off. She seems once more, with her childish attitude to money, to have gone well over the top, but Gray was satisfied. He showed no interest at all in the birth of his daughter Mary – which was trouble-free, and took place at Gibside in August 1777 – and retired from the stage.

Meanwhile, Bowes had discovered that the accomplishment of his plans was not as complete as he had believed. Far from his wife's fortune now belonging to him as entirely and unquestionably as her person, he had no control over it whatsoever. He was furious when he heard of the meeting that had taken place just before the wedding between Mary Eleanor and her solicitor, Joshua Pride, whom she had instructed to prepare a deed placing all her worldly goods in trust. Pride and his fellow trustee were to administer all her income, and any payments she had to make must be made through them. The Ante-Nuptial Trust decreed that money paid to her was to be 'for her separate and peculiar use and disposal, exclusive of any husband she should thereafter marry with; and wherewith he should not intermeddle, nor should the same be anyways subject or liable to his debts, controul [sic] or management'.[3]

One has to admire Mary Eleanor's sagacity. She has been called 'a silly woman' in so many words;[4] the description is surely mistaken. She may have been unwise in her choice of men, and had no idea how to manage her money, but certainly in this case she was far from foolish. She wisely commissioned two copies of the trust deed: one to be left with her lawyers, one for herself. One is almost tempted to suspect that at the last minute – as with her previous marriage – she feared she was marrying the wrong man. Indeed, in her *Confessions* – written at Bowes's command – she admits (first assuring him that she never had a moment's doubt but that he would 'chearfully supply [her] with what sums [she] might want') that 'it struck me that having taken such precautions on my children's account . . . with a man who I knew I could trust [Gray]; I ought not to be less cautious with one whom I could not be so strongly assured of; but I would not tell you of the paper, lest it should look like mistrust'.[5]

Of course it *did* look like mistrust – and Bowes made up his mind that he must get his hands on the deed and destroy it. When he brought the matter up, Mary Eleanor said that she had instructed her footman and confidant George Walker to destroy it, together with a mass of unrelated manuscripts.[6] Bowes's temper was not improved by the news that his wife's second trustee was none other than George Stephens, who perhaps had already demonstrated more familiarity with the Countess than was strictly proper. He often went into her room when her maid was doing her hair, on several occasions found some good reason to kiss her, put his arm about her waist, and at least once seated her on his knee.[7] She also admits that she took him into her bedroom once in a while after, years before, having first invited him into her room to speak to him privately about his plans for his elopement. Bowes was not ready to give up his rights to such a man without a fight, and was determined – either by the exercise of his charm (which by now may have been spread a little thin) or by threats – to persuade Mary Eleanor to sign a deed revoking the ante-nuptial agreement.

Meanwhile, he began to take precautions lest she should take any more steps which might result in his being permanently deprived of the command of her income. He ordered the servants to bring the daily post to him immediately it arrived: he would see that his wife received her letters in due course. On one occasion Walker brought her a letter, and she said 'I dare not open it!' and told him to take it to Bowes. Bowes's valet, Mahon, was told to bring him the names of every person who entered or left the house (he refused: it was, he told Bowes, 'beneath him and no part of his business'[8]). When, one day, the Countess went out in her coach, he also instructed Mahon to follow it and carefully note every address at which it stopped. Shortly afterwards, perhaps to prevent clandestine meetings with her solicitor, he informed her that should she require a carriage, she should order it through him, rather than sending for it herself – and when she took the liberty of ordering her own barouche one day to visit Stanley House in order to inspect her greenhouses and hothouses, he positively countermanded the order. She was never able to go freely to Chelsea again, and her botanical pleasures there were to all intents and purposes ended.

The speed with which Bowes revealed his temper and took complete control of his wife and her household was extreme. A few days after his marriage he flew into a rage when he sent for champagne at dinner, and was told there was none in the house. He immediately ordered one of the footmen to go to a tavern and fetch some, and his wife and her guests must wait until it arrived. Then at one of the earliest of his dinner parties, overhearing a guest – a fellow Irishman called O'Burne – speaking to the Countess in French and Italian he sent a footman to her with a note instructing her that in future she should not use any language other than English. He gave orders that only the maids should answer the door-bell, and that nobody should be admitted unless by his orders. Not more than a fortnight after the marriage, Mrs Bowes sent a message via her lawyer asking if she could see her daughter in private. This was certainly somewhat tactless, but in any case she received a peremptory refusal from her son-in-law. She was never to see her daughter alone again. He finally forced Mary Eleanor to dismiss Walker and those other servants with whom she was on friendly terms, and did his best to make sure that no one else employed them.

The dismissal of Walker had something curious about it, as two letters written by the Countess to Henry Stephens show – Stephens was to produce them later when Mary Eleanor was accused of adultery with her footman.[9] The first was written from Gibside to Grosvenor Square on 20 March 1777:

Mr Bowes told me yesterday he had written to you, that day, about ye dismission of George, who has behaved very ill and convinced me but too fully how much I have been mistaken in the good opinion I had of his Honesty, and created doubts which never before entered my head. As there is nothing of which he can be guilty, that I have not reason to suspect he would, with ye most distant prospect of its answering any purpose, I beg the favour of you before he comes to Town, to open his Boxes and Drawers, and take out and seal up against I return, all ye papers on which you either see my handwriting, or have reason to think are in the least belonging to me, and then fasten up the locks again as if no violence had been offered. . . . As soon as George has got his cloathes, tell him I join with Mr Bowes in desiring and *insisting* that we may never see him more.

Three days later, on Good Friday, she sent a second letter, promising to take Sunday dinner with the Stephenses on 6 April, announcing that she has now 'discharged *trusty* George this morning in great disgrace, which information I think it necessary to give you that in case he should go to Grosvenor Square before my arrival in town, you may, after allowing him to take anything that is *really* his Property, discharge him from ever presuming to enter the Doors again – my Reasons for this step are many, but the principal is, his expressing in company with his fellow servants and *others*, that he was too well acquainted with his Lady's *secrets* ever to be dismissed from my Service. This keep to yourself.'

What papers could Walker have hidden away which could be damaging to the Countess? Could she have written him any indiscreet notes? Was she referring to the copy of the ante-nuptial trust deed which with 'a heap of papers and letters and an old lease or two' she had given into his keeping on the eve of her marriage? Why should she want to take these back from him at this particular moment? And did Stephens recover any material from the footman before he left Grosvenor Square for good? We must remember that it was on Bowes's instructions that Walker was dismissed – there is no reason except the letters to suppose that Mary Eleanor mistrusted her servant. Had she and Walker really fallen out, or was she placating Bowes and exercising caution in keeping the truth from Stephens?

But to return to the main theme. For some time after the wedding, though he showed his true colours by the restrictions he placed upon his wife, Bowes had other things to think about than devoting his time to his marriage. The death of the sitting MP for Newcastle-upon-Tyne made it possible for him to persuade the radicals of the constituency to adopt him as their candidate to stand against the Whig, Sir John Trevelyan. He was not in the least interested in politics, but there was money to be made from public office. There was a general apprehension that everyone – from poor law overseers to magistrates, to Members of Parliament and the Prime Minister himself – was either taking bribes or in other ways illicitly enriching themselves.[10]

Bowes had very little of his own fortune left, but his wife would of course support him in his candidacy to the tune of the several thousand pounds it would cost him to persuade the voters to elect him. He made little effort at the hustings, and did not even appear in the constituency on nomination day, asking a friend to appeal to the electors in his place. William Scott, a reader in ancient history at Oxford (his brother Henry was Bowes's election agent), told them that they should remember that Bowes was very recently married, and encouraged them to extend their understanding to an eager bridegroom unwilling to leave his bride. His election address was, for the period, relatively restrained, merely alluding to his opponent in general terms as one of the oppressors of the poor. Sir John replied with a broadside concentrating on Bowes as an insignificant whipper-snapper who had nothing to commend him except marriage to an heiress. Should Lady Strathmore die, her husband would 'go back to his original insignificance'.[11]

The pages of the two local newspapers, the *Newcastle Courant* and the *Newcastle-upon-Tyne Chronicle or General Weekly Chronicle*, reveal Bowes and Trevelyan as no better and no worse than any other pair of politicians competing for a seat; there is no serious political debate, and a great deal of name-calling. Bowes and Mary Eleanor came up to Newcastle a fortnight before election day, and a local dignitary described the Countess as sitting all day in the window of a local inn, 'from whence she sometimes lets fall some jewels or trinkets, which voters pick up and then she gives them money for returning them – a new kind of offering bribes'.[12] If the story is true, the ploy was an ingenious one – and there is no reason to disbelieve it.

The reported speeches of both candidates were almost completely lacking in anything which could be called political discussion – and this, like the allegations of bribery, is not unusual. In *Barry Lyndon*, the eponymous hero also stands for Parliament, and it is difficult to believe that the author had not listened to anecdotes still remembered in Bowes's constituency:

> Though I lavished sums of money in the election, though I flung open Hackton Hall, and kept champagne and burgundy running there and at all my inns in the town as commonly as water, the election went against me. The rascally gentry had all turned upon me . . . it was even represented that I held my wife by force, and though I sent her into the town alone, wearing my colours, with Bryan [his baby son] in her lap, and made her visit the mayor's lady and the chief women there, nothing would persuade the people but that she lived in fear and trembling of me, and the brutal mob had the insolence to ask her why she dared to go back, and how she liked horsewhip for supper.[13]

Neither Bowes's speeches from the hustings nor his ingenious efforts at bribery brought him success: at the poll he discovered that while he had attracted 1,068 votes, his adversary had polled 1,163.

As a matter of form he protested, registering a petition to the House of Commons; Sir John replied with a counter-petition. Henry Scott and his brother William recommended their barrister sibling John, who agreed to represent Bowes's case in Parliament, assisted by another barrister, John Lee. If Bowes had any chance at all of convincing MPs that the election had been fraudulent, he could scarcely have been represented by two abler men: Lee was to become Solicitor General in a future government, and John Scott, as Lord Eldon, was to become Lord Chancellor – that same Lord Chancellor whom Shelley was to castigate in his great political poem *The Mask of Anarchy*.

Bowes had no reason whatsoever to suppose that the election was fraudulent, and certainly not a scintilla of proof to support the argument. But we need not wonder why the brothers, highly intelligent as they were, took on what from the beginning seemed a hopeless case. Bowes had already paid John Scott 300 guineas for his advice during the election – and what modern advisor would not be pleased with a fee of £21,600, which is what the sum would represent today? This, together with an additional fee plus a retainer for Lee, ensured that the two men did their best, though John Scott at least had no illusions: before the case was ever raised in the House, he told his brother that Bowes had no chance of reversing the return, but that he would probably be content with the publicity the action would bring him. He was right. The case failed.

Bowes was left with a bill of £12,000. Where and how was he to raise it? The answer was simple: his wife's money.

By the time the bill was due Bowes had 'persuaded' the Countess to revoke the trust deed. Mary Eleanor's fortune was now his own, together with all her income and property. At the time, most men considered this to be an admirable outcome. It was highly improper for a wife to have taken such an underhand action to deprive her husband of his rights. During their courtship, quite apart from the passionate nature of their relationship, Stoney had given the impression of having an open purse and an open heart. He had made himself agreeable to her children, bringing them small presents and making much of them; he seemed to have an equable temper, and to be the stuff of which an ideal husband might be made. She was speedily disillusioned. But precisely how he managed to persuade her to cancel the trust deed is something of a mystery.

With hindsight, one might suspect physical violence, but it was early days for that. There could have been suggestions of separating her from her children, though she showed so little devotion to them that that threat seems unlikely to have succeeded. One might remember that by 1 May, when Mary Eleanor signed the document nullifying the deed, she was seven months pregnant, and very probably obviously so. She may have thought she had concealed the pregnancy from Bowes at the time of their marriage – it should have been quite possible, for the child would have been conceived sometime during the middle of November. But even if he did not realise that she was pregnant then, it would be unrealistic to suppose she could have concealed it until the sixth month of her pregnancy. Perhaps he held his fire on the subject, believing that there was more capital to be made from pretending ignorance and saving ammunition for a time when he could profit from the resulting 'shock'.

It is more likely that he took advantage of his wife's distress at a major quarrel between herself and the Stephenses, which blew up in April, a quarrel which Bowes may have provoked. Not long after the election, Thomas Mahon, Bowes's valet, got up very early one morning intending to visit another servant, a girl he was later to marry. She had however locked her door, and as he made his way reluctantly back to his own room, he heard a creaking coming from Mrs Stephens' bedroom – then, as he looked over the bannisters, saw his master come out onto the landing. The night before, he had not, as usual, helped Bowes undress, and he noticed that when he left Mrs Stephens he had on the same clothes which he had been wearing at midnight.[14]

The Countess speaks in her *Confessions* of her 'madness' in allowing Eliza Stephens to stay on in the house after their marriage, and says that had she truly known what she was like, she would have asked Bowes to turn her out of the house directly, for 'such a wretch was not fit to live on the earth'; as for the Revd Stephens, she had taken him for an honest man, but now 'thought only with horror of his ever being near my sons or in my house'.[15]

Those are strong words, especially when one remembers that they were spoken about a couple who had been the Countess's intimate friends and had lived in her house on the most amicable terms for the best part of a year. Various conjectures have been made by both of Mary Eleanor's previous biographers as to the basis for the quarrel; but neither seems to have homed in on Mahon's story, which surely offers a probable solution. Suffice to say that the couple was unceremoniously sent packing, and only surfaced again to give evidence on behalf of Bowes when he was accused of adultery; so they felt quite as bitterly against the Countess as she did against them.

When his wife's pregnancy began to be obvious, Bowes took a house in Hammersmith – a house, Foot points out, that was 'quite secluded from the busy preying eye of curiosity, and where Bowes might hear the cuckoo in the merry month of May, the time they went there, without it being unwelcome to the married ear'.[16] This rather arch statement seems to hint strongly that Bowes had already embarked upon a career of serial adultery, though precisely why he thought it would be easier for him to deceive the Countess in Hammersmith than in Grosvenor Square is a mystery. It also begs the question that there is no evidence that she was not from the first fully aware of his many affairs. Perhaps Foot got it wrong, and the move was for some other reason.

The couple spent two months at Hammersmith, during which the town gossip was enlivened by another squabble between Bowes and the Fighting Parson. Bowes had been talking rather too freely in his cups at the Cocoa Tree Club and accusing the Revd Bate of having been less than enthusiastic in the recent duel. Bate naturally responded, and called several times at the house in Hammersmith, to find Bowes not at home. When Bate wrote a letter to the *Morning Post* accusing Bowes of drunkenness and slander, the latter replied with a letter marked more by incoherence than temperance:

> Sir, I have known bad men, I have heard of many, and have been a dissipated man myself, but of all the diabolical wretches that since the beginning of the world God thought expedient to introduce upon earth, as a detested example of vile prodigality, you are the first. . . . Providence, when we last met, thought you too proper a subject for public justice, to allow you to fall for the satisfaction of an individual, has therefore, I presume, detained you as an example and partner in clerical reprobation; else what devil could have instructed you to have made a second attack on me, when you know I wish to relinquish every part of the world that can produce so infernal and black a book, AS YOUR COUNTENANCE.

He added a postscript pointing out that he had not been at home when Bate called because he did not wish to get into another quarrel with him, but he would make a point of being at home until six o'clock the following evening, and after that at the theatre.

Bate replied by return of messenger:

Sir, I have just received a letter signed R.B. which, from its bedlamite strains, I conceive to be the genuine effusions of your extraordinary head and heart. The man, however, who dares to hold the language to me, which I have been able to collect from the only intelligible part of it, is a liar and a scoundrel. What you mean by expecting me at your house this evening, after the very singular line of conduct you have lately pursued, I neither know nor care; but I am now advised not to be imprudent enough to enter under the roof of an assassin. I shall therefore take the opportunity of expressing my sentiments of you in the face of the world. . . . Your going to the theatre this evening may possibly be in order to raise a fresh disturbance at that house. I shall be there likewise, though with no such intention.[17]

Bowes was not at the theatre that evening, and the affair petered out after the combatants' solicitors had exchanged more polite and restrained insults. It is a curious exchange, especially if one believes that the earlier duel was rigged. Would Bowes have taken the chance that Bate might reveal the nature of the arrangement? But then, would Bate have been happy should Bowes have revealed that the parson had received payment for taking part in a masquerade? At all events, when, shortly afterwards, Bowes advertised for a private chaplain, Bate did not apply.

EIGHT

Damned for a Bitch

The Confessions *is of that vile and abominable nature, which will
not admit of public inspection.*

Jessé Foot

George Gray's child, a girl, was born in August 1777 at Gibside,
and christened Mary. The Countess, with Bowes and Dr John
Scott had travelled north earlier in the month. According to Foot, Dr
Scott had been appointed Bowes's private physician. Foot did not think
much of Scott (professional jealousy?), describing him as smart but
'plausible' and 'a useful new instrument to Bowes'.[1]

Foot tells us that on arrival at Gibside, though Dr Scott was in
attendance, Bowes sent for a male midwife to supervise the delivery, but
that by the time he arrived Mary Eleanor had successfully given birth,
the child was alive and well, and the mother sleeping comfortably. The
midwife took his fee and left. What Dr Scott was doing all this while is
not explained, but the presence of a male midwife is not in itself
surprising: they were rather in favour at the time, and at childbed were
generally thought to be more efficient and sympathetic than women.[2]

For the next several years, Bowes settled down in the North Country
and cultivated an image as a country gentleman with country interests.
The Countess lived in the same house, but had little to do with his life.
He hunted – sometimes from Gibside, sometimes from Cold Pike Hill
(for he still owned and occasionally used his first wife's house) – and
went out and about on the Countess's estate, interfering with its
running. He had a perfect right to do so; but the random, crude and
often mistaken nature of his interference did not endear him to those
who had been running the place perfectly efficiently before his arrival.
He was desperate for money, and from this period on continually
attempted to persuade Child's Bank to raise more funds for him
through the agency of its employee William Davies, who had known
the Countess well for many years (he gave her away at her wedding to
Bowes) but must already have begun to regret having anything to do
with her husband, and was later to regret it even more.

Nor did Bowes make himself popular on the Gibside estate where he reduced staff and raised tenants' rents. As our poet complained:

> Her Ladyship's tenants first gained his attention,
> Whose treatment was cruel – most shocking to mention;
> He rais'd all their rents, which if they could not pay,
> He crav'd them, and seized them, then turned them away.
> The helpless dependents – the labouring poor,
> He removed from their work, or horse-whipp'd from his door.
> Free-schools he condemn'd, and of course did suppress,
> As tending to cause and promote idleness!
> The yearly, the weekly, the daily supply
> To Orphans and Widows, he next did deny;
> Those acts of benev'lence, whence Gibside was famed,
> Are wholly forbidden and must not be named!
> How lonely the neighbouring village appears,
> No more the poor cottager chearful we hear;
> The old and infirm, the lame and the blind
> Are fled a more hosp'table spot for to find.[3]

Gibside was remarkable for the quality of its timber, and among Bowes's first actions was an order for a violent acceleration of deforestation. He sent for merchants and interviewed them about the price of timber, then berated them for not offering a sum which matched his expectations ('I will see myself and them damned before I agree to the price you mention,' he wrote to an agent[4]). He pleaded poverty and complained about being in debt ('I have given up all idea of going this winter to London', he wrote to one correspondent in December 1778, 'as I can live here for half the expence'[5]). He continued however to entertain neighbours and others he thought might be useful to him, and kept a table as laden with expensive food and wine as that he had offered his friends in London.

Life for Mary Eleanor must have been extremely dull. No evidence survives to tell us how she passed her time, how she filled the interminable hours of neglect and loneliness. There were occasional visits to London – though we do not know how often or for how long they moved between Gibside and Grosvenor Square. Deprived as she was of the interests she had enjoyed in town, she still had little contact with her husband except during his energetic attempts to beget a son. These proved successful. On 8 May 1782, his wife gave birth to William Johnstone Bowes. But this did not mean that she must give up several years to attend to the child, as it does today; wet-nurses, nursery-maids and other servants meant that a wealthy woman need only give such attention to her babies as she felt was necessary, desirable or pleasant. The Countess was never a devoted mother (indeed, had she lived a couple of centuries later she might have been one of those women determined not to breed). But with no necessity to work at motherhood, how was she to pass her time? – for she was not so much discouraged as positively forbidden to follow her own interests. Bowes made himself responsible not only for the running of the estate but for domestic affairs also, and – as she was discovering – he was not a man it was wise to contradict or question.

It was at this time that she began writing her *Confessions*, an account of her 'imprudencies' written at Bowes's request, or more likely demand. This remarkable document, of about fifteen thousand words, is the source of much of what we know about her life. It raises many questions, the answers to which we can only guess at. Why did Bowes ask her to write it? Was he already thinking of a time when he might use it against her, either to blackmail her or in the event of a possible divorce? And why did she accede to his request? He may already have been offering her violence, but that would not necessarily have been enough to persuade her to write the memoir if she had serious objections, for though she was intimidated by him, she was perfectly capable of standing up to him.

He already knew about her relationship with Gray, and she could not have avoided writing about it. But he may not have known of her earlier attachments, nor need she have hinted that they were perhaps more than sentimental – as she did, confessing for instance to admitting 'many improper declarations' from James Graham, and to giving him reason to think that she had 'more than an affectionate friendship for him'.[6] She played directly into her husband's hands, presenting herself with perfect frankness as a woman who had been tempted, and had fallen – so frankly that her first biographer, Jessé Foot, spoke of her *Confessions* as 'of that vile and abominable nature which will not admit of public inspection'. This was a comment bred of the time, though even Ralph Arnold, her second biographer, writing in 1957, was uncomfortable with some passages which now seem harmless enough, but which he suppressed as 'matters which are seldom discussed in print'.

Though he relied on the Countess's book for information, Foot condemned it as inaccurate: 'I feel no disposition to awaken curiosity by laying [the *Confessions*] before the public. . . . Not but they contain among Many falsehoods some truths, yet these are scattered and entangled with falsehoods, and when found and separated, like a few grains among the chaff, are not worth the search.'[7] Did Foot's long familiarity with Bowes, whom he saw so much more often and came to know much better than Mary Eleanor, cloud his judgement? He was surely wrong in his assessment.

The Countess's narrative not only contains no obvious fabrications – at least none which we can identify – but has a tone which rings remarkably true. One hears her voice again and again in the artless document, and it is not the voice of the duplicitous woman Foot believed her to be. It is as though she was dictating the text to an amanuensis – she stumbles, repeats herself, makes chronological slips and corrects herself. There are sentences without subjects, without verbs – and she is sometimes interrupted by Bowes as she is writing, and says so. The narrative is frank and artless enough to arouse sympathy in the reader, and a sense of identification with a confused and unhappy woman. And, for what it is worth, at the end of the document she gives the most solemn assurance that it is a truthful record: 'May I never feel happiness in this world, or the world to come; and may my children meet every hour of their lives unparalleled misery, if I have, either directly or indirectly, told one or more falsehoods in these narratives; or if I have kept any thing a secret. . . .'[8] She was not a religious woman, but it is a serious declaration all the same.

What is still a puzzle is that Mary Eleanor should have thought for a moment that Bowes had any motive for inviting her to write the document other than being able to hold it over her. She knew perfectly well what a risk she was taking: 'I have, under my own hand, furnished you with a perpetual fund for unkindness and even good excuse for bad usage', she tells him; 'If you think my sincerity and unreserved confession of my faults may entitle me to ask a favour, let me beg your promise to burn these papers, at least, that you will destroy them when I die, that I may not stand condemned and disgraced, under my own hand, to posterity.'[9] It was an idle request.

While Mary Eleanor was probably still writing her brief auto-biography, Bowes appointed a new chaplain; the first vanishes from the story almost as soon as he appears, and without explanation. Clearly Bowes thought the household of a country gentleman of his pretensions incomplete without the attendance of a clergyman. Davies recommended the sixty-two-year-old Revd Samuel Markham, of Parliament Street in London, who lived with the Bowes family both in town and in the country from May 1778 until early February of the following year. His employer, he speedily found, was 'of a very savage and tormenting disposition' who behaved to his wife 'in a very crusty and savage manner'. The chaplain too came in for the rough end of his employer's tongue. One evening in January he said grace at supper, and when he thanked God for his mercies, Bowes cried: 'Damn your mercies, I want none of them!' Later that month when Bowes thought that Mr Markham had sat a little too long in the parlour after dinner, he called him a villain and a rascal and knocked him down. Markham had had enough, and resigned his position.[10]

Meanwhile, Bowes had made some money by selling Stanley House and his wife's beloved hothouses there, but spent it again by buying another residence in the North Country: he still had his first wife's house at Coal Pike Hill, and now added Benwell Tower, nearer to Newcastle, which cost him £24,000 – almost £1¼ million in today's currency. He also bought several race-horses. Meanwhile, he sought to further establish himself in the area by contriving to get himself made High Sheriff of Newcastle and continuing his lavish entertainment of the local gentry – the feasts he gave were celebrated for their richness and the quantity of wine which went with them – and decided again to stand for Parliament. This time he was successful, and in February 1780 became MP for Newcastle. He never took the slightest interest in Parliament, and was scarcely ever seen in the House which, people said, was because his only motive in becoming a Member was to gain an Irish peerage. If that is so, he failed.

Though he continued to share his wife's bed adultery became a way of life with him, and no female servant was safe from his attentions. Seventeen-year-old Dorothy Stevenson was engaged as a nursery-maid, and shared her bedroom with little Mary and the new baby, who slept with his wet-nurse, a Mrs Houghton. The latter was one of those countrywomen much used to suckle the babies of the upper classes, especially at a time when fashion decreed severe strait-lacing, which was said to affect the quality of the milk produced by a mother. Houghton, in her mid-twenties, had sworn to sexual abstinence while feeding the baby (this was thought to have a positive affect on the quality of the milk). But Dorothy became aware that Bowes would come into their room at night and slip into Houghton's bed, where presumably the wet-nurse's vow was broken, for later she bore Bowes's child – and persuaded Jessé Foot, who delivered it, to explain to her husband that a six-month pregnancy was not at all unusual, and that the child had certainly been born in lawful wedlock.

Shortly after he started visiting Mrs Houghton, Bowes removed the key from the bedroom door and forbade Dorothy to lock it, even after

Houghton had left: the door of her bedroom had always to be left open, whether they were at Gibside, St Paul's Waldenbury, or Grosvenor Square. Inevitably, one night Dorothy awoke to find Bowes in her bed. Thrusting a handkerchief or the corner of the sheet into her mouth, he raped her. She in turn became pregnant, and about a week before their child was born, Bowes took her to a house in Hanover Square run by a respectable widow, telling the woman that Dorothy had been seduced by his chaplain, a married man whose wife must not know of the affair. That might well have been true, for one of Bowes's stable of chaplains – this one a Mr Reynett, whose wife also lived with the family – fumbled with Dorothy on many occasions, and once, when Mrs Reynett was pregnant, tried to throw her down on his bed. She hurled a heavy candlestick at him, and he did not go near her again. But her child was certainly Bowes's. (There was a strong suspicion that Bowes was also the father of Mrs Reynett's child.)

Another servant who was the object of Bowes's extravagant sexual appetite was nineteen-year-old Elizabeth Waite, who had worked in a brothel kept in King's Place by a Mrs Matthews, then in another kept in the same street by a Mrs Duberly, but hoped to better herself by responding to an advertisement for a nursery-maid at Grosvenor Square – salary £8 a year. Bowes rather than the Countess interviewed her, using the opportunity to take 'improper liberties with her person'. He then told her that her appointment must be approved by the Countess, but when she returned for an interview with the mistress of the house, it was Bowes who answered the front door. He took her upstairs, plied her with wine and raped her. The girl resigned herself to Bowes's approaches (she later said, because her father was in prison for debt and she hoped to persuade Bowes to help them). She would never want for anything, he promised; but sent her away, and she never got anything out of him.

The fact that a young woman was happily married was no bar to Bowes's approaches, especially if she was a servant – servants were not people. The wife of one of his serving-men, herself a maid in his household, had great difficulty in rebuffing him. He professed not to know that she was married, accused her of having an affair with a fellow-servant and, in order (he claimed) to prove that that was the case, one night set up a ladder to the girl's bedroom window at Gibside, mounted it, and watched her and her husband making love. He then rushed indoors, thundered on the door of their bedroom, and turned the pair out naked into the night. Next day, when he discovered that the porter in the lodge had taken them in, he promptly dismissed all three.

Jessé Foot was witness to Bowes's voyeurism. He met him one afternoon at a jeweller's in Cockspur Street, where Bowes readily confessed that he was buying gold trinkets with which to seduce young women. He asked Foot to come down to Gibside to innoculate his young son. The doctor did so, and was given an excellent dinner prepared by a new cook his host had just employed. Among the other guests at his table was a neighbour, a farmer, and his particularly beautiful young daughter. She, Bowes told Foot in an aside, was one of those for whom the trinkets were intended.

After dinner, when the guests had gone, Bowes took Foot to the nearby farmhouse where the girl lived and, concealed by the dark, peered through the bedroom window where she was preparing for bed – 'everything, in her innocent custom, was undoing', as Foot wrote.[11] A barking dog scared Foot, who retreated; but Bowes remained until the show was over – the dog, he later said, was no threat because he had accused the animal of killing sheep, and insisted on it being tied up so that he could return to the bedroom window every night. One cannot but smile to read that on the next occasion Foot met Bowes, the man was limping heavily: the farmer, hearing continual barking, had suspected thieves and let the dog loose – and the animal had fixed its teeth firmly in the voyeur's leg.

Foot thought, on that visit, that the Countess was clearly not at all well. Pale and nervous, she ate little of the excellent food provided, and deferred to her husband even more diligently than was usual in an eighteenth-century marriage, looking to him for assent when the servant offered to refill her glass, and never speaking unless he spoke to her or invited her to speak. She only brightened up when showing Foot around the gardens at Gibside, pointing out improvements she had made, guiding him around the walks, showing him flower beds and shrubs she herself had planned and laid out.

Mary Eleanor must speedily have realised that she had married an inveterate roué, and had that been all she might have reconciled herself to his continual adultery, as did so many wives. Unfortunately, matters were worse than that, for Bowes was showing himself to be pathologically violent – a vicious and unreasoning wife-beater.

The servants, themselves subject to Bowes's sexual peccadillos, saw how he treated his wife, and were later to testify in court. Susannah Church, a middle-aged woman who was employed as a kitchen-maid in May 1783, was surprised that the Countess should be dressed more like a servant than the mistress of a large estate: her stays 'were in so very bad a condition that [Church] although a servant would have been ashamed to wear them'. Dorothy Stevenson confirmed this: she had heard Mary Eleanor ask Bowes from time to time for a little money to buy clothes, but he had told her she must wear what she had so the Countess 'was obliged to wear very ragged and shabby clothes' and 'frequently had scarcely a shift or a pair of stockings fit to put on, and therefore went worse clothed than any of the servants'. She even occasionally borrowed clothes from her servants.

Kept short of money for clothes, she was also often deprived of food. Bowes gave instructions in the kitchen that no food or drink – not so much as a glass of water – should be served to his wife without his knowledge. One day at Streatlam, Mary Eleanor told Church that she thought she might be able to eat a little boiled chicken. The woman served her, and was instantly dismissed by Bowes when he discovered it.

Then there was the violence. Stevenson first became conscious of this when she heard Bowes complain angrily that Mary Eleanor was making too much noise when playing with the children, and saw him actually strike his wife. Thereafter, she often saw him hit her in the face, and punch and pinch her in various parts of her body. On one occasion when the nursery-maid was in her mistress's bedroom helping her to pack for a journey, her master came in and asked the Countess what she was doing. When she said she was looking out some clothes to pack, 'he damned her for a bitch, and told her to get into the closet, which was in the same room, and while he was pushing her across the room to the closet, he gave her several blows with his doubled fist over her arms and shoulders, and kicked her'.

On another occasion, Mary Eleanor was taken ill while at the dinner table. Bowes sent her to her room, and though a doctor was dining with them, refused to allow him to examine her. He himself followed his wife upstairs, went into her bedroom and locked the door. Screams were heard; and after the man had left the room, a girl went to her mistress, and found her badly bruised. When one evening the couple was dining alone and Bowes discovered that his wife had been walking in the garden at Gibside without his permission, he threw a dish of hot potatoes at her; then made her eat them until she was sick; and finally threw a glass of wine over her 'to wash off the potatoes'. When she protested, he held a table knife to her throat and threatened to cut it if she spoke another word.

It would be a mistake to think that Mary Eleanor suffered alone in this way among married women in Georgian England. On the contrary, marital violence was relatively widespread, linked often to drunkenness on the part of the husband. Take the case of Elizabeth Shackleton, whose letters give us a harrowing picture of another failed marriage.[12] Among the epithets she applied to her husband were wild, beastly, barbarous, brutish, nasty, dirty, odious, hideous, stinking, horrid, rude, surly, cross and vulgar – and, if anything, these fail to give a full picture of his behaviour: he beat her with a horse-whip, smashed wine bottles and china, turned over the card-table when he found her playing with some friends, and when she asked a servant to go to enquire about a sick acquaintance, 'Cursed & D——d swore no servant of his sho'd run about the country with such foolish messages'.[13]

In mixed company, it was necessary to show civility to the wives of other men – just as one would not trample down one's neighbour's crops, or criticise his personal appearance. Similarly, single women with whom one had no connection – by family or by some other relationship – might properly be treated with politeness, especially of course if one was courting them. In the privacy of their own homes, however, men like Shackleton and Stoney Bowes seemingly needed to prove that they bore no resemblance to those effeminate foreigners who treated their wives with simpering respect. One's wife was in a very real sense oneself, and if a man's behaviour did not offend himself, why should it offend his wife?

The Countess must in some ways have been extremely relieved that her two daughters, Maria and Anna – Lady Maria and Lady Anna – did not live at home. In 1784 they were sixteen and fourteen, respectively, and were boarding at different schools in London (the boys, certainly John and George and possibly Thomas, boarded in Middlesex). It seems unlikely that Bowes's decision that it was time the girls came to live with their mother was based entirely on his sympathy for his wife's wish to see her children more frequently; in view of his adventures with the young servants of the house, a darker purpose cannot be ruled out. Mary Eleanor must surely have suspected it. Moreover, she cannot have been convinced that his brutality would not be exercised upon them.

The late Earl's family had not been inactive where the children were concerned, and had succeeded, in 1780, in getting them made Wards in Chancery, with Mary Eleanor's old enemy Thomas Lyon appointed as one of their guardians. The girls were allowed to visit their mother from time to time and on 21 May 1784, she wrote to the two women who ran the school in Queen Square where Anna, her younger daughter, was boarding, to let them know that she would send for the child the following day so that she could spend a few hours with her mother before she and her husband set out for Bath. The girl was fetched by Mr and Mrs Reynett (not perhaps the ideal people to put in charge of an adolescent girl) and taken to Grosvenor Square. Later, her sister Maria was brought to her mother's house from that of Lady Ann Simpson, the late Earl's sister, by Mrs John Ord, Lady Ann's sister-in-law. When they entered the house, Mrs Ord asked if Anna was also in the house, and was told that she was. On some specious excuse, the Countess took her elder daughter into another room. When they had been absent for some time, Mrs Ord became suspicious – and rightly so, for when it was time for her to take Maria back to the school, there was no sign of her, or of the Countess. Instead, a servant handed her a letter from Mary Eleanor complaining that she was never allowed to talk to her daughters alone, and suspected that Mr Lyon had given instructions to that effect. She had had enough, and now intended to keep both girls until she could appeal to the Lord Chancellor for mitigation of the Strathmore family's control over them. She wrote:

> However inhuman may be the BEHAVIOUR I have experienced from those who never paid the slightest attention to my feelings as a mother and whose professed regard for my children ought to have taught them a very different lesson; yet I hope you will be so obliging as believe that nothing can be further from my wishes than to treat you with the most distant degree of impoliteness, especially in my own house; but that goodness of heart which I have the pleasure to know you possess, will, I doubt not, fully excuse the liberty I now take, and lead you to sympathize in the sufferings of a parent, whose children have, for many years, been entirely secluded from her sight, an affliction which, though you have never been so unfortunate as to experience, yet you may easily conceive the severity of; and from your own sensations upon inferior occasions, you will form a just idea how impossible it must be even to exist under such cruel and unnatural controul.[14]

Bowes dictated many, even most, of the surviving letters ostensibly written by the Countess; but this one has a genuinely touching tone, and it sounds as though the Countess is speaking in her own voice. However, Mrs Ord had been entrusted with the care of Maria – and had just finished reading the letter when she heard the girl screaming, somewhere in the house. She called out to her, and shortly afterwards the child was brought to her 'led by a gentleman without whose interference she would have been a VICTIM'.[15] Foot, who recounts the story, stops short of accusing Bowes of molesting the girl, saying merely that he and the Countess argued very forcibly that she should leave her aunt's house and stay with them. But would Maria have screamed had that been all that occurred?

Meanwhile, the Misses Carlisle and Este, who ran the boarding house where Anna, the younger sister, was living, were surprised to receive, instead of their pupil, a letter from the Countess. In it she announced that since the child had said she wanted to spend the holidays with her mother, she had taken the liberty of keeping her at home – as (Mary Eleanor wrote) 'the only means to make myself some recompence for what I have endured for several years from Mr Lyon's constantly refusing me the company of my children in such a manner as humanity and propriety seem to demand'.[16]

The girls' guardians applied to the Lord Chancellor to have Anna returned to their care; but it was too late. Bowes, his wife and the fourteen-year-old girl had already left England for Paris.

NINE

The Most Unhappy of Men?

Her person, accustomed only to distress and confinement, found no alleviation of the bitterest sorrow.

Jessé Foot

In March or April of 1784, Mary Eleanor employed as lady's maid Mary Morgan, a woman in her early thirties. It was one of the wisest things she ever did. Mrs Morgan was to stay with her for the rest of her life, and became as staunch a friend as she proved a faithful servant.

Only a few weeks after she had been engaged, she accompanied her mistress, Bowes and Lady Anna to Calais, and on to Paris. Though not uncommon among those who could afford to travel, the journey was not one to be undertaken lightly. First, there was the drag down to the coast – along the Old Kent Road to New Cross, over Black (or Bleak) Heath and up Shooter's Hill (the shooting usually done during spats with highway or footpads, among whom this was a popular hunting-ground), then to Gad's Hill (not a great deal safer), and through Rochester and the Medway marshes to Canterbury, where it was often the custom to pass a night before pressing on to Dover.

Then there followed the crossing itself, more or less stormy – perhaps only four but on occasion over twelve hours of tossing about on the unpredictable waters of the English Channel. It may be that Bowes paid the 5 guineas which would have hired him a private boat (the usual charge for passage on a packet boat was half a guinea for a lady or gentleman, and 5s for each servant). At Calais the customs officers did not detain them long: a traveller some years earlier described being 'examined immediately on landing, before an officer (to whom you are carried by a couple of soldiers), who only requires your name, business in France and occupation, you are dismissed, and may go where you please; only the baggage is sent to the Custom House, with your servant and porters, to be searched for contraband goods'.[1]

The party put up for the night at the Lion d'Or in Calais, a posthouse run by the estimable M. Grandsire, well used to catering for English travellers. At the Hôtel d'Angleterre M. Dessein ran the rather more fashionable house – but that was reason enough for Bowes, hoping to pass unnoticed, not to stay there. When she helped the Countess to undress that night Mrs Morgan was surprised to notice a large bruise on her arm between the elbow and the shoulder. When the maid commiserated with her mistress, Mary Eleanor told her that she had been bruised by hitting her arm against the side of the coach on the ride from London to Dover. At the time, the maid did not think that very likely, but she accepted the explanation.

Next day Bowes hired a four-wheel coach for the journey on to Paris – a closed vehicle with a hard leather-covered top and leather strap suspension. There was little chance of blaming the roads for any bruises the Countess might sustain, for French roads were far better than English ones – the best in Europe, with a stone pavement wide enough for two carriages to pass, and a *parterre* on each side of natural earth, kind to the wheels and thus to the passengers. It was as comfortable a journey as anyone could expect.

However, Mrs Morgan noticed very strange behaviour on the part of Bowes. Whenever his wife went to look out of the window, he violently drew the blind up, and in a half-doze Mrs Morgan thought she saw him slyly pinch and kick the Countess without the slightest provocation.[2] Later, at the Hôtel de Luxembourg, she saw plain evidence of the man's brutality towards his wife for he treated her always 'with the greatest indignity possible'. His behaviour 'was one continued scene of abuse, insult and cruelty . . . she was seldom free from bruises upon face, neck or arms'.[3]

Bowes was clearly beginning to panic at the possibility of their being recognised by some agent of the Lord Chancellor. He forbade Mary Eleanor to look out of the window of the hotel – he once beat her severely because he saw her doing so – and if she was ever permitted to walk in the streets, she was instructed to keep her face covered. On one occasion, Bowes beat her again, because he thought her bonnet was not pulled far enough over her face. It was in fact rare that she was allowed out – the door of her room was usually locked, and at least once Mrs Morgan was ordered to place a chair against it so that her mistress could not get out – she was not, Bowes asserted, capable of taking care of herself.

The maid became seriously worried that her mistress might be murdered, so ungovernable seemed Bowes's temper. One day she saw Mary Eleanor standing with her face in her hands, crying and holding a towel with which she was trying to staunch the bleeding from her mouth and one ear. Her face, neckerchief and the sleeve of her gown were covered with blood. Bowes explained that his wife had 'let the wind blow open one of the doors upon her, and has by that means run a pin through her ear'. The damage to the ear did not seem to Mrs Morgan likely to have been caused by a pin, and indeed Mary Eleanor later confessed that her husband had clawed at her face because she wanted to look out of the window.

Despite his nervousness, Bowes seems to have had a rather pleasant time in Paris. The first thing he did was to buy a quantity of fashionable clothes, for Parisians were more concerned with appearance even than Londoners, and he found that 'when an Englishman comes to Paris, he cannot appear until he has undergone a total metamorphosis. At his first arrival he finds it necessary to send for the tailor, perruquier, hatter; shoemaker and every other tradesman concerned in the equipment of the human body'.[4] Bowes felt the need to be in the fashion, however much it cost him – and it must have cost him dear, for the materials for even a modest suit would have set him back at least £25 (£1,750 in 2006 terms), while twenty years previously the Duke of Bedford had paid 64 guineas to have a crimson velvet suit made and embroidered. The city also suited his temperament, for he found the men of the town as devoted to gambling and womanising as he – and there was plenty of scope for both. Gambling was the most convenient and enjoyable way of passing the day, and while he may not have availed himself of the multitude of available prostitutes – even more numerous than in London – we have some evidence that he spent at least part of his time enjoying the gentle art of seduction. Mrs Morgan recalled that he beat his wife on one occasion because, though she had a good command of French, she unkindly refused to translate for him a letter he had written to a woman he admired. The letter ran:

Madam – Though I have not the satisfaction of being known to you, and though I was so happy, the want of even the least knowledge of your language would prevent me from enjoying of your acquaintance; yet I cannot resist the sentiments of a disinterested love and affection so far, however improper the confession may be as to quit Paris without declaring in the most express and direct terms that you have rendered me the most unhappy of men, and that my fortune, which is more than ample, and everything honourable which I can confer, shall be for ever devoted to your service and happiness.[5]

Written at a time when he had no intention of quitting Paris, this was an obvious stratagem; whether or not it succeeded we have no means of knowing.

And what about Lady Anna? We have no information about her, either. The Countess must have been worried about her daughter. No adolescent girl was safe where Bowes was concerned, and Mary Eleanor may have been disconcerted to discover that the age of consent in France was fourteen. To do Bowes justice, there is no shred of evidence that he had any intention of seducing or raping his step-daughter – and there can be no doubt that the Countess would have used it against him if it had existed. Lady Anna never made any complaint at all against Bowes – on the contrary, she seems rather to have liked him – which suggests that he was careful to keep his cruelty to her mother a secret from her.

What might have been an entirely enjoyable interlude was spoiled for him by anxiety about the consequences of what he now saw had been a very rash action in bringing the girl abroad – and one may well wonder why he had done so in the first place. He was not in the business of making life pleasant for his wife, and her melancholy at not seeing her daughters as often as she wished would not have weighed with him. It is difficult not to put his attitude down to the simple desire to upset the girls' guardians, the relatives of his wife's late husband, and in particular Thomas Lyon. Together with his sister Lady Anne Simpson, he had made himself offensive to Bowes by attempting to interfere in the business of his marriage, issuing a Bill of Complaint against him and his wife in the matter of the late Earl's marriage settlement, and contriving to get all her children made Wards in Chancery.

Bowes now began to try to get some kind of defence together against the time – which he realised must come – when he would have to account to the Lord Chancellor for his actions. He turned to William Davies, the banker who had known the Countess since he had helped with the financial arrangements for her marriage with Lord Strathmore and had given her away at her marriage, for advice and help. On 13 June he wrote to Davies complaining at the apparent prejudice of the Lord Chancellor: 'I am perfectly well satisfied that the same diabolical and unfair artifices would have been successfully practised upon Lady Anna Maria that have deprived Lady Strathmore for ever, I believe, of the company of her eldest daughter. Besides, his lordship has been applied to upon two former occasions, without giving redress, though no circumstances could be stronger than those brought against Mr Lyon.'[6] He was extremely rude about Mr and Mrs Ord (the former was, he said, the commander-in-chief of the schemes to keep her daughters from the Countess, and he would make him pay for his insolence the moment he met him).

What was needed, he suggested, was to show that Mary Eleanor's state of mind was in such confusion and her health so damaged by being deprived of her daughters' company that her husband must be forgiven for the action of kidnapping the girl. John Hunter, a famous surgeon whom the Countess had met through his wife, a prominent Bluestocking, would surely help, for 'he told me . . . before I left town, that Lady Strathmore's disorder was entirely occasioned by the agitation of mind she underwent by the cruel absence of her children'. Dr John Scott, his personal physician, would testify in the same vein, while William Scott – no relation to the doctor, but a friend who had spoken for Bowes on the hustings at Newcastle and was a well-known lawyer practising in the Ecclesiastical Courts – would be eager to assist him, as would the barrister John Lee. More evidence on the Countess's behalf might be given by the chaplain, Mr Reynett, 'a blundering poor fellow that would do all in his power to serve us, but has no head'. However, because Bowes had always been careful to keep him in the dark about everything concerning Mary Eleanor's daughters, Reynett could be counted on to say anything he was told to say.

A month went by, and Bowes heard nothing to his comfort. Eleven letters written to Mr Scott remained unanswered, and those from Davies were devoid of anything which bore on his case. On 26 July he wrote Davies rebuking him for his inaction, asking him to have accounts of any transactions relative to his case published in 'ALL THE PAPERS', to send clippings from any newspaper that mentioned anything to do with Lady Strathmore and her children, and suggesting he might have a few paragraphs inserted 'relative to Mr Lyon's conduct. I will be answerable for them ALL'. Davies, a wiser man, did nothing of the sort. A fortnight later Bowes was complaining that his enemies were putting it about that he had 'taken off a child under thirteen years of age, for the purpose of getting her married to some improper person UNKNOWN TO THEM'. Davies should please put down all his work, and come immediately to Paris for a consultation.

Davies had troubles of his own, however. He had appeared on Bowes's behalf at preliminary proceedings in the Chancery Court, and the Lord Chancellor had been scathing in his criticism of Bowes, and of Davies for representing such a reprobate without being able to offer any assurance that his client would comply with the Court's instructions. When he reported this to Bowes, the latter penned a letter in which criticism and mock sympathy were equally mixed:

Paris, August 30, 1784.

I lament most exceedingly that I have been the involuntary cause of
the troubles you have lately experienced, and are still likely to
sustain, as far as I can judge by your own representation. However I
cannot conceive how you are thought culpable, except it was from
your being the entire author of preventing Lady Strathmore from
gratifying her feelings, when I think, in regard to her eldest daughter,
an exertion of them might have been exacted, and I will venture to
add, ought not to have been left short. As to our immediate return,
no man ever took greater pains than I have done to convince Lady
Strathmore and her daughter of the propriety of that step. But it is
not in my power to succeed, without extracting from their minds
every dread of what may follow, by the death of my wife, and equally
her daughter, their affections are so much interwoven. At all events,
however, you must not suffer for me. Every experiment was tried to
soften the conduct of Mr Lyon. You have neglected me much, by not
keeping your promise of visiting me. I shall set out from hence to
Calais early tomorrow morning. By your meeting us, you will have
an opportunity of stating matters in their true colours to both ladies.[7]

Fourteen letters, he stated, had now been sent to Mr Scott, and none of
them answered. It was too bad.

The following day, another letter to Davies: would the lawyer please
not wait at Calais, but go on to Lille, where Bowes would wait for him
at the Hôtel de Bourbon in the Grand Place. Calais was too
dangerously near England, and if Davies met anyone there who knew
either of them, he should tell them he was on his way to Paris.

When Davies got to Lille, there was no sign of Bowes. He returned,
in some irritation, to London, where he found a letter dated
12 September reporting that Bowes was in bed with rheumatic fever,
but would be on his way to Lille the following morning. Four days later
came another from Lille rebuking him for not waiting. The rheumatic
fever had subsided, but Bowes had been again delayed by 'the gout in
the head'. The lawyer should now once more set off immediately for
Calais. Bowes would leave Lille for the same place, and they should
meet there. Davies should also be so good as to bring with him
£17,000, borrowed against Bowes's estate at Benwell, for he 'must get
clear of all little demands'. Not perhaps so little, if they required the
present-day equivalent of over £1,224,000. Gambling debts, perhaps?

In Calais, three days later, Bowes was waiting impatiently, grieved by
'the perpetual agonies of distress that attend Lady Strathmore and her

An anonymous drawing of Andrew Robinson Stoney Bowes used as a frontispiece to Jessé Foot's biography, published after Bowes's death in 1810. *(Author's collection)*

2. Mary Eleanor, Countess of Strathmore. This anonymous sketch was made perhaps at the time of her divorce. *(Author's collection)*

3. 'Cruelty Displayed' – the frontispiece of a published report of Bowes's trial for adultery, showing him assaulting his wife at the dinner table. *(Author's collection)*

4. A portrait by Enoch Seeman of George Bowes, the Countess's father. He was 'uncommon handsome, and a great rake in his youth'. *(Glamis Castle)*

John, 9th Earl of Strathmore, 'a hearty Scotchman, and a good bottle companion . . . not exactly calculated to make even a good learned woman a pleasing husband'. This portrait was painted in 1762, five years before his marriage to Mary Eleanor Bowes. (Glamis Castle)

. Streatlam Castle, where Stoney Bowes imprisoned his wife in 1786. The house was demolished soon after the Second World War. (Country Life Picture Library)

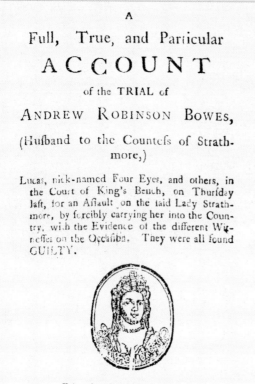

A

Full, True, and Particular
ACCOUNT

of the TRIAL of

ANDREW ROBINSON BOWES,

(Husband to the Countess of Strathmore,)

Lucas, nick-named Four Eyes, and others, in
the Court of King's Bench, on Thursday
last, for an Assault on the said Lady Strathmore, by forcibly carrying her into the Country, with the Evidence of the different Witnesses on the Occasion. They were all found
GUILTY.

Printed and Sold in London,

7. The trial of Bowes and the following divorce proceedings were eagerly read when the details were published as books and pamphlets soon after the events. *(Author's collection)*

8. 'He was too well acquainted with his Lady's *secrets* ever to be dismissed from my service.'
A quote from the Countess's letter to the Revd Stephens about the dismissal of her favourite footman, George Walker.
(National Archives – DEL2/12)

9. A nineteenth-century etching of Gibside by T. Allom and T.A. Prior. *(Author's collection)*

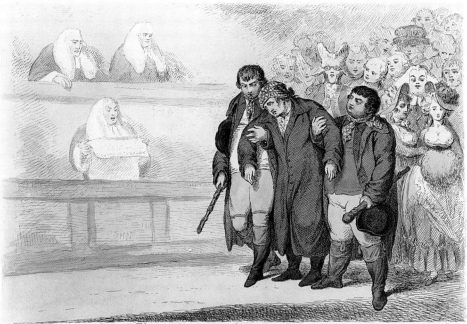

ANDREW ROBINSON BOWES Esq.ʳ as he appeared in the Court of Kings Bench, on Tuesday the 28.ᵗʰ Nov.ʳ 1786, to answer the Articles exhibited against him, by his Wife, the Countess of Strathmore. —   Pubᵈ Dec.ʳ 2.ᵈ 1786, by E. Jackson, Maryboner Street, Golden Square

10. James Gillray's drawing of Bowes supported by two tipstaffs and 'saluted with hisses' as he was brought before the justices in Westminster Hall on 28 November 1786. *(National Portrait Gallery, London)*

11. Gillray's caricature of the Countess carousing with her servant, Mrs Mary Morgan, and nursing two cats, while Lord Strathmore waits, with a candle, to go to bed, and their son turns away crying 'I wish I was a cat – my mother would love me more'. *(National Portrait Gallery, London)*

12. A libellous drawing by Gillray of the Countess's son being held out towards her by her servant Mary Morgan, apparently to be offered her breast. *(National Portrait Gallery, London)*

13. St Paul's Waldenbury, photographed in the 1860s. *(Hertfordshire Archives and Local Studies)*

14. A portrait of the Duchess probably drawn in 1784, the year in which she escaped from her husband's brutality, but before he abducted her. Portrait by J.C.D. Engleheart, after George Engleheart. *(Bowes Museum)*

15. A contemporary drawing by John Dowman of Andrew Bowes. *(Fitzwilliam Museum, Cambridge)*

16. An unattributed portrait of the Countess of Strathmore: the only full-length portrait, showing her in one of the monstrous headdresses. *(The Hon. Simon Bowes-Lyon)*

daughter, from the dread of being parted from each other.' *Where was Davies?* This neglect of a friend and client was extremely distressing.

Meanwhile, the case came forward in London, but although Foot tells us that Lee and Scott 'pleaded with their eyes full of tears', protesting that Bowes had only acted as a loving and attentive husband should in helping Lady Strathmore to be reunited with her daughter – and may well have believed it – the unfeeling Lord Chancellor ordered Davies to go to France and without delay bring the child back within the jurisdiction of the court. Davies obeyed. Mary Eleanor was only too eager to return – but Bowes was terrified of what might happen to him, and for three days managed to keep the lawyer and the Countess apart, making her write Davies a note complaining of his 'barbarity' in attempting to take her back to England. When Bowes finally allowed Davies to see her, he ordered her to pretend to faint with fear at the prospect of leaving Calais for Dover.

By this time so sick was Davies of the whole business that he 'was almost disposed to return the second time without [the Countess] and Lady Anna, and take all the consequences with the Lord Chancellor'.[8] But in the end he prevailed, and by the middle of October the three runaways were back in England, first at St Paul's and later at Buxton,[9] where Bowes's ill-treatment of his wife continued to distress Mary Morgan – and in retrospect distressed Jessé Foot, who for once allowed himself some colourful, if turgid, prose:

All the delight of the fond heart of a woman of fashion, possessing an immense fortune, high education, and strong propensities for figuring in the *beau monde* and for displaying the resistless ornamental appendages of exalted rank, was by Bowes suppressed. The rich, the gay and fashionable equipage, the well-disciplined and flirting fan, the proud and nodding plumage, the brilliant and superb diamonds, the conspicuous opera box, the love-exciting dance, the soft and extatic [*sic*] endearments of the Italian song, which was better tasted by the Countess than most ladies, from her perfect knowledge of the language and of music, were all compressed, and totally obliterated. Her person, accustomed only to distress and confinement, found no alleviation of the bitterest sorrow. Mind and body jointly submitted to receive the pressure which Bowes, like a MANGLE, daily rolled upon them, and both were grievously collapsed.[10]

The lack of opportunity to wear her diamonds to the opera was the least of the Countess's troubles, as Mary Morgan continued to observe.

One of the first things which happened at Buxton was that in the presence of Lady Anna, Bowes thrust a lighted candle into his wife's face – wax stuck to her burned skin. Mary Eleanor's daughter also saw her step-father thrust a quill pen so violently into her mother's face that it stuck in her tongue. In November 1784 Mrs Morgan saw Mary Eleanor with her clothes torn to pieces and her mouth bleeding, allegedly because she had failed to make proper arrangements (as Bowes thought) for some dinner guests. During the following month, Mary Morgan observed Bowes beating the Countess severely with his fists and a stick, and shouting that he would teach her to be beaten without crying out; then he threw the fire tongs at her. Mary Eleanor told Mrs Morgan she wished 'it would please God either to take her or Mr Bowes, that her sufferings might in some measure be put to an end'.[11]

In January, the final straw broke her back. She and Bowes were in London, where people were given the impression that she was unwell. Bowes sometimes saw to it that she was starved for several days, and she certainly looked pale and wan. Some evenings, the knocker of the front door of the house was seen to be tied – something usually done to prevent an invalid being disturbed at night. Meanwhile, the Countess was again worried because Bowes seemed intent on getting both her girls under his control.

In January 1785, she told Mrs Morgan that Bowes had threatened to strangle her. A friend had come to tea, and she had asked her to bring her little dog with her. Bowes was furious, had made her go down on her knees and swear that she would never bring another dog into the house. After taking his hands from her throat, her husband had threatened to have her locked up for life. She decided that if she really wanted her torture to end, she must take the initiative herself. Towards the end of January, she sent a message to Mrs Morgan by a friendly housemaid, Ann Parkes, saying that she was seriously in fear of her life, and wanted her maid to help her escape. Mrs Morgan was all too ready to help.

TEN

Wringing of the Heart

Beating, scratching, biting, pinching, whipping, kicking, imprisoning, insulting, provoking, tormenting, mortifying, degrading, tyranizing, cajoling, deceiving, lying, starving, forcing, compelling, and a new torment, wringing of the heart.

Action for Divorce

The escape was well organised. It took place while the family was at the house in Grosvenor Square – it would have been difficult for the Countess to cover her tracks had she made her move at St Paul's Waldenbury or at Gibside, where she would have had to make her way over open countryside leaving tracks that would have been relatively easy to follow.

She was never left unguarded and was always watched now by a servant Bowes could trust; no doubt he suspected his wife might attempt to leave him. But on the evening of 3 February 1785, while her husband was dining with a friend in Percy Street, a couple of miles away, she asked her guard to go around the corner to a stationer's and buy her a magazine – the *Ladies' Diary*, perhaps, or the *Bon Ton Magazine* – with which she could while away her time. He unwisely agreed. She and three sympathetic servants – Parkes, Ann Dixon (the housekeeper), and a footman called Thompson – contrived to send the remaining male servants on errands which occupied them in other parts of the house, and the Countess slipped away, locking the doors of her rooms so that it would seem that she had shut herself in and gone to bed. Accompanied by Dixon, she made her way north up Duke Street to a hackney coach stand in Oxford Street. It was empty, and they had to wait anxiously for some time before a coach came along. Eventually one appeared, and they gave the driver well over the set rate of 1s to take them to Cursitor Street, off Lincoln's Inn Fields, and the apartments of one of Mary Eleanor's cousins, a lawyer called Shuter.

The delay in Oxford Street was almost fatal, for as they drove towards the junction with Tottenham Court Road another coach passed them at a rattling gallop, going in the opposite direction, and they saw

Bowes's head thrust out of a window. Happily, he did not see them, but the shock threw the Countess into one of her fits. Comforted by Dixon, she had recovered by the time Mary Morgan and Ann Parkes had made their way to Shuter's rooms, from which they accompanied her to a lodging house in Dyer's Buildings, Furnival Street, off High Holborn.

There she installed herself as 'Mrs Jeffries', and four days later took out Articles of Peace against her husband, alleging physical cruelty. The Kings Court Bench moved swiftly, and Bowes was bound over to keep the peace on a surety guaranteed by two friends, John Lee and the Duke of Norfolk, the 11th Duke and a companion of the race-track. But Bowes was quick to discover his wife's whereabouts, and took rooms nearby. If there was any way in which he could recover her, he was determined to do so. She requested a tipstaff to guard her, and the request was granted.

The Bishop of London's Consistory Court now dealt with the action for divorce which she laid before them. Her citation contained a long list of her husband's alleged cruelty: 'beating, scratching, biting, pinching, whipping, kicking, imprisoning, insulting, provoking, tormenting, mortifying, degrading, tyranizing, cajoling, deceiving, lying, starving, forcing, compelling, and a new torment, wringing of the heart'.[1]

Bowes cannot have been surprised by anything his wife alleged; but pretended to be astonished and aghast at her action. Cruelty offered by husbands to their wives was such a common occurrence that it showed considerable effrontery for a wife to complain of it. Husbands possessed considerable legal authority to torment and even physically chastise a wife, sometimes as a result of drink, sometimes simply for sadistic pleasure, sometimes to force her to do something she was reluctant to do. Sometimes the violence was offered in the hope that the wife would leave the marriage – if she did so, she immediately put herself legally in the wrong. Many wives simply put up with the violence for fear of losing their children and being left penniless. It was possible to appeal to the Court of Chancery for protection or to sue in an ecclesiastical court for separation on grounds of cruelty. Mary Eleanor had now done both.

Her cousin, Mr Shuter, was clearly a competent adviser. In an attempt to cut short what would certainly be an expensive and possibly a prolonged battle in the courts, he suggested that she might ask Bowes if he would submit their dispute to arbitration. He agreed, but then reneged on his agreement. On 16 July the Countess exhibited a Bill of Complaint against him in the High Court of Chancery, protesting that she was destitute and asking for the re-establishment of the Ante-

Nuptial Agreement, made just before the wedding, restraining Bowes from receiving any rents or other income from her estates, and the appointment of a receiver to collect and administer them. The court was asked to direct that she should be paid £1,500 (about £108,000 today) to house, feed and clothe her and help her with the costs of her action. This request granted, it enabled her to move to rather more salubrious lodgings, first in Hart Street, not far from the Tower of London, and then in Bloomsbury Square, where she was able to maintain her own carriage.

Her children, happily, were well out of the way during the brouhaha of the next year and a half. Lady Anna was back at school in Queen's Square, and the girl's sisters and brothers – as far as we know – continued their education at the schools to which Bowes had sent them. He, meanwhile, claimed that the deed executed by the Countess before her marriage should be declared null and void because he had not been told about it, and because it interfered with his rights as a husband. The Countess responded by appealing to the Consistory Court of the Bishop of London for a divorce, on the grounds of cruelty and adultery.

The mills of the Court of Chancery always ground slowly. *The Times* had recently complained of its appallingly slow and expensive procedures, its obstructionism and obscurantism, the obstacles raised to its reform by professional interests, the way in which it wasted the lives of those who came within its grasp. 'Ask why such a family is ruined,' its leader writer demanded, 'ask why such a one drowned himself, and another is disgraced – you are just as likely as not to hear that a Chancery suit is at the bottom of it. . . . A suit in that court is endless, bottomless, and insatiable.'[2]

But the Countess had little option but to place her affairs in the court's hands. She must recover her fortune, and she could only hope that the process would not be too prolonged, or she would be reduced to bankruptcy and poverty while the Lord Chancellor and the Master of the Rolls, the two judges of the Court, considered her case and the Cross Bill submitted by Bowes's lawyers, reading their leisurely way through the massive bundle of documents placed before them – complaint and rejoinder, statements on one side and on the other, the testimony of witnesses, all recorded, collated, repeated not once but two or three times.

In a cross-suit brought early in 1786 Bowes asserted once more that the pre-nuptial deed should be declared null and void. His argument was that she had not told him of her intentions, and had never shown him the deeds – which was certainly, he claimed, an unfair and illegal act by a wife against her husband. He should, he went on, be sent regular statements of the income from his wife's estate, and should during their lifetime be entitled to receive it. The couple presented to the court a delightful, weirdly obscure tangle of litigation for the lawyers to hack their way through. Marriage law was still an amalgam of canon law, which laid down the rules of marriage, and customary law, which had jurisdiction over matters arising from debt and credit. There was a huge volume of litigation in this area, much of which laid down precedent to make the path forward rockier, slower, and extremely profitable for the lawyers concerned.

With yet another housemaid pregnant by him, Bowes sought for ways of contributing to what he trusted would be the downfall of the Countess. He sent the court a copy of the manuscript of her *Confessions*, which among other things showed her to be an adulteress, pregnant by a lover while her husband, the Earl, was still alive. But the incidents she described had all occurred before her marriage to Bowes, and had no legal force where the court case was concerned.

He had plenty of other things to occupy his time: bribing or trying to bribe those servants who knew of his treatment of his wife and might be called on to give evidence against him; finding the servants he had raped, and bribing them to keep quiet about his illegitimate children; and all the time keeping watch on his wife – following her movements from Dyer's Buildings to Hart Street, and then Bloomsbury Square, but never daring to approach her.

For thirteen months the Bishop's court turned and re-turned the pages of depositions from the Countess, her servants, her doctors and the chaplains, and from Bowes and his supporters. Finally the case was set down for hearing in May 1786. It was in that month that two scurrilous engravings of the Countess were published. One, which came out on 25 May, bears the title *LADY TERMAGANT FLAYBUM going to give her STEP SON a taste of her DESERT after Dinner, a scene performed every day near Grosvenor Square, to the annoyance of the neighbourhood*. It depicts Lady Strathmore, in an advanced stage of décolletage, lying back in a chair, with a nurse holding out a young boy towards her, one hand undoing his breeches. In the second, *The Injured COUNT . . S*, she is shown lolling at a table, clinking glasses with a decrepit and possibly diseased old man. Two cats are sucking at her breasts, and a small boy at her knee is exclaiming 'I wish I was a cat – my Mama would love me then'; over her shoulder hangs a handsome young man in a night-cap, holding a candle, and saying 'My Lady, it's time to come to bed'.

The two drawings were the products of the most famous of all English caricaturists, James Gillray. Gillray was then not quite thirty, and for seven years had been delighting the public with the earliest of his long series of over 1,500 caricatures. The two dealing with the Countess were put out by W. Holland of 66 Drury Lane, who had already published some of his engravings, and C. Morgan of Holles Street (a street in which the Countess was later to live for a time). Gillray's work was published by a number of people, though by 1786 he was already living in the house of Miss Humphrey. She brought out his work almost exclusively until his death in 1815, but her shop was not yet famously associated with him – later, it became almost impossible to walk down St James's Street once word had got out that a new Gillray caricature was in her window.

By 1780 Gillray had already turned from the social caricatures which had first brought him to the public's attention to the political ones for which he became most famous. The fact that he produced two focusing on Lady Strathmore may have had less to do with the fact that her case had caused considerable public comment and gossip, than that he had been primed and probably paid by Stoney Bowes. There is no proof of this, but the suggestion seems supportable when one considers the caricatures themselves. While the fact that she loved cats may well have been public knowledge, as perhaps was her neglect of her eldest son, the first drawing on the face of it is pure malice – and inaccurate to boot: she had no step-son, and the implicit allegation that she might have a sexual interest in young boys – let alone in her own son, for presumably that is the boy referred to – is, on the face of it, ludicrous.

One might almost think that the drawing did not refer to our subject at all: yet it has always been firmly identified as alluding to her.[3] The explanation may be that Bowes commissioned Gillray to draw the caricatures to blacken his wife's name and, presumably, to influence any jury before whom he might have to appear. The idea was not particularly original: open accusations of sexual misconduct were often made in order to point up alleged moral shortcomings (not necessarily sexual). Examples which spring to mind are the campaign against George III's widowed mother Augusta, alleged in cartoons to be having an affair with the first minister, John Stuart, Earl of Bute; and, indeed, the even more scurrilous case of the libelling of Marie Antoinette, later in the century accused in cartoons of having committed incest with her son.

Whether the Gillray caricatures actually did the Countess any real harm is doubtful – though the public, as usual, reacted with delight to this and any other allusion to the splendid scandal which was entertaining them. For her part Mary Eleanor, while she had learned by now that she had to put up with everything the press or public gossip threw at her, cannot but have been outraged by them, even while others were buying them as delightful examples of the artist's barbed wit. But there was nothing she could do but sit tight and do her best to ignore the ordure.

The Bishop's Court found against Bowes. A separation was granted, and he was ordered to pay his wife £300 a year in alimony. He immediately appealed to the Court of Arches, and the case was stalemated while the appeal was put in motion. He decided to make good use of the pause, and take matters into his own hands.

ELEVEN

'Can You Keep a Secret?'

A place where no woman who regards delicacy would appear so late as the hours of ten or eleven at night, yet at such a place and at such hours Lady Strathmore often visited Captain Farrer.

Mary Farrer, *The Appeal*

Bowes had decided that if he was to continue to enjoy the fruits of his labours – the pursuit, capture and marriage of Lady Strathmore – he must persuade or cajole her to return to him as his wife, at least for a short period of time (if he could prove that they had cohabited even for a few days, her suit would collapse), and to sign a paper agreeing to drop her divorce suit. This last was vital – if a decree nisi were granted, much of the £10,000 a year he was still receiving from her estate would revert to her.

The Countess was perfectly aware of this, and her experience of Bowes's brutality and persistence had prompted her, just after her escape from Grosvenor Square, to write to the Chief Justice, Lord Mansfield:

My Lord,
The authentic information I receive from all quarters, of Mr Bowes's repeated declarations that he 'will have Lady Strathmore, let the consequence be what it may', has at length driven me to a step which I have long wished to take, but could not, till now, prevail on myself to risk, from an apprehension that the very incompetent idea which a man of honour can form of Mr Bowes's deep, wicked, and dangerous scheme should induce your Lordship to think my intrusion merely impertinent, and my fears entirely visionary. I am now, however, irresistibly urged by my too justly grounded terrors, most solemnly to entreat, in that name of a God who abhors every act of cruelty and oppression, that your Lordship will force Mr Bowes to restore me, should he put his threats into execution by seizing me himself, or by the crew of ruffians whom he has hired to watch incessantly; for there is the strongest reason to believe that he intends carrying me off, either by forcibly entering my lodgings, or at any of the very few

opportunities when an indispensable attention to my health obliges me to take an occasional airing.

As a preparation against such accidents, I therefore beg to declare upon my oath, in this manner, or in person (if your Lordship and the forms of the law permit it,) that I never will, except by force, return to Mr Bowes; and that if he should, after he has thus seized me, produce any paper signed by my name which contains a declaration that I am willing to live with him, it must either be an absolute forgery, or extracted by the immediate danger my life would be in, if I refused to comply; and your Lordship may be assured that I should joyfully snatch the first moment after I was produced in Court, or in your presence, to make my recantation, and expose every fraud and violence which has been practised upon me. As habeas corpus would, I hope, have the same effect in my case as in that of the *poor girl** whom Mr Bowes carried off, and I have given a written sanction to sue for one, under such circumstances.

I am, and not without much concern, sensible that I now trespass on all form, and even on that respect which is due to your Lordship, and which no heart is more justly penetrated than mine; but fear, like death, tramples on all etiquettes, and surely never fear was more excusable than that under which I at present drag under my existence, in the hourly expectation of losing it, or, what is ten thousand times worse, of being reduced to endure Mr Bowes's cruelties 'til their excess has put a period to my sufferings, which it was very near doing when I quitted him.

I have the honour to subscribe myself, with the greatest respect and esteem, My Lord,

Your Lordship's much obliged and devoted humble servant,

M.E. Bowes Strathmore.[1]

The letter gives us some idea of how sure the Countess was of her husband's intentions. By the autumn, though beset by various troubles – the chief of which was her apprehension about Bowes's determination in one way or another to get her to withdraw her divorce suit – she was living in reasonable comfort in Bloomsbury Squaee, attended by a number of servants – including the faithful Mary Morgan, as upper servant and companion, a footman (Robert Crundel) and a coachman (Daniel Lee). She had also a new protector, one Captain Henry Farrer, brother of James Farrer, her solicitor.

---

*   Dorothy Stevenson

It was James Farrer who paid her rent. Bowes had no intention of honouring the order to pay alimony of £300 a year, and in any case that would not have gone far in keeping the Countess in the style to which she intended to become accustomed, now she was out of his grasp and no longer subject to his meanness. However, until a legal settlement was reached she had no access to her income, hence it was convenient to rely on an attorney who was sufficiently confident of the firmness of her legal situation to consider it a safe gamble to support her until her case against Bowes was won.

James Farrer's home was in Carlisle – he travelled to London when a consultation with his client was necessary – but his brother Henry lived in London, and was introduced to Mary Eleanor, who was no doubt pleased to have some agreeable male company.

The Farrer family was not a wealthy one – indeed, the brothers' father had been a bankrupt. James seems to have made his way fairly rapidly in the law; Henry went to sea, and eventually became a captain in the service of the East India Company. In 1781, in London, he met and secretly married a young woman called Mary Goldsmith – she suggests that the secrecy was because she was of lower station than the Farrers[2] – and for some time lived with her and her mother at Nonesuch Park. His wife supported him, for he could not find a command at the time, and was completely without means. She made a small income first as a milliner and mantua maker, and then when that business failed by cleaning silk stockings and starching muslin for ladies.

Farrer spent much of his time travelling about the country looking for some form of profitable occupation, leaving his wife in London to make enough money to support herself, and send some to him. She had a hard time of it, living in a single room in Stafford Street, off Piccadilly, reduced to selling the small amount of family silver she possessed, and falling prey to rheumatism, she says, from washing linen in a damp place.

At last, Farrer managed to get a berth as captain of the East India Company's vessel *True Briton* and he and his wife were reunited for a week or so at Portsmouth before he sailed for the East. He left her with £30, and swore that he had given instructions to a relative to collect £10 from India House for her every six months. However, when no money turned up and she called on her husband's kinsman at Deptford, the man not only refused to help her, insisting that he had no instructions to do so, but attempted to assault her.

Eventually, some money did come through. She went to live with her brother at Ramsgate, and eventually, when the *True Briton* returned, was happily reunited with her husband at Deal. They then took rooms in Kensington.

Henry Farrer, however, had returned complete with a mistress, a Mrs Parks. She was not (he assured his wife) *currently* his mistress. He had taken her to India with him in that capacity some seven years earlier, but had lost her to another captain, Parks, who had given her six children and then deserted her. Farrer had found her living in poverty. Mary Farrer was cautiously sympathetic, and believed her husband when he said that his intention in bringing Mrs Parks (as she called herself) back to England was to force her ex-lover to make a settlement on her.[3] Eventually, he seems to have managed that.

Mrs Farrer soon realised that she had not married an uxorious husband. He continually entertained Mrs Parks at expensive rooms which he had taken in the Temple, and when she called on Mrs Parks his wife found them in a compromising position. Later, he invited Mrs Farrer's young unmarried sister to his rooms and violently assaulted her: she defended herself with spirit – for three hours, Mrs Farrer tells us, after which 'he being fatigued with the contest gave it up'. A little later, when the same sister was sleeping in Mrs Farrer's house, he forced his way into her room and again made an attempt on her – he was violent, his wife claimed, to the point almost of madness, and cursed his wife for intervening.

Her discovery of some love-letters written to her husband by a woman who at least could not be accused of ignorance or illiteracy – Mary Eleanor, Countess of Strathmore – may not have surprised her, even if she did not already know of their friendship. The letters hoped for 'a repetition of those pleasures [the Countess] had contributed to entertain him with' and contained 'warm solicitations to visit at her house or other places of assignation'.[4] It was not difficult for Mary Farrer to confirm that Lady Strathmore frequently called at Farrer's chambers, that they often made excursions into the country. It was the last straw, and the couple separated.

The Countess certainly had a talent for falling for the wrong sort of men: the cold, indifferent Strathmore; the energetic but dim Gray; the violent, deranged Bowes; and now another potentially violent, ambitious and, as it turned out, spineless man, Farrer. It seems likely that he had his eye on a possible marriage, after his friend had achieved her divorce and recovered her income. Was he her lover? If we are to believe Mrs Farrer, then certainly. We know that soon after they had been introduced, the Captain regularly called at the house in Bloomsbury Square. Mrs Farrer says that the couple visited Tunbridge

Wells together, and that Mary Eleanor called on Farrer at his chambers, 'a place where few modest women venture to visit even their lawyers or counsel, unless under the protection of some male friend, a place where no woman who regards delicacy would appear so late as the hours of ten or eleven at night, yet at such a place and at such hours Lady Strathmore often visited Captain Farrer. A woman called Morgan often attended, as I presume for the purpose of keeping up appearances.'

A sexual relationship seems probable. Mary Eleanor was a spirited and warm-blooded creature, for too long deprived of affection. A lover who could also act as a protector was extremely desirable, for she continued to fear that Bowes was planning some dastardly scheme against her.

TWELVE

'Ready, my Boys'

Can you arrest a Countess as you can a common person?
                                    Mary Morgan, *The Trial*

For the moment Bowes remained in the North Country, and our only evidence of what he got up to is *Paddy's Progress*, which suggests that he attempted to stage his own suicide. The evidence is slender, but the ballad's author lived near Gibside and knew Bowes and his servants well, so though on the face of it the action seems ludicrous we can probably believe it. At all events, he set the scene for

                                    A deep tragedy
Perform'd by known actors, whose number was three:
The first was that scheming, and deep plotting Paddy,
The next Joe the groom – a fly and smooth laddy;
Then Charley, a Collier,[1] did bring up the rear,
Because to a falsehood he boldly would swear.
Now, in the first act, the scene was well known,
To be at the house of the late Doctor Brown;[2]
And also the time that was fix'd for performing,
Was early (you'll find) on a good Sunday morning.
When Charles on the stage his appearance first made,
With countenance grave, to the Doctor he said,
'May't please you, good sir, I come to relate
And give you account of poor Bowes's sad fate . . .
At Gibside (said Charley) this morning I've been,
I ask'd for my master – but none had him seen;
A report like a pistol they heard in his room,
But the door being locked, they could not get to'm:
Desirous to know how this matter would end,
By means of a ladder, I then did ascend,
Thus in at his window I got with all speed,
But as for the rest, I can hardly proceed!
The floor I observed with blood covered o'er,

On the bed lay my master extended in gore!
On a table hard by, swords and pistols I see'd,
With which I suspect, he accomplish'd the deed!'[3]

Brown was clearly suspicious, for he declined to ride over to the house to confirm the suicide's death. But in the meantime 'Charley' went to the colliery nearest to Gibside and told the same story to the pitmen there, and was evidently believed, for a number of men downed tools and tramped over to Gibside, anxious about their jobs and their pay, if it proved to be the case that their employer had done away with himself. Finally, the door of his house was opened and Bowes appeared:

then came amongst them, when smiling he said
'Well, Lads, did you really think I was dead?'
Then placing himself right before them, he cries
'Well, I hope you will now believe your own eyes?
I cannot think who could have raised this report,
Nor yet what the devil such villains had for't!'[4]

The pit workers were not impressed by his joke, and together with his regular displays of meanness, the episode further racked up their general mistrust and dislike of him. What did Bowes hope to gain by such a pantomime? Martin Brown, the author of the ballad, suggested that he hoped the news of his death would delay or even prevent his coming to trial, but this seems unlikely. He may rather have had some crude idea of engaging Mary Eleanor's sympathy when the story got about in London.

A few weeks later, in early October 1786, he left Gibside, travelling south under the pseudonym of 'Colonel Medison' and taking back roads to the west of the Peak district. On 14 October he stopped for the night at the Crown at Stone, 7 miles or so north of Stafford. A young post-boy, Peter Orme, was riding one of the horses drawing the coach in which Bowes left that town, and at one of the stops was asked whether he wanted a place. He was delighted to be engaged as a groom at 20 guineas a year, and 1 guinea in his hand.[5] Bowes rode on down to London, leaving Orme to follow immediately and make his own way to the Swan with Two Necks in Lad Lane, which ran west from Milk Street to Wood Street, in Cripplegate. There, the boy found two of Bowes's men: a coal merchant from Newcastle called Francis Peacock, who had for years been a friend of Bowes, and the latter's French valet, Mark Prevot. They took Orme off to the Grand Hotel in Covent

Garden, where he stayed on the night of the 15th, before being taken next day to 18 Norfolk Street, off the Strand, a house which Bowes had taken under his assumed name of Colonel Medison. Orme was told that Bowes's horses had not yet arrived, and he wouldn't be wanted for work until they did; but he was to stay in Norfolk Street and not budge.

He did so, curiously watching Bowes's comings and goings, which seemed rather odd. Sometimes his employer sallied forth as Medison, a large black wig thrust over his own hair; sometimes as an old man, perhaps a Justice of the Peace, in grey wig and with spectacles on nose; sometimes – and here farce seems to creep in – as a sailor (sadly, we do not know whether this means an officer's uniform or an impersonation of a Jolly Jack Tar – the fact that he wore 'sailor's trowsers' is the best information we have, which suggests the latter).

After his horses arrived, Bowes almost daily ordered his carriage to be driven by Orme, invariably with the blinds up, either to Bloomsbury Square or to the nearby streets – Russell Street, Southampton Street, Bloomsbury Way, Bury Place or Galen Place, where it loitered so that any appearance by the Countess could be observed. Occasionally there would be two coaches, Bowes and Chapman (the pitman, who sometimes called himself Cummins) in one, Bowes always armed – usually with both a horse-pistol and a small-sword – with Peacock and Prevot in the other. By the way of explanation, Orme was told that Bowes had been robbed of some plate, or sometimes he claimed of some jewellery, and that he was going about in disguise to see if he could catch the thief. Soon, the Countess's servants became suspicious. It would have taken a cleverer man than Bowes to mount such a close observation of the house without being noticed. The Countess began to have her own suspicions, while her servants were quite sure that something was afoot. Daniel Lee saw the same carriage returning again and again to the square, pausing outside the house, often for several hours at a stretch; sometimes the blinds would be drawn aside and an eye would be seen, looking out. One morning Thomas Crundel, one of the footmen, noticed a coach standing just outside with the blinds up and thought he recognised Bowes himself, peeping out.

Sometimes, Orme later said, they drove to Hyde Park Corner and down to the King's Road and Chelsea, 'looking about to see if they could see the persons they wanted'.[6] (One wonders if on these occasions Bowes was actually following the Countess on some of her expeditions with Farrer.) After a time, Bowes got bored with continually watching the house without the opportunity for action, and decided to show himself again for a while in the North Country, which might have the effect of making his wife relax her vigilance. Taking Orme, Prevot and John Bickley (his coachman) and leaving Chapman, Peacock and William Pigg (another pitman he had recruited) in Norfolk Street, he retired to Gibside, and was soon seen prominently displaying himself at the cattle market in the blackened, shabby town of Barnard Castle.

It was important to him that everyone should know that he was in Durham minding his own business, and being seen at Barnard cattle market was scarcely news likely to be reported in the London papers. Some more dramatic incident was necessary. On 24 October he sent for Dr Robert Hobson, who had attended both himself and the Countess at Gibside.

'I have a secret to trust you with,' he told the doctor.[7] 'Can you keep a secret?'

The doctor said he could.

'The situation of my affairs is such,' Bowes continued, 'that I wish to be secret for a while, for I am afraid some trouble is coming upon me. The thing is this: I will fall off my horse tomorrow, between Streatlam Castle and Barnard Castle. You will be sent for, and you must say I have fallen off my horse and broke three of my ribs – you must attend me at the Castle the next morning.'

The doctor agreed. Whether or not he disliked or mistrusted Bowes, wealthy patients were thin on the ground in his practice, apart from which Bowes seems to have convinced him that he had devised the ruse as a harmless way of evading his creditors.

So on 25 October, Bowes went out riding with Henry Bourne, the steward at Streatlam. The order of the following events is rather confused, but at some stage Bowes got off his horse and lay down on the ground while Bourne rode off to fetch Dr Hobson. A Mr Colpits, who knew both Bowes and Bourne, later happened on the scene, and Bourne told him that Bowes had had a bad accident – his horse had fallen, and 'pitched over him'. He had 'broke his leg, and everything but his neck'. Colpits later said that he was rather suspicious, because Bowes had the reputation of being something of a practical joker, but when he came up he saw him 'lying near the turnpike, apparently dead, with his head on a heap of stones and a little hay under him'. Prevot and one or two other men were there, and were tying up Bowes's arm – the doctor had presumably bled him. There was no sign of a broken leg, and Bowes's neck seemed intact.

After a while, a post-chaise appeared and Bowes was placed in it. Colpits gives a curious detail: he says that Bourne took money out of Bowes's pocket and he and his associates counted it – 'I heard it jingle in their hands' – and turning to the doctor Bourne asked him to witness that it amounted to £14,000. Colpits must have wondered, as well we may, what Bowes was doing riding about the country with the modern equivalent of £1¼ million in cash in his pockets. *Could* one get that amount of money in cash in one's pockets? The current coin of the highest value was the gold 5-guinea piece, and Bowes would have had to carry 3,200 of them. The jingling would have been considerable. What can be the explanation? The story was clearly a fiction yet both Colpits and the doctor confirmed it, under oath, in court. The incident remains a mystery, unless the story, when it got about, was meant to convince the neighbourhood that Bowes was a wealthy man who did not need to pursue his wife in a desperate attempt to keep her money.

Bowes was taken to Streatlam Castle, whence (Colpits says) 'a great deal of pains was taken' to spread the news of the accident. A number of people called to pay their respects, but were turned away; the only person allowed into his bedroom was his solicitor, Thomas Bowes (no relative), who rode the 18 miles from Darlington for the purpose. The castle was shut up, and anyone who called was told that the invalid was a little better, but 'too bad to be seen'.

If the news that her husband had been injured in a fall and incapacitated gave the Countess sufficient reason to relax her caution, this was a mistake. On 28 October Bowes was seen at the Cock at Eaton Socon, 14 miles from Cambridge – well on his way back to Norfolk Street.[8] His plans for his wife's immediate future were beginning to come together. A few days later Bowes, Chapman, Pigg and Peacock met at a pub called the Pyed Bull, in Russell Street – all in disguise, Bowes in his sailor suit and the others dressed as servants. They drank a pot of beer each, and then called for 1*s*'s worth of gin and the landlord, one Edward Crooke. They said they wanted beds for the night. Crooke said he had no room. Bowes suggested they might come back the following day and dine at the inn – bread and cheese would suit them fine.

Next day Chapman and Peacock returned in a hackney coach, and over their bread and cheese told the landlord that they had travelled some 500 or 600 miles from the North Country in pursuit of thieves. They hoped he might be of service to them, and told him to clean himself up, put on some decent clothes, and report to the house in Norfolk Street. There, he was introduced to Colonel Medison, whom they addressed as a Justice of the Peace (Bowes complete with wig and spectacles, sitting in an impressive chair, with Pigg in attendance as his clerk). The Colonel produced an impressively bound book and swore

Crooke to secrecy on it, offered him money, and asked if he knew of a dependable constable.

It would have taken an extremely stupid man not to have realised that there was something untoward about the situation, and Crooke said yes, he did know of a reliable constable, and would certainly introduce him to the Colonel. His confidant was Edward Lucas, known as 'four-eyes' because of the spectacles he always wore. Crooke had known Lucas for two or three years, and told him the tale. Lucas agreed that an introduction to Colonel Medison might be profitable, and a meeting was arranged.

Lucas was one of eighty voluntary constables employed in Westminster, ostensibly chosen from among the respectable, honest citizens of the parish. Parish constables drew no pay, and were expected to do their constabulary work in their spare time. This was fine in theory, but in practice the chosen tradesmen were usually not eager to give up their time to voluntary work and work which might be dangerous at that, and considered it well worth their while to pay substitutes to do their duty for them. The result was that many of the constables were dishonest, and so badly paid that they were happy to take bribes from anyone with something to hide or something to gain.

If Crooke did not tip him off, Bowes probably realised the moment he saw Lucas that the latter was susceptible to bribery, and offered him a large sum of money to get himself introduced into Lady Strathmore's house as a 'peace officer', one who knew she was in danger, and could protect her. Lucas bargained for a while, and in the end was offered not only money down but, once Bowes had regained his proper authority over his wife, some houses the Countess owned, at a peppercorn rent, and the promise of employment at the Custom House, which Bowes assured him he would be able to procure.

It took Lucas no time at all to gain the confidence of Lee, the Countess's coachman. Lee had a particularly fine dog and the constable, who knew about dogs, congratulated him on the animal, fell into conversation, and walked back with him to the rear of the house in Bloomsbury Square. There, Lucas remarked on how strongly the rear entrance was protected – all those locks and bolts!

'We have need of that,' said Lee, and when Lucas asked why, the coachman explained about the mysterious carriages which had been lurking in the area. Moreover, he said, a day or so ago he had followed three or four men down Little Russell Street and seen them looking at the Countess's house and pointing at the stable doors as though they were thinking of breaking in.

On 1 November, on Lee's recommendation, Lucas was introduced to the Countess. He had taken the liberty of watching the house for two or three days, he said, and had seen some rough fellows lurking about.

'My lady, they are very ill-looking fellows,' he went on; 'they look as though they deserve to be hanged. They must have something very infamous in view.' He suggested that he should be hired to protect the house and herself, 'to go backward and forward and give her notice' of anything untoward.[9] Mary Eleanor agreed, and he was employed on a retainer of 12s a week.

The first thing he discovered, to his chagrin, was that the Countess had somehow contrived to find herself an honest night-watchman. Bribes were often paid to night-watchmen or 'Charlies', who were usually happy to supplement their average income of 1s a night, but the Countess's man was not only being paid 10s a night, but was clearly honest so Lucas persuaded her that the sum she was paying him was exorbitant, and in any case no longer a necessary expense. He then went about finding a trustworthy accomplice and introduced himself to another constable, one William Saunders. Over several glasses of punch, they chatted for a while. What was Saunders doing tomorrow, 10 November? Saunders said he was going to Smithfield on business – nothing very important. Lucas winked, and told him that if he would give that up and come with him instead 'on some particular business', he could earn himself 1 guinea. Saunders agreed. Lucas also engaged the services of three other constables, none of whom was any better than he should be.

Meanwhile, Chapman went before a magistrate, Mr Justice Walker, and swore that he went in danger of his life from three servants of the Countess of Strathmore – a footman called Crundel, a coachman called Lee, and Mrs Mary Morgan, an upper servant. Really? asked the magistrate. Yes, said Chapman. He had been threatened, and 'it's time to be afraid when a pistol is put to my head'.[10] He offered no evidence to support his allegation, but unpaid parish magistrates were as susceptible to bribes as constables (one, Sir Thomas de Veil, boasted that he made £1,000 a year, in that way[11]), and money may have changed hands (the fact the Lucas had worked for Walker is perhaps suggestive). A warrant was granted against the three servants.

Next day, Bowes ordered Orme to fetch two horses from a stable at Water Lane, off Lower Thames Street. He came back with two stalwart bays, and was told to take them to St Giles, hire a chaise and drive it to the turnpike at Tottenham Court, on the road to Barnet. Arriving there between ten and eleven in the morning, he settled down to wait for

Bowes. Meanwhile Lucas went to the Countess to pick up his retainer. He asked whether she meant to go out that day. She said yes, she was going out, but that Captain Farrer would be accompanying her as her protector. Lucas bowed and left, making his way to the Yorkshire Grey in Hart Street, where Saunders was waiting with another constable, Broad. Upstairs, they ordered a pint of purl.[12] Lucas was nervous and impatient, 'pacing backwards and forwards about the room, and began to damn and swear that other people did not come'. Eventually Meacham, one of the other constables, was seen in the street, and Lucas leaned out of the window and called him up. Then at last Saunders appeared, and a coach rattled up and Chapman got out of it. He and Lucas conferred for a while in a corner, then they went down into the street, where Lucas summoned a hackney coach.

'Come down – we are all ready, my boys,' he said, and they all piled in.

They loitered near Bloomsbury Square ready to follow the Countess's coach, driven by Daniel Lee with Crundel at his side, as it left the house and drove to Forster's ironmonger's shop in Oxford Street. One might wonder what Mary Eleanor wanted with an ironmonger until one recalls that then ironmongers often acted as nurserymen, selling plants and trees and 'all sorts of Garden Seeds flower seeds and flower roots; fruit trees flowering shrubs evergreens and forest trees. Also shears, rakes, reels, hoes, spades, scythes, budding and pruning knives, watering pots, mats, sieves and all sorts of materials for gardening.'[13]

Mrs Morgan and Captain Farrer got out and went into the shop. Immediately they were inside, Lucas and Saunders were out of their coach and into the street, and Saunders stretched up his hand and grasped the rail of the box of the Countess's coach, making to climb up. Lee hit out at him and told him to get down.

'No, damn you, I will not get down,' said Saunders. 'I have a warrant against you!' At which he waved a piece of paper at the coachman, took him by the arm and pulled him from the box. Meanwhile, Lucas had arrested Crundel, and one of the rogue constables took the two of them, who were intimidated by the warrants produced, off to Justice Walker. There was never any question of their being prosecuted; they were merely conveniently detained for an hour or two and then, since Chapman, who had laid the complaint against them, did not appear, they were released.

Farrer, hearing the argument and seeing Lee and Crundel taken off, came out of the shop to see Broad on the box of the Countess's coach. Somewhat ineffectually, he merely asked Broad what he was doing there, and when Broad answered, pistol in hand, that 'he should know', held his peace. Perhaps we need not blame him too much: he had left his pistol in the Countess's coach, and it was now stuck in Lucas's belt.

The fracas in the street was clearly audible inside Forster's shop, and Mary Eleanor and Mrs Morgan, seeing the two servants arrested, rushed upstairs, where they locked themselves in a store-room, shouting to Mr Forster to go and fetch assistance. In a while there was a knock on the door.

'Who's there?' asked Mary Eleanor.

'My dear lady, here is your friend Lucas.'

'Oh, Lucas – open the door!'

She turned the key, and Lucas entered. He told her not to be afraid, but there were a hundred people collected in the street, and her coachman and footman had been arrested and taken away. However, he reassured her that she might depend upon his taking care of her, even at the peril of his life.

Nervously Mary Eleanor and Mrs Morgan accompanied him downstairs, where his deception was revealed when he told the hapless Countess that he had a warrant for her arrest.

'I must carry you to Lord Mansfield's at Caen Wood,' he said (the Lord Chief Justice's house stood between Hampstead and Highgate).

'Can you arrest a countess as you can arrest a common person?' asked Mary Morgan.

Lucas turned on her.

'As for you, Mrs Morgan,' he said, 'I advise you to go away – there are more warrants against you!'

Morgan whispered to the Countess that she would go out by the back door and make straight for the office of James Farrer, her solicitor. As she left, Lucas pulled out his constable's staff, took Mary Eleanor by the arm, and said: 'By God, my lady, you are my prisoner, and at peril of my life I must take you!'

Outside, the Countess refused to get into the coach unless Captain Farrer was allowed to accompany her. They rattled away down Oxford Street to Tottenham Court Road turnpike, where Orme was waiting with the chaise. Inside it, now, sat Bowes. The three vehicles pelted along towards Highgate – first the coach with Lucas, the Countess and Farrer, then a hackney carriage carrying Chapman, Prevot and Pigg, and finally the chaise with Bowes. Lucas continued to keep the Countess in a state of nervous fear: there would be 'terrible work', he said, if any resistance was offered, and he was afraid that lives would be lost.

At Highgate, the coach stopped at the Red Lion Inn where the Countess was taken into an upstairs room. She looked out of the window and for the first time in months saw her husband. She cannot have been altogether astonished, but nevertheless threw up the sash and shouted 'Murder! Murder!' No one took any notice. Bowes followed Farrer inside the inn, and asked who he was.

'I am a gentleman,' he replied.

'Well that is my wife,' said Bowes, pointing upstairs.

Farrer attempted to leave, to raise the alarm.

'Sir,' said Bowes, 'if you do not be quiet I will knock you down.'

'Mr Bowes,' said Farrer, on his dignity, 'remember what you have said.'

'Sir, I will give you satisfaction,' snapped Bowes.

It was an exchange between two not overly courageous men, and led nowhere. Farrer later said: 'I did not think myself bound as a gentleman to take notice of Mr Bowes; there was very great confusion in the place.'[14]

That was certainly true. Lucas and his confederates were taking advantage of the stop to have a drink or two, Farrer and Bowes were quarrelling at the door, and upstairs the Countess was still shouting 'Murder!' out of the window. The landlord, William Broughton, was understandably alarmed but thought the row probably had something to do with 'a runaway match to Gretna Green', and went about his business. Eventually Lucas went up and pulled Mary Eleanor away from the window, and he and Pigg took her downstairs and bundled her into her coach. She pulled Farrer in with her, and Bowes and Lucas climbed in after them. As they drove off the Countess clung desperately to Farrer.

'Damn you, madam,' said Bowes, 'are you not ashamed of yourself?'

Mary Eleanor was silent for a while, and then began to protest that they were not driving in the direction of Caen Wood. Farrer agreed, but when they both continued to protest, Bowes threatened to throw the captain out of the window.

A little further on, he stopped the coach.

'Sir,' he said to Farrer, 'you may get out of the carriage.'

Farrer showed some hesitation, but when Bowes pointed his pistol at him, he detached himself from the Countess, got down into the road, and more or less disappears from the story. Later he gave evidence for Mary Eleanor against Bowes, but does not seem ever to have spoken to her again. Hardly the knight in shining armour she had believed him to be.

Onward the procession went. At one in the morning of the next day, 11 November, it reached the Bell Inn at Stilton. The Countess succeeded in breaking the window of the coach, and was heard to shout 'Murder! Murder! Help for God's sake! Murder! Murder!' Bowes, exercising all his charm, told the landlord that she was a poor madwoman, and he allowed himself to be persuaded.[15] The party entered the inn.

William Barker, who was living at the Bell, heard Bowes call for pen and paper, and – an inquisitive fellow – saw him write out a document which he wanted his wife to sign. She refused: 'I will not sign it for you or anybody,' she said. Bowes struck her in the face, and Barker heard her 'hallowing out murder'. Her husband then threatened her with a pistol: 'Say your prayers, for I shall kill you.' Still she refused, and told him to fire. Barker heard Bowes mutter grudgingly, 'By God, you are an astonishing woman!'[16] He then forced her outside and tried to push her again into the carriage. She wriggled away from him and ran down the street, calling 'Murder, murder! – is there nobody to assist me?'

Lucas ran after her, took hold of her, and pushing her into the carriage cried out: 'Yes, I will assist you! – I will jump up behind.' He did so, Bowes climbed in beside his wife, and they drove off. As they did so, he was observed to strike his wife once more on the face, and hit her on the bare upper part of her breast with his watch-chain wrapped around his knuckles. When she complained, he thrust a handkerchief into her mouth.

On they drove – to Barnby Moor, where the Countess was allowed briefly to leave the coach, with Bowes protesting all the time at the delay; then on to the dirty and unpleasant Angel Inn at Doncaster, for fresh horses – they had already come 195 miles. The innkeeper, a Mr Woodcock, sent some grubby cakes out to Mary Eleanor, which she gratefully ate. At Ferry Bridge she needed urgently to leave the carriage; Bowes ordered it to stop, and pushed her into a field, where she relieved herself.

The weary prisoner made only one more attempt to raise the alarm: at Greta Bridge, the penultimate stop on her long journey, where she was once again allowed to get out, this time at a decent inn. She called out: 'I am brought here by force, and desire it may be made public.'

No one heard or, if they heard, none answered her.

By nine o'clock that evening, after a helter-skelter journey, Bowes and his wife reached Streatlam, followed by a second coach carrying the gaggle of other conspirators – Chapman and Prevot, Pigg and Peacock and the ubiquitous Lucas, who seems to have joined them on the permanent pay-roll. The journey, on which a traveller would normally expect to spend at least three days, had been accomplished in thirty-three hours.

THIRTEEN

'Her Ladyship Does Not Speak'

Lady Strathmore is a little woman, a longish Face, with fine dark brown Hair, rather Bulky over the Chest – Mr Bowes gives out that she is Dumb, and sometimes Disordered in her Mind – Her Ladyship does not speak.

Advertisement, *The Morning Post*

Mary Eleanor was almost faint with hunger and exhaustion after a journey which had seemed almost endless. At Streatlam Castle the door under the forbidding portico was opened by Henry Bourn, Bowes's steward, a man thoroughly in his employer's pocket. Standing behind him to welcome the Countess was Mary Gowland, the housekeeper, whose duties included personal services to Bowes which had resulted in her giving birth, very recently, to yet another of his illegitimate children.

Thinking to take advantage of his wife's fatigue, Bowes hurried her into the dining room, took his pistol from his belt, and laid on the table the document which he had written at the Bell at Stilton. Once again, she refused to sign. Bowes struck her. Then while the other men unpacked the luggage from the coaches, which included a quantity of firearms, he instructed Chapman and Pigg to carry her upstairs, following them into her bedroom.

'Are you reconciled to a dutiful domestic life?' he asked.

She hardly knew how to reply. Ordering Chapman and Pigg to remain in the room as witnesses, he threw off his clothes and attempted to rape her. Despite her weakened state, she successfully fought him off. Later, Chapman testified that she told her husband: 'I know your purpose well – I know your object – if you cannot compel me by force to give up my suit, you may notwithstanding compel me to that which is called cohabitation, and if you do, I will indict you for a rape.'[1]

Her threat seems to have frightened Bowes. It need not have done so – there was no such thing as marital rape; a husband had the right to have sex with his wife whenever and however he wished. He later claimed that she had willingly had intercourse with him between 12 and

20 November 1786. But on this occasion he abandoned his attempt and let her sleep.

Within a few hours, next morning, word got about that the Countess was being held at the castle against her will. The news had probably been spread by a coachman, Wade, who had been employed to drive the last few miles to Streatlam, and had overheard her cry for help at Greta Bridge. At the castle, and realising that the driver must have been aware that there was something strange about his passengers, Bourn attempted to allay his suspicions by suggesting that the Countess had been crying out because of the roughness of the roads.

'No,' said Wade; 'she didn't cry out until she was out of the coach.'

Bourn asked why he thought she had cried out; and Wade answered, 'Very like you may know as well as me.'

Whether Wade talked or not, within two days a crowd of men collected with the object of releasing her. Orme, looking out of an upper window, saw what he said was 'a great mob' – actually, about two hundred people, some of whom lit fires to keep themselves warm as they awaited developments. Late on Sunday evening, 12 November, Thomas Bowes, the solicitor with a practice in Darlington who was not related to Stoney Bowes, by whom he had been engaged from time to time to deal with minor legal matters, arrived and was admitted. The doors were locked behind him, and servants closed and barred the shutters of the fourteen large ground floor windows. It is probable that towards midnight that day Bowes took his wife quietly away through a back entrance, bundled up in her own clothes with a greatcoat over them and wearing 'an old bonnet belonging to some servant'. She was mounted pillion behind Chapman, and they rode off into the darkness. Thomas Bowes was under the impression that his namesake meant to get his wife out of the country, perhaps to Ireland. Lucas appears to have started back for London that morning, before the siege started, presumably with Saunders and Meacham.

On the Monday morning Ridgeway, a tipstaff, arrived at the castle with a writ of habeas corpus made out by the Lord Chief Justice at the behest of James Farrer's partner (Farrer was in Carlisle at the time) requiring Bowes to deliver the Countess up to the court. On the evidence of Mrs Morgan and Captain Farrer, Lord Mansfield had no hesitation in granting the writ, together with a 'Rule for Information against the persons concerned in seizing and carrying off by force the Right Honourable the Countess Dowager of Strathmore', instructing all Persons to 'give their Assistance in having her Ladyship produced to the Court of King's Bench.'

When Ridgeway knocked at the door, the solicitor, Thomas Bowes, shouted from behind it that he could not open it to anyone.

'Then open a window,' Ridgeway demanded.

This was done, and Ridgeway asked if Bowes was in the castle. The solicitor said no, he was not.

How long had he been gone?

'I cannot hold any conversation with you,' the solicitor replied.

Ridgeway later told the court, 'I waited there a long while – I shoved the rules under the door, and there I left them. I called out at the same time, "Mr Andrew Robinson Bowes, I have shoved a Habeas Corpus and a copy of the original Rule under the door, and I deem it a good service."'[2]

Young Orme later found the documents ('a paper with some writing on it' – he was illiterate) lying where they fell. He picked them up and handed them to solicitor Bowes, who the moment he saw what they were hastily dropped them, and told Orme to put them back where he had found them. Bowes later swore that he had not seen them.

By this time the men outside were laying siege to the castle, calling out for the Countess. Almost all were pitmen from the Strathmore collieries, particularly from Norbanks, about a mile and a half from Gibside, and mustered by one of the managers, John Langstaff, whose sympathies lay with the Countess. The low grumbling noise of the mob could be heard inside the house, with an occasional shout and a report which might have been a firework, or perhaps a pistol shot. This frightened Robert Peverill, a grocer who had called there in the ordinary way of business and now found himself trapped in a most unpleasant situation. 'The people were very violent,' he later reported, 'calling out for the Countess. . . . They were so threatening I scarce durst to have ventured out.'

Orme too peered out from a darkened window at the mob 'of many hundreds, nay thousand of colliers and people who remembered the father of the family and worked there' and who 'were assembled for the purpose of dragging her from the hands of ruffians'. They 'swore they would have Lady Strathmore, living or dead'. Jessé Foot writes that a couple of female servants were made to put on some of the Countess's clothes and show themselves at the window, to placate the crowd; but the stratagem, if indeed it was employed, did not succeed.[3]

The speed with which so many men arrived at the castle and their enthusiastic interest in the Countess's welfare perhaps reveal as much about Bowes's bad reputation as about any efforts Mary Eleanor may have made to be pleasant to the colliers or their wives; but clearly they thought more of her than of her husband. He was known to have ill-treated her, and Wade's story of her arrival at Streatlam may have lit the fuse which had burned with such alacrity.

On 15 November, James Farrer arrived at the castle, and was turned from the door. He was insistent, and when he threatened to summon the police, and it looked in any case as though the men now crowding around the house would be quite willing to break down the door, Thomas Bowes responded with 'I will let you in with one or two friends.' Farrer asked if the Countess was there. Bowes hesitated, then said she was not. Farrer rejoined: 'I presume you have *seen* Lady Strathmore?' Bowes said he had not. Farrer then insisted on searching the house, suspecting that she was in fact there. He and two constables he had brought with him conducted a thorough search. Finding no sign of Mary Eleanor, Farrer told Bowes 'You *must* know where she is.' Bowes did not answer, declaring he had no intention of saying anything on the matter.

'I then mentioned to Mr Bowes,' said Farrer later, 'that I would not be in his skin, knowing, as I conceived he did, where Mr Bowes and Lady Strathmore were, for the whole county of Durham.'

After a while, now apparently convinced that neither Bowes nor Lady Strathmore were any longer in the castle, the colliers reluctantly left.

While his solicitor, at least some of his accomplices and the unfortunate grocer were beset by the angry colliers, Bowes himself, together with Chapman and Pigg, were at a house belonging to the father of his housekeeper-mistress, Mary Gowland. Mary Eleanor was there also, but while Bowes enjoyed the moderate comfort of the living-room, such as it was, he had thrust her into a tiny, cold compartment where the bed was stored; when she protested, he threatened to put her in a straitjacket and confine her to Bedlam.[4] According to Jessé Foot, he again attempted to rape her, 'behaving to her in a manner shocking to the delicacy of civil life . . . and finding threats in vain, throwing her on the bed and flogging her with rods'.[5]

The party remained in Gowland's cottage until midnight on 16 November, when they set out into the darkness on horseback, ice cracking under the hooves until the falling snow smothered the tracks. Mary Eleanor was mounted bareback behind Chapman, sitting astride and clinging on as best she could. They wound their way over Bowes Moor in the direction of Appleby.

Even today, guides to the area describe Bowes Moor as 'remarkably wild and empty', and 'not the place to be in bad weather', and the winter of 1787 was one of the coldest winters of one of the coldest decades of the eighteenth century: snow had fallen in County Durham in early September and, far south, the Thames was frozen hard. In mid-November it was almost suicidal to venture out in such weather. The travellers fumbled their way through the darkness, the wind blowing stinging flurries of snow against their faces, until at five in the morning they reached a house at Argill belonging to a man called Shields. There, on the night of the 19th, the Countess was forced to sleep in the same room as Chapman and Pigg, though she was probably too exhausted and cold to trouble about any such embarrassment. They had a rough and ready meal, and at three in the afternoon set out again. In three hours they reached the turnpike at Brough Corner.

Bowes called out 'Gate! Gate!' and the turnpike-keeper, David Kirk, came out. Bowes asked what the charge was for three horses to pass through. Kirk said 3d, and Bowes paid it. Then he asked if the lady could warm herself before the fire. Kirk said she would be very welcome, whereupon Bowes lifted Mary Eleanor down and led her out of the snow and sleet into the house. Kirk, a sharp young man, remembered that she had been wearing a man's greatcoat with yellow buttons on the sleeves.[6]

Bowes took out 1s and threw it on the table. 'Maybe this lady will drink a dish of tea,' he said. The keeper's wife prepared some tea, and Mary Eleanor drank a cup. So did Mary Gowland, who was still with the party. Mrs Kirk was perplexed to see that her lady visitor had lost a shoe and stocking, and was not only cold and faint but more bedraggled and ill-dressed than her speech and behaviour would seem to suggest.

'Sir,' said Kirk, 'you have a very bad night to travel in.'

'It is a point of necessity,' Bowes replied; 'she has a daughter lying-in, at the point of death.'

'At the point of death!' said Kirk, 'what, at Appleby?'

'Yes, Appleby. Are there any good inns there?'

Kirk recommended one, and they prepared to leave. Mary Eleanor was still so cold and weak that Bowes bought a pennyworth of gin and forced her to drink it. Though she had never tasted gin before, and did not like it, it did warm her a little.

Kirk offered them a lantern to light their way.

'No, we want no light!' said Bowes.

'Oh, yes you do!' said Kirk, and they took it with an ill grace. The turnpike-keeper watched as they 'chucked' the Countess onto the horse behind Chapman and rode off. Later, at the trial, Kirk was asked by Bowes's defence lawyer whether her husband had not been 'very civil to the lady, and wanted to accommodate her.' 'Well,' he replied tartly, 'I think the gentleman wanted more to accommodate her than she wanted to be accommodated by him.'

Following what is now the A66, but was then a very minor road, they reached an inn at Appleby after another hour and three-quarters. There they gratefully ate supper and slept. In the morning Bowes took two post-chaises and the party set out at ten o'clock, pushing through the bustle of market day and on towards Penrith in the direction of the coast.

Bowes had been growing increasingly nervous, aware that sooner or later he must be pursued. They were not more than an hour out of Appleby when a lone rider overtook them and told him that a group of men seemed to be chasing them, and were only perhaps a mile behind. The chaises were too slow to outrun men on horseback. Bowes leaped out of his, pulling his wife after him, unbuckled the horses, and once more she found herself mounted bareback behind Chapman. They rode on 2 or 3 miles to Brampton.

There Bowes, calling himself 'Dr Hopper' and describing himself as 'a mad doctor' escorting an unfortunate female patient, complained that his chaise had broken down, and asked Ann Harrison, a woman of the village, for a horse to take him on to Coupland Beck, where he was expected. From there they rode on to Esplan Moor, where they found a cottager, John Lamb, to guide them over high moorland to Burton. By this time the Countess was in such a state – shivering from the cold and almost hysterical with exhaustion – that Bowes stopped at a cottage and allowed her to go in for a time and warm herself, explaining to the cottager that she was out of her mind. When she was reluctant to leave, Mary Gowland slapped and pinched her until she once more climbed up behind Chapman.

Bowes now seems to have lost all sense of purpose, and turned the party back to Shields's house at Argill. The snow was falling faster than ever, and was so deep on the moorland tracks that had it not been for Lamb's guidance they would have been lost. It was Lamb too who helped to lift Mary Eleanor when Chapman's horse stumbled and she fell into a snow-drift. As he carried her, she weakly implored him to help her: 'Tell them I'm here, tell them I'm here!' But 'Dr Hopper' had convinced the man that she was deranged and subject to hallucinations.

After three days on and off the road it was at four on the morning of Sunday 19 November that the party reached Bowes's solicitor's house at Darlington, where Thomas Bowes's wife gave the Countess a bed (taking the precaution of not allowing her servants a sight of the prisoner, lest they give the game away). Here, Bowes again attempted to get her to sign the by now dog-eared document he continued to carry about with him, threatening her with a red-hot poker; still she refused to sign.

After a few hours of warmth and uneasy sleep, Bowes and his captive drove on through Durham to Newcastle. At least the snow had stopped, but only to be replaced by heavy rain and bitter winds. Bowes bespoke four fresh horses, and drove off through the night towards Chollerton, just north of Hadrian's Wall. He was now on a road which led nowhere except the wilderness of Black Fell. Again, he apparently had no real object other than the hope that the purposelessness of his random journey would throw off any pursuers.

At Harlow Hill one of the coach windows broke, or Mary Eleanor managed to break it, and the chaise was stopped. There was a sort of rude shack nearby, a poor farmhouse. Bowes got out, the horses were uncoupled from the chaise, and the conveyance was pushed into a yard where it stood for some time with pigs rooting about beneath it. The Countess was still in it, with Mary Gowland to guard her, both shivering in the draught from the broken window. It was parked there from 10.30 p.m. until three the next morning. Bowes then ordered the postboys to drive on to Morpeth, being careful to keep to back roads. The 'boys', actually two elderly men, refused: 'Good God, sir, it's as much as our lives are worth – we can't go – we *won't* go!'[7] The roads were treacherous at the best of times, and in this weather they believed no one could survive such a journey. Eventually, Bowes ordered them to drive back to Newcastle, instructing them not to mention him, the Countess or the journey to anyone, and tipping them 1 guinea apiece (about £75 in today's money) to harden their hearts and close their ears to any enquiries.

And enquiries were by now well afoot. A notice had been inserted in the papers announcing that anyone 'who shall bring the said Countess of Strathmore to James Farrer Esq., now at Carlisle, shall received a Reward of FIFTY POUNDS from that gentleman. The like Reward will be paid by Mr Farrer on bringing the said Andrew Robinson Bowes Esq. and his armed ruffians to him at the city of Carlisle aforesaid.'[8] It was followed up the following day by a second advertisement describing Bowes, the Countess, and the known accessories to the kidnapping:

Mr Bowes is above the middle size, sallow complexion, large Nose which stands rather one side, and lisps in his speech.

Lady Strathmore is a little woman, a longish Face, with fine dark brown Hair, rather Bulky over the Chest – Mr Bowes gives out that she is Dumb, and sometimes Disordered in her Mind – Her Ladyship does not speak.

Edward Lucas, one of Mr Bowes's Ruffians, is a Middle Aged Man, looks quick, an acquiline Nose, a striped second Mourning Coat, and a light coloured Great Coat, a light two or three Curled Wig, in general wears spectacles.

Francis Peacock, a very tall and stout Man, above six feet four inches high, dark Complexion, a little pitted with Smallpox. Lucas and Peacock were yesterday at Carlisle, lurking about and looking for Intelligence.

A number of men were hired to find, follow and capture Bowes. One of them, Abraham Dunn, came upon him one afternoon halfway between Durham and Darlington, and recognised him, but as Bowes had pistols in his hand and Dunn was unarmed, the latter merely retired and reported. The futile, pointless trek continued for another week, until on 26 November at Aycliff, 5 miles outside Darlington, Robert Thornton, another pursuer, saw Bowes being driven past him in a carriage with Mary Eleanor. Bourn, the steward, who was riding some way behind the carriage, realised that Thornton had recognised Bowes and the Countess, and galloped on to warn his master. Meanwhile, Thornton went to Neasham, a village now part of Darlington, and called on the parish constable, Christopher Smith, to arrest the kidnapper. Smith summoned his brother, and joined by Anthony Claxton, John Wainton and one or two other villagers picked up some stout staffs, and went forth.

Bowes had now forced the Countess out of the carriage and had her lifted on to a horse behind him. He left the road and galloped off across frozen ploughed fields and over icy ditches. The constable and his men cut him off and, deciding to brazen things out, he stopped and faced them. He had two loaded pistols, one stuck in his belt and the other in his hand. Smith gave a vivid account of the sequel.[9]

Bowes reined his horse up short and faced the constable.

'What do you want?' he said.

Smith said, 'The country is alarmed with a bad report. We are come to take you.'

Bowes pointed his pistol and said he would blow out the first man's brains that dared touch him. Smith promised that if he surrendered, he would not be hurt. Bowes repeated that he would shoot at anyone who came near him, and then offered to pay handsomely to be shown the way to Northallerton and allowed to ride away.

Smith warned him not to move until he had been arrested. If he would not submit they would set upon him and take him: 'You are a suspicious person, and have surely done something bad, or you need not be riding through the country in such a way.'

Bowes turned his horse around, and seemed to be about to make off, when the woman sitting behind him slipped down, ran towards the constables and said: 'I am Lady Strathmore – for God's sake assist me.'

'Are you indeed Lady Strathmore?' asked Smith.

'I am,' she said, 'and am forced away contrary to every inclination by that man.'

Smith said that if she really was Lady Strathmore, they would take care of her, and arrest Bowes. He told the others to pick up their sticks, and prepare to set upon Bowes. Claxton made to take hold of his horse. When Smith saw Bowes point his pistol at Claxton, he reached up to take hold of his arm. John Wainton took hold of the horse's head while Smith struggled with Bowes, and managed to seize his pistols (badly cutting his hand on the trigger guard of one of them). He then struck Bowes on the head with his staff, and the man fell from his horse.

'Fearing he had more pistols about him,' Smith later said, 'I gave him another blow upon the back part of his head and cut it about two inches. Lady Strathmore asked if he was killed, and desired we would not strike him again, and several times bade us search his pockets for pistols and take care he did not shoot some of us.'

But Bowes was in no condition to shoot anyone. He lay still until he was placed on a hurdle and carried to a nearby cottage. A surgeon was called to dress his wound, Thomas Bowes eventually appeared, and Bowes was carried to his house in Darlington, and thence to London.

Mary Eleanor 'put herself under the protection of the peace officer, and being on horseback, in a kind of womanish exultation, bid Bowes farewell, and mend his life, and so left him weltering in his blood'.[10]

Mary Morgan had travelled to the north to be on hand when and if her mistress was found. She was aghast at the Countess's appearance.

'I can scarcely describe her condition, she was so altered,' she told the court at Bowes's trial, 'so full of mud, and dressed in an old bed gown, a red petticoat, a coloured apron and an old bonnet. She had several black bruises on her breast, and on her temple. She was so feeble she could not write.'[11]

Morgan escorted Mary Eleanor to London and James Farrer's house in Bread Street Hill. On the way they stopped at the Red Lion at Highgate, and Broughton, the landlord, scarcely recognised her; she was, he said, 'an object of pity . . . in a bonnet and an old handkerchief, like a woman that was sifting cinders in Gray's-Inn-Lane'. She had been a reasonably healthy woman of thirty-seven, though not particularly active; she now felt like a woman of sixty. But one must wonder at the courage with which she had sustained her trials. She had been hardened somewhat by Bowes's treatment of her during the previous nine years and no doubt her anger at this, and at her husband's attempts to lay hold of her fortune, fuelled her determination not to give way to him. All the same, many women might well have done so. Now her determination that he should not have his way had prevailed.

FOURTEEN

Ipecacuanha and Pine Apples

*There is not the least reason to imagine that [he] conducted himself
in any manner towards Lady Strathmore but what was absolutely
necessary to protect her from her pretended friends.*

Universal Register, 1 June 1787

The inveterate gossip Horace Walpole wrote to a friend in
November 1786 that 'the town was ringing about . . . Countess
Strathmore and the enormous barbarities of her husband'.[1] Her
adventures provided the finest material for gossip since, fifteen years
previously, Lord Grosvenor had sued the Duke of Cumberland for
£100,000 in damages for seducing his wife. Now, the town once more
had plenty of material for prattle and chatter.

On 23 November 1786, two days after she returned to London, the
Countess again swore Articles of Peace against Bowes, briefly
summarising his treatment of her during the past weeks. The court had
no hesitation in supporting her, and moreover was outraged that a
lawyer appearing for Bowes was so impertinent as to apologise for his
not appearing before the court earlier because the River Dee was so
swollen that he and the Countess could not possibly ford it with safety!
The Judges ordered that Bowes's affidavit to that effect should be filed,
and he should be prosecuted for perjury if it was not proved to be true.

Bowes had been escorted south by court officers. From Barnet, he
wrote incoherently to Jessé Foot:

My dear Sir, I beg to see you immediately, as I am in real necessity for
your professional abilities, and I am so distressed in body, that
nothing but a mind fully convinced of its own rectitude could
support it. Before the cock crows thrice, my enemies shall be
convinced that I paid more attention to my late movements than their
present *éclat* gives them an idea of . . . I am ever yours, A.R. Bowes.[2]

On reaching London, he summoned Foot to meet him at Atkinson's
Hotel in Dean Street. He clearly regarded Foot as a friend, though the

latter was advisedly cautious about the relationship – Bowes had already attempted to persuade him to rent a house for him in London, and Foot had said he'd be damned if he took a house for Bowes, lest he should have to pay for it.

At the hotel, Foot found Bowes in a poor state, and could not but pity him: '[He] was dressed in a drab-coloured great coat, a red silk handkerchief about his head', he wrote; 'he was supported by two men, yet nearly bent double with weakness, in consequence of his wounds; he frequently appeared in the point of fainting, and his appearance, on the whole, was the most squalid and emaciated that can possible be imagined. . . . His beard was a week old, his head bound up with a bloody handkerchief, his boots dirty, his shirt and cravat stained with blood, and he looked as pale as ashes.'[3]

Bowes was summoned to appear immediately at Westminster Hall, in a corner of which the court sat. He was desperate to avoid this, and tried to persuade Foot to go in his stead, and plead that he was too ill to appear. Foot summoned a second doctor to give his opinion; Dr Kennedy shared the view that Foot was perfectly able to appear, and they went down in the coach with him. He was sick twice during the short journey, and Foot began to wonder whether perhaps he had not been mistaken, that his patient's skull might be fractured.

At Westminster Hall, a small crowd had gathered to hiss Bowes as he walked in. He was a pitiful figure – there is a sketch by Gillray showing him staggering in supported by two tipstaffs.[4] The depiction is almost sympathetic (though the onlookers behind Bowes, craning for a look at him, are caricatures). But if the artist showed some sympathy for the prisoner, no one else did. People did not go to the courts of justice to show sympathy for anyone; they went for a good show, and those who had previously sneered at the Countess now laughed at her husband. There was plenty of rough humour to be had and on this occasion, when a plea was made that Bowes should not be remanded in custody because of his injury and the Marshal loudly remarked that he could accommodate the gentleman, there was much laughter. Bowes was taken off to Southwark, to St George's Fields and the King's Bench prison. He was never to be a free agent again.

By now the Countess had learned that while it might be easy to ignore gossip and publicity, they resulted in certain inconveniences: they often attracted friends who proved to be false, lovers whose focus was one's wealth rather than one's personality. The lesson both of her second marriage and of her relationship with Captain Farrer was well taken, and while she was happy to accept his brother's hospitality at his house in Bread Street, she seems to have severed all ties with the Captain. She began to recover with remarkable speed from her ordeal, for three days after her return to London she wrote to John Langstaff to thank him for organising the pitmen who had mustered at the castle to protest at her detention there:

Lady Strathmore returns her very sincere and particular thanks to Mr Langstaff for his most judicious and active exertions in her favour, which she must always remember with heart-felt gratitude. . . . Lady Strathmore has the pleasure to add that she is greatly recovered within these last three days, having regained the use of her limbs in what at first seemed to threaten a mortification, so far as to walk the floor with a stick.[5]

Meanwhile, Bowes had settled into prison life, which was not as unpleasant as one might suppose. The first King's Bench prison, which had been established in the fourteenth century, was several times burned down – finally and completely during the anti-Catholic Gordon riots of 1780. Rebuilt, it was now used chiefly for the imprisonment of debtors or those convicted of libel. Southwark was not one of the more salubrious quarters of London: tanneries, vinegar makers, dye manufacturers and makers of soap and tallow rendered the air of the area rank with pungent and unpleasant smells, and the place as a whole had an almost obscene reputation – the local press reported that some of the inhabitants 'made a trade of digging up the bodies of the dead: they made candles of the fat, extracted volatile alkali from the bones, and sold the flesh for dog's meat'.[6] Many others actually fled the area, so noisome did it become.

It seemed a natural place for a prison, and over the centuries half-a-dozen sprang up, flourished, and more or less fell to pieces within a mile or so of each other – the King's Bench, the Clink, the Borough Compter at St Margaret's, the Marshalsea, the White Lyon (a small prison, originally an inn), and Horsemonger Lane gaol. King's Bench prison itself stood on four acres of land – it comprised two four-storey houses and a chapel, with a yard in which there were three pumps for washing and providing drinking water, and racket and fives courts for recreation. Behind its enormously high walls – even from the top floors of the houses there was no view of the outside world – the prison had the reputation of being filthy and overcrowded, and certainly there were from time to time outbreaks of typhus fever.

None of this troubled Bowes, who had enough money to rent a suite of 'state rooms' in the Marshal's house, and later one of the eight 'superior' rooms facing on to the yard of the prison, which received a great deal more light and air than the 225, 9-foot-square inside rooms or cells which faced on to blank walls. He could also afford to pay for 'Liberty of the Rules' and was thus, after his trial, allowed outside the walls as long as he restricted his wanderings to within 3 miles; he could and no doubt did find plenty of amusements at such pleasure-palaces as the Temple of Flora and the Dog and Duck Tavern, described as 'certainly the most dreadful place in or about the metropolis . . . the resorts of women, not only of the lower species of prostitution, but even of the middle classes'.[7]

Bowes shared the privileges of the 'Politic Debtors', wealthy men who had deliberately or recklessly run up debts without any intention of settling them. Outside the prison walls these men – often the profligate younger sons of the aristocracy and gentry – would have had to live within their restricted means; inside the walls they were rich, and for them King's Bench was more like an hotel than a prison – despite its situation, it was called 'the most desirable place of incarceration in London'. For the poor, on the other hand, it 'rivalled the purlieus of Wapping, St Giles and St James' in vice, debauchery and drunkenness'.[8]

For the first month or so, Bowes kept himself very much to himself. Foot visited him regularly, and found him making 'those adjustments which are necessary for all who seek for comfort in such abodes of accommodation'.[9] At first the doctor was rather worried by his patient's condition, until he discovered the reason for Bowes's constant dizziness and nausea – at Barnet he had bribed his guards to buy for him a dose of ipecacuanha,[10] and had been taking it at intervals ever since, to make him appear much more ill than he really was.

Bound over by the justices to keep the peace for a term of fourteen years on his own recognisances of £10,000 and two other securities of £5,000 each, Bowes now awaited trial for abduction. Reconciling himself to what might prove a prolonged residence in prison, he sent out for his tableware, linen and plate, and began to spend some of the income which was still coming to him on small, select luncheon and dinner parties. As Jessé Foot puts it, 'he had the best room within the walls of the prison, and as birds do, when they are reconciled to the cage, he began to plume himself up, to peck, and meditate upon the possible smiles the place could afford him. He took an analysis of the inhabitants, and particularly all those he could make useful to his purpose, he tempted by his dinners.'[11]

Meanwhile, the Countess was continuing to recover her strength, and in January 1787 became relatively independent. Though still supported by James Farrer, she moved out of his house and into one in Holles Street, a few steps from what is now Oxford Circus.[12]

In order to prepare the minds of those who would try him, her husband bought an interest in a newspaper, the *Universal Register*, and began inserting small paragraphs here and there, all naturally pointing out what a reasonable man Andrew Robinson Bowes was – how there was 'not the least reason to imagine that [he] conducted himself in any manner towards Lady Strathmore but what was absolutely necessary to protect her from her pretended friends',[13] and how he was 'perfectly happy to reach a reasonable accommodation' with the Countess.[14]

He also began a campaign to blacken Mary Eleanor's reputation as thoroughly as possible, in order to excuse his own actions against her. On 5 February 1887 there appeared in the *Universal Register* an account of the allegations against the Countess made in the Court of Arches in Doctors Commons, charging her with treating her husband with 'insolent contempt and disobedience' and asserting 'that previous to her marriage with him, she carried on a criminal intercourse with George Grey [*sic*] Esq., and promised him marriage'. On the night before her marriage to Mr Bowes, it was alleged, the Countess had 'slept all night in the same bed with Mr Grey' and 'was five months gone with child when she married Mr Bowes'. This was followed by the accusation that 'George Walker, her Ladyship's servant, carried on a criminal correspondence with her, and acknowledged that he had as often been connected with her as Mr Bowes, that she had 'also carried on a criminal correspondence with one Thompson, her gardener, and was detected in adultery in the green house and various parts of the garden; that she had an adulterous connection with Edward Llewellin Esq., and was detected on a bench in the garden. . . .'

Not a shred of evidence was offered in this farrago. Bowes's intention was to paint her as 'a woman of the most extravagant, lustful, wicked and abandoned temper and disposition'. He may to some degree have succeeded in suggesting this sufficiently strongly to turn against her those readers of the popular newspapers who were disposed to believe anything against the wealthy and aristocratic; but the minds of the future jurymen who were to try him were clearly not sufficiently swayed.

Fascination with the Bowes and Strathmore affair now gripped the whole town – everyone was talking about it, and interest was fuelled by comment and correspondence in the press, in particular a series of letters signed 'Justus', 'Truth', and 'Vindex,' published in the *Register* between November 1786 and April 1787. Bowes has been accused of writing all these himself,[15] but it does not seem likely – the writers' styles are very different from letter to letter, and there is no special reason for Bowes to have written the reasoned condemnation of his actions which appeared, signed 'Justus', in the *Register* of 29 March 1787.

The correspondent addressed himself directly to Bowes, sketching out his career from his position as 'a subaltern officer' to his marriage to 'a Lady with one of the largest and most powerful properties in the country'. Perhaps immediately after his marriage, he might have shown some regard for his wife, but 'the gentle sentiments of tender regard and grateful affection seem not to have been congenial to your character. Inebriated with wealth, vanity and ostentation, you thought only how you should display yourself in the parade of fortune, the affectation of greatness, and the splendour of superior life'. Bowes's bullying of his wife was common knowledge – he had made his house a prison for Lady Strathmore and a brothel for himself. There might be, unlikely though it seemed, an explanation for his actions and behaviour, and if there was the correspondent would be glad to hear it, but (in a final and somewhat low-key paragraph) he confessed that 'I do not think well of you, and augur ill of your cause'.

Bowes was still, as best he might, 'displaying himself in the parade of fortune', for although at first he had looked 'like a petty debtor rather than the lord of the Bowes Estate', as an anonymous contributor to the *Universal Register* put it, there were soon complaints from the paupers in the King's Bench prison that it was not pleasant for them in their starving poverty to see displayed in the windows of his rooms, 'turkies, fowls and pine apples' as well as the silver plates and dishes on which later he was wont to enjoy them.[16] Nor was he in any way cowed by the position in which he found himself. He took out a warrant at the Old Bailey indicting the Countess for perjury, allegedly committed during the late trial: James Farrer and Mr Forster, the ironmonger from whose shop she had been snatched, stood bail for her and on the day before his trial was to begin, Bowes cheekily placed in the *Universal Register* a paragraph alluding to the efforts of a 'Mr B.' to defeat 'the strange machinations of his amiable lady' and proposing 'a subscription in honour of the meritorious services [of James Farrer] to the enemies of *petticoat government* and the friends of matrimonial subordination'.

At the end of November, Bowes impertinently handed in to the court an 'allegation of mutual forgiveness' on the grounds that he and his wife had cohabited between the 12th and 20th of the month. Indeed, he had attempted it, but been thoroughly repulsed; and in any case, as one of the lawyers for the prosecution was to point out at his trial, it was extremely unlikely that he and the Countess would have had any kind of carnal connection while tramping over the moors in wind, snow and sleet. The Court of Arches was quick to dismiss his plea, and he was ordered to pay costs of £1,742 14s 2d.

And now he had to face trial: on the morning of 30 May 1787, he appeared, with Lucas, Peacock, Prevot, Chapman, Pigg, Bickley, Bourn and Thomas Bowes, in His Majesty's Court of King's Bench, Westminster, before the Hon. Mr Justice Buller, on a charge of conspiracy against the Right Hon. Mary Eleanor Bowes, commonly called Countess of Strathmore.

FIFTEEN

The Trial

For a man to treat a woman thus, what must be every honest man's sensations?

James Mingay, 30 May 1787

Sitting on the bench on 30 May 1787, Mr Justice Buller was flanked by a jury, and between him and the dock in which Bowes and his fellow-conspirators sat, was a half-dozen of distinguished advocates: the Hon. Thomas Erskine, Mr Chambre and Mr Fielding for the accused, and Mr James Mingay, Mr Law and Mr Garrow for the prosecution. In the well of the court, Mr E. Hodgson, the official shorthand writer, busily prepared his notebooks and sharpened his pencils.[1]

Bowes may well have thought himself lucky when he first set eyes on the Judge. Sir Francis Buller, a squat Cornishman with a piercing eye and a short temper exacerbated by gout, had been the youngest man ever to have been created a judge, at the age of thirty-two. He was notorious for his hasty and prejudiced judgements, of which his most notable had asserted that any husband had the right to thrash his wife provided the stick he used was no bigger than his thumb. Now forty-one years old, he was delighted to be known as 'Judge Thumb', a nickname given him in a Gillray caricature which had made him famous.[2] Presumably Bowes would have heartily concurred with Judge Buller's view of matrimonial justice, just as he would have sympathised with his love of cards (Buller once said that 'his idea of heaven was to sit at *nisi prius*[3] all day and play at whist all night').

But the Judge's temper was not improved by the sight of Mr Erskine seated below him. He and Erskine had had a celebrated clash five years earlier, when Buller was hearing a libel case against the Dean of St Paul's. Erskine had not only rebuked His Honour for omitting an important word in his address to the jury, but had then moved for a new trial on the ground of misdirection. He had failed, but the Judge had not been amused, and Erskine was not his favourite advocate.

A judge in favour of wife-beating, but at odds with the counsel for the defence. So far so inconclusive. What was perhaps more interesting, and a great deal more chilling, was the sight of the leader for the prosecution. James Mingay at thirty-five had taken silk three years previously, was at the height of his abundant powers, and by his success at the bar was already laying the foundations of the fortune which was to allow him to enjoy early retirement. He was a figure to command awe, as much for his loud voice and blustering manner as for the grappling hook which replaced his right hand, and which he deployed with great skill and to considerable effect.

The public, unsurprisingly, continued to take a great interest in the case, and those who could gain entry to the court were pleased to do so. The Countess, however, stayed well away – as far as we know. There is certainly no indication that she attended, though naturally her interest was keen, and she carefully cut out of the press every report or piece of gossip that appeared relative to the case, which she kept in scrapbooks in Holles Street, and later in the house out of town, in Fludyer Street, near Blackheath, to which at some time she removed.

It was Mingay who opened the case against Bowes, alleging that he, learning that his wife had instituted a suit for divorce, had determined 'by force, violence and imprisonment of her person' to compel her to drop it, and had with his fellow defendants 'forcibly seized her, in the middle of the day, and in one of the most public streets in London, dragged her servants before a Justice of the Peace under a warrant objected by gross perjury, and carried the unfortunate Lady, against her will, near 300 miles through the heart of this kingdom'.[4] He went on to summarise the facts of the case: Bowes's calling together of his confederates; the disguises and subterfuges employed to observe the Countess's movements; the laying and execution of the plot to abduct her; and what followed.

He was graphic and melodramatic in his description of the travails Mary Eleanor underwent, especially on the bare hills around Appleby – but no man, he asserted, could talk of the events with patience!

Informed that he was pursued, [Bowes] immediately stopped and forced her out of the chaise, he put her behind Chapman on the horse's bare back and hid her in a cow-house. They bundled her in as a bale of goods. . . . He then took her and dragged her over the top of some mountains that were covered with snow, till she was very near perished . . . she was put into a pig stye, and put into a stable – the fact was, she was kept in a dark passage, frozen almost to death, and perishing, her mind distracted, she was taken into a stack yard where pigs were kept – not in a pig stye, but I shall call the farmer to prove there was a large herd of swine grunting round her – she was kept with hogs, pigs and sows round about her – what could she have thought? I will, for a moment, suppose her the most abandoned prostitute that the earth ever produced, but for a man to treat a woman thus, what must be every honest man's sensations?[5]

Mingay was confident, he concluded, that the jury would treat the accused men as they deserved, and would 'teach them that such glaring and audacious violation of the laws cannot in this country escape with impunity'.

The witnesses now presented themselves. First, Bowes's marriage to the Countess was proved, and the presentation of her case against her husband for divorce 'by reason of adultery and cruel treatment'. Then came Peter Orme, who gave evidence of what he had seen and heard of the preparation for the abduction, and of the event itself. He was clear and definite, and Bowes could very well have been convicted of the abduction on his evidence alone. Robert Crundel, the Countess's footman, and Daniel Lee, her coachman, were followed by the constable William Saunders, who had turned his coat, and the magistrate Mr Walker, who gave evidence of the false accusations that had obtained the warrant for the arrest of the Countess's servants.

Mrs Morgan was conclusive about the same events, and about Mary Eleanor's state of mind: the Countess had always been in perfect command of her reason. When Mr Fielding, for the defence, brought up the matter of 'conjurers and sorcerers' he got no satisfaction; he had hoped no doubt to show the Countess as a gullible and foolish woman, but (as he admitted when the judge asked him whether his questions were material) was 'disappointed in the answers [he] expected'.

Erskine then attempted in a very roundabout way to suggest that it might be proved that Bowes had a perfect right to abduct his wife, and that that was the important factor, rather than the degree of violence offered. Mr Justice Buller gave him short shrift on that account. Erskine was possibly on firmer ground, if he only knew it, when he turned to a question of Mary Eleanor's relationship with Captain Farrer, and asked Mrs Morgan how long the Countess had known him. Mrs Morgan replied that the Captain had known Lady Strathmore from her childhood and, rather foolishly, Erskine did not pursue the matter, taking the witness's perjury at face-value.

Farrer stepped into the witness box a few minutes later. His evidence was confined to the actual circumstances of the abduction, supported Mingay's opening statement, and added nothing of interest or value.

Erskine failed to cross-examine. Other witnesses added some smaller details to the account of the abduction: the Countess's cries for help, the desperation with which she attempted to escape and the violence offered to her by Bowes, in particular at the Bell at Stilton.

Dr Hobson spoke of Bowes's 'accident', and swore he thought it was a more or less innocent attempt to mislead his creditors. Then came Ridgway, the tipstaff, and the others – the lawyer James Farrer and the grocer, Robert Peverill, among them – to describe the events at Streatlam Castle, implicating Bourn in the attempted deception of those who were seeking to discover the Countess's whereabouts.

The description of the trek of Bowes, his captive and his associates over the snowy moors was gradually elaborated as the turnpike-keeper David Kirk, the Brough innkeeper James Angier and others gave evidence. The story was wound up by the courageous constable from Neasham, Christopher Smith. When he described how Bowes was carried unconscious to the nearby cottage and was asked whether he had surrendered, Smith replied: 'There was no occasion for a surrender when he was knocked off his horse, I think.'

The procession of witnesses over, Mr Erskine was left to make what bricks he could out of a very small amount of unwholesome straw. His opening was sufficiently turgid and obscure, one would have thought, to try Mr Justice Buller's patience:

May it please your Lordship, Gentlemen[6] of the Jury, no man can possibly lament more than I do that such a connection as subsists or rather ought to subsist between the gentleman who sits by me and the prosecutrix of this indictment should be productive of such consequences that the husband and wife, which is most undoubtedly instituted by society to be the solace of human life, and for the production and the protection of posterity, from which so many real enjoyments ought to arise, and in which the public is so very much interested in the preservation of, should be in this manner turned into bitterness and gall. . . .'[7]

He did his best to suggest that the Countess had brought the whole incident upon herself by her behaviour, but was nevertheless forced to agree that 'the wife has a right to the protection of the law to keep herself from violence, even against the husband; and, although he may have a right of possession of her person, he can neither seize or detain that person by force'. In long pages of tumid prose he attempted to obfuscate what he was unable to deny – that he had 'no evidence by which I can protect Mr Peacock, Mr Prevot, Mr Chapman, Mr Pigg and Mr Bickley, and the defendant, Mr Andrew Robinson Bowes', although he was 'prepared with a great deal of evidence to mitigate the conspiracy of which they have undoubtedly been guilty against the law'. This, he sought to argue, was connected to the Countess's own ill-conduct: 'If a wife squanders the property of her husband, or runs into debt, or lives in improper company, there can be no sort of doubt that he may take his wife into his possession, provided she is not either separated by consent, or by the act of law.'

The judge was rather doubtful about this: no evidence had been produced, after all, that Mary Eleanor had in any way squandered her husband's property or run into debt; as to 'improper company', though he may have heard, outside the court, gossip about the relationship between her and Captain Farrer, nothing material had been heard to suggest that any such thing was more than idle tattle.

Erskine attempted too to make something of the influence of Mary Eleanor's friends:

> It may be highly humane to take a woman out of the hands of persons that are conspiring to ruin her by amusing her with lies of fortune-tellers in order to widen the breach with the husband, and to prevent that union which is much to the honor of all persons; if Mr Bowes had taken his wife into his possession peaceably, he would have been protected by the law.[8]

But Erskine must have realised that all that was beside the point: there was no defence should a jury believe that Bowes had acted illegally by abducting his wife. In seeking to demonstrate that the husband had had 'honourable, just and pure motives' for his actions, he was really speaking in mitigation before a verdict had even been considered, let alone delivered.

He did attempt a serious defence of the attorney Thomas Bowes, a man 'of fair and honest reputation', who though he was employed by Stoney Bowes was innocent of the charge against him. It was the now familiar plea that he was 'only obeying orders': 'because a gentleman, for reasons best known to himself, we will suppose improper ones, chooses to lay hold of his wife by violence, and carry her down to his house at the distance of two hundred miles, if it was to involve every servant or every attorney employed, what would be the consequence?' Moreover, there was 'no proof of any sort or kind which can leave you to fancy that Mr Thomas Bowes knew that my Lady was under any restraint . . . if he has been guilty of any act at all, it is in not raising the country, and not assisting in the liberation of Lady Strathmore'. Bourn, the steward, Erskine suggested, was in the same case: 'it would be very severe and very harsh if whatever reason you may have to punish Mr Bowes, you are to involve every man who is at all connected with [him]'.

It is difficult not to believe that an experienced barrister like Erskine did not sit down perfectly confident that Bowes and probably all of the other defendants – with the possible, slender exception of Bourn and Bowes – would be convicted, and that he had been able to do very little for them.

Mr Justice Buller's lengthy summing up can have done nothing to dispel that view, and certainly offered no comfort to the defendants.[9] Bowes, he concluded, had obviously planned to abduct his wife in order to attempt to halt the progress of the divorce suit which was before the Ecclesiastical Court, and at last had carried her off 'by means that must shock every man in this country who has the smallest regard for his personal liberty or safety'. She had then been dragged about the country 'repeatedly crying murder, and intreating assistance and none could be obtained'.

As for Mr Erskine's argument that the other defendants were innocent because they might have been unaware of Bowes's intention, or of anything about the divorce suit, he directed the jury firmly that if persons joined in a conspiracy to do an illegal act, even if they did not know precisely what its aim was, each must be answerable in law. He went at some length into the cases of Bourn and Thomas Bowes. Wade's evidence, he said, told against Bourn: it seemed clear that the latter knew perfectly well that the Countess was in fear of her life. He had also been part of the feigned riding 'accident', which seemed to indicate that he was thoroughly in the confidence of his employer. 'In my opinion,' Buller advised the jury, 'the true rule is this – if these defendants Bourn and Bowes were privy and assenting to the design before Lady Strathmore was taken away – if they are proved to have advised or concurred in it, they are all equally guilty with those who acted on the spot.'

The jury had little doubt about their duty. They did not trouble themselves to retire. After hearing almost eight hours of conclusive evidence, they brought in an immediate verdict: all the defendants were guilty as charged.

At this stage, Erskine rose to announce that his client had decided to drop the indictment of the Countess for perjury which was set down to be heard before the same court. He was 'reluctant further to wound the lady's feelings'. The jury, whether or not impressed by this merciful act, automatically brought in a verdict of not guilty in the case. Bowes's charity ended there, for on 20 June an advertisement appeared in the *Universal Register* announcing that there would shortly be published 'AN ACCOUNT of the life of M.E. Bowes, including a narrative of her Conduct from the age of 13 till a short time previous to her elopement from her present husband. Written by herself.' When it came out, it bore beneath the title a quatrain contributed by Bowes himself:

> *When hoary age the lustful passions bend,*
> *Compunctions oft the matron's bosom rend;*
> *Then comes CONFESSION, eager to disclose*
> *The* Source *and* Cause *of all her present woes.*

This was the short autobiography Bowes had insisted Mary Eleanor write for him some time before. Bowes's motives in publishing it were mixed: it was first of all an act of revenge; but no doubt he also hoped that her revelations of her adulterous relationship with Gray would have their effect on the judges, who had still to sentence him. He had already on 23 January submitted it in manuscript as evidence of his wife's adultery; but Dr Calvert, sitting in Doctors Commons, had ruled that it was not admissible, as the Countess 'had made such confession under a promise of seeing her children, in consequence of her compliance'.[10]

Bowes and his fellow conspirators waited almost a month in the King's Bench prison for news of their fate, then on 26 June the Marshal escorted them again to court for sentencing. Mr Justice Buller sat with two other judges, Mr Justice Grose and Mr Justice Ashurst. Buller opened the proceedings with a few observations on one or two of the five accused, in particular Peacock and Lucas:

Francis Peacock, I think, appears by the evidence to have been with Mr Bowes so early as October, [and] is proved to be a man acting in the business from that time to the moment Lady Strathmore was carried off. . . . Lucas is proved to be a constable, a peace officer, and minister of the public justice of the country; he availed himself of that character, in order to carry this plot into execution – it is not probable that any man but a peace officer could have carried this plan into execution, which we have heard of.[11]

Lucas had 'insinuated himself into the confidence' of Lady Strathmore and was 'the contriver of the whole business'. There was strong reason to suppose he was privy to Chapman's perjury. 'It seems to me,' the judge sternly remarked, 'that there never was any conduct in which the character of a peace officer has been so abused as by him; at the voice of a constable, and at his appearance, every man opens his doors with perfect confidence, knowing that both his person and property will be protected from violence – the most hardened offender submits to his authority, because he is sure that as far as concerns the security of his person he shall be protected; this man, who in words had mocked and insulted Lady Strathmore, by pretending to protect her, was the very man who took her in this manner till he saw her locked up safe within the walls of her own castle.'

Mr Erskine half rose to begin his plea in mitigation, but Mr Mingay struck the table with his hook and intervened: 'On behalf of the Crown, my lord,' he said, 'I pray that you will pass a very heavy sentence on these persons now before the Court, if my learned friend Mr Erskine has nothing to say in mitigation.'

There was little Erskine could say in defence of Bowes. With his colleague Mr Chambre at his side to pass the occasional note of advice, he made as good a fist of things as he could for the others, arguing for instance that the evidence against Bourn was very slight – that Bowes himself had sworn that he had told his steward nothing of his plans, and that when the latter had seen the Countess at the castle 'he saw nothing that led him to believe her to be there, otherwise than by her own consent'. But that was a horse which the barrister could surely not have expected to run? He went on to make a personal appeal: Bourn had a large family, and would be absolutely ruined if sent to prison, deprived of bread and his family turned out of doors. The look on Mr Justice Buller's face was very probably not promising; it was the kind of appeal every defence lawyer made on behalf of every convicted prisoner. Erskine was no more persuasive in respect of Prevot: 'a foreigner, a stranger to our constitution and laws, and observing literally what his master commanded'. (Surely he knew by now that that argument, too, would not hold water?)

But it was now time for Erskine to employ a little hyperbole. He attempted again to turn to the Countess's reputation; it was, he argued, germane to the case, for 'if a man is so sorely pressed, it is not a wonder if he should turn in his own protection, and strip this lady of the mask in which she has so long walked, that of an oppressed and persecuted woman'. In Erskine's view, Bowes could rely on the judgement of an earlier court, that 'if a husband saw his wife conducting herself improperly, it was part not only of the power and authority of her husband, but part of his duty also to rescue her, and bring her back to that control which, by the law, he has over her as a protector.' Then there was of course the financial aspect of the case: Erskine was sorry to say ('I am sure I speak every thing of her with reluctance', he piously observed) that Bowes discovered after his marriage that the Countess had 'conveyed away her estate to trustees for her own separate use'. This 'did not place the Lady in a very honourable light'. But that, Erskine said, was nothing to what he was about to reveal.

What he wanted to do was to rely on an affidavit Bowes had provided, detailing his wife's alleged misbehaviour during the years leading up to the abduction – in particular her adultery with Gray. But Mr Justice Buller had had enough. Erskine must stick to the point, and not drag into the case events which had occurred ten years previously.

Erskine attempted to insist. All he wished to do, he said, was to show the true relationship between the Countess and her husband – to show, 'in answer to that cruelty which is imputed to him, the various acts of tenderness of which his whole life has been composed, since his marriage, and the particular reasons why he was bound in honour and in compassion to her, to do the act which he has done'.

All three judges forbade him to go further in attempting to prove Bowes the kind of husband who might have been sponsored by the angels. Erskine's colleague Mr Chambre intervened on his behalf: surely, he argued, the Countess's whole attitude before the abduction was relevant?

'How does that mitigate the enormity of this crime?' asked Mr Justice Grose.

'To show the absolute necessity Mr Bowes was under of securing her in some way or other,' said Chambre.

'That,' said Mr Justice Ashurst, 'is neither more nor less than abusing the situation to take advantage of publishing a gross libel.'

Erskine was beginning to lose his temper.

'Is not a husband bound to protect his wife?' he asked. 'And if she is not capable of governing and protecting herself, is he to suffer her to be in the hands of conspirators and servants?'

'But you should confine yourself to the facts that were the immediate cause of his conspiring,' said Mr Justice Grose.

'They are so coupled and blended together that I cannot state a part of the circumstances that led Mr Bowes to do this, without stating the whole together.'

'Then,' said Buller, 'the consequence is that no part of the affidavit can be read.'

'It would have been improper anywhere,' agreed Mr Justice Grose.

Erskine was now furious. He had actually made a bad mistake. Previous to the hearing for sentencing, he had been given the opportunity to read through Bowes's affidavit about his wife's behaviour, in order that he could weed out material the court would find offensive or libellous, and make use of the rest; he had failed to do so. The knowledge that it was his own fault did not improve his temper.

'I have now discharged part of my duty to Mr Bowes,' he said impertinently, 'and he will see that it is the Court that have prevented my concluding that duty.' He went on to assert that Lady Strathmore and Mr Bowes were living together 'in perfect harmony and peace' until she was 'carried off' to the apartments of a Mr Shuter, where she was 'exposed to most cruel hardships by those people that kept her as if she had been a lunatic, that she was so confined that she was hardly allowed to go from one room to another . . .'. It was all nonsense, whether Erskine knew it or not – Bowes may have successfully pulled the wool over his attorney's eyes; the latter may well have believed Bowes when he claimed that he 'never threatened Lady Strathmore, never treated her with any indecency or violence – that the great object he had was to conciliate her affections'. But it seems unlikely.

It was Erskine's duty to defend his client, and he certainly did his best to show that Bowes was as innocent as a new-born babe or at least was 'not as criminal as he appears', which was rather different. He made another spirited attempt to quote from the affidavit, which Mr Justice Ashurst stamped on with equal vigour. And that, as far as pleas for mitigation of sentence on Bowes were concerned, was that.

Mr Chambre then made his appeal on behalf of the rest of the guilty men. He made rather a good case for Bourn as a man seriously misled by his employer, while Prevot, he said, was simply a stranger to the laws of England, who did not think he could be prosecuted for simply serving his master. Peacock had sworn he knew nothing of the plot against the Countess, and indeed had reason to suppose that his friend intended a reconciliation – 'so far from perceiving any disinclination, he perceived expressions of fondness and endearment' between the married couple. As for the lawyer Thomas Bowes, the judges really must show leniency to him – he had acted indiscreetly, even wrongly, but he had done so from the best motives in the world; he had believed that the Countess, when parted from her husband, was in a melancholy state of distress, and had been aware of nothing but the appearance of reconciliation between her and Mr Bowes.

Erskine had done what he could, but even he shrank from seeking to excuse the behaviour of the constable, Lucas, leaving that impossible task to his junior, Mr Fielding, who simply pleaded that Lucas was intent on helping Bowes take control of his wife – something to which no Englishman could surely object? Certainly he had committed perjury, but that was surely excusable under the circumstances?

Mr Mingay had been almost, but not quite, reduced to speechlessness by the impertinence of these arguments. The bench should take no notice at all of this nonsense about servants 'only doing their job'. 'Servants ought to be taught by your Lordships that, in breaking the laws of their country, whoever teaches them to break those laws, it is certainly penal. . . . Suppose Lady Strathmore had been murdered in the heat of this violence – how would the people concerned have been able to escape? What, by saying, I am a servant, and my master bid me do it? My lords, I do hope servants will be taught better today!'

Bourn had been an actor at every stage of the game: he had heard the Countess protest that she was being held against her will, he had heard the coachman tell how she had cried out in the same way. And his excuse? – that he was an old servant of the family! Then, take Peacock, 'selected perhaps by his being eight feet high, strong, boney and athletick' – he must have known that Bowes 'was about some bad purpose'. Lucas's actions were simply indefensible – he had been 'the heifer with which they ploughed'.

And what could he say about Bowes himself that had not already been said? Only that 'he has the character of a husband. But are the powers of a husband in this country such that women that are ill-used are not to complain? Are they so subjected that she has not as much right to complain as the husband?' Bowes had attempted to cover his tracks well. People had been deceived: 'He took care to ill use her so much in private, he had no occasion in public.' As for his talk of attempts at conciliation and cohabitation: 'Good God! – Cohabitation and forgiveness! – Cohabitation on the mountains, in snow!'

Mingay yet again went through the story of the abduction and what followed, emphasising every detail – no doubt the hook was again wielded for emphasis. It was a long, long speech, and doubtless the judges had had enough by the time he came to his conclusion. Buller left his colleague, Judge Ashurst, to deliver the sentences:

> The crime of which you have all been found guilty is of as atrocious and daring a nature as ever appeared in a Court of Justice, and had not the facts been made out by the most incontestable proof, one should hardly have thought that in a civilised country, governed by law, any set of men would have been found hardy enough to take

away a Lady of rank and fortune from one of the most public streets of this great town, at mid-day, in defiance of all law, order and government, and to drag her through the heart of the kingdom.

He rebuked each man individually – Lucas, whose duty was to preserve the law, not to break the peace; Peacock, a man of fortune and education, who should have known better; the servants, who should have known perfectly well that 'it is no part of their service to enlist themselves into the illegal concerns of their masters'. As for the verdicts, Bowes would pay a fine of £300 and go to prison for three years, after which he must 'give security for good behaviour for the space of fourteen years'. Lucas was fined £50 and sent to Newgate for three years; Prevot was to be imprisoned for a year; Peacock for two years (with a fine of £100); Bourn for six months (fined £50).

SIXTEEN

Bowes Unrepentant

He thought every day lost / In which he made none wretched.
                                    Mary Eleanor Bowes

Returning to King's Bench prison, Bowes was welcomed by his own obituary, composed and sent him by his wife:

> HERE RESTS
> Who never rested before,
> The most ambitious of men:
> For he sought not virtue, wisdom, or
> Science, yet rose by deep hypocrisy,
> By the folly of some,
> And the vice of others,
> To honours which Nature had forbid,
> And riches he wanted taste to enjoy.
>   He saw no faults in himself,
> Nor any worth in others.
>   He was the enemy of mankind;
> Deceitful to his friends,
> Ungrateful to his benefactors,
> Cringing to his superiors,
> And tyrannical to his dependants.
>   If interest obliged him to assist
> Any fellow creature, he regretted the
> Effect, and thought every day lost
> In which he made none wretched.
>   His life was a continual series
> Of injuries to society,
> Disobedience to his Maker,
> And he only lamented in despair
> That he could offend them no longer.
>   He rose by mean arts

To unmerited honours,
Which expire before himself.
    Passenger, examine thy heart,
If in aught thou resemblest him;
And if thou dost —
Read, tremble, and reform!
So shall he, who living
Was the pest of society,
When dead, be, against his will,
Once useful to mankind.

The Countess was gathering strength and gradually recovering from her ordeal. She had already inserted a notice in the papers:

Lady Strathmore returns her sincere and hearty thanks to her friends for their humane and spirited exertions towards the restoration of her liberty, and the preservation of her life. She is able to inform her friends that she is at length in a fair way to recovery from the painful and alarming effects of her late sufferings, and gains strength daily.[1]

Bowes settled down to permanent imprisonment, though he cannot have suspected at the time that he would never be completely at liberty again. Jessé Foot described him as 'a tree struck by lightning', and the *Universal Register* remarked that he 'looked like a petty debtor rather than the lord of the Bowes estate'. But he gradually collected some of his belongings around him, and was able to live in considerable comfort in the 'state rooms' of the prison. At first he shared these with Mr and Mrs Peacock and their daughter and four-year-old William Johnstone Bowes, his son by the Countess. Why or how William was living with his father in the not uncomfortable but certainly not especially congenial surroundings of the prison, we cannot say; the Countess appears to have made no effort to have him removed from his father's influence. It may be that she simply did not want to subject the child to a parental tug-of-war, or give Bowes the excuse to use his custody of the boy as a weapon against her.

As Foot observed, Bowes's days were spent in two pursuits – in determining how to pull down Mary Eleanor as best he might, and in his continued interest in young women.[2] He had a number of servants and while we do not know how many, we do know that they included Mary Gowland (who, incidentally, was never prosecuted for her part in the abduction). She, however, was now getting a little old to satisfy his carnal appetite. Jessé Foot describes her as 'a good-hearted, hard working woman, . . . [who] possessed more than a common share of the homely and useful qualities'. She does not sound especially seductive, and in any case for Bowes familiarity had by now bred contempt. He was ready for younger and more agreeable female company, and set his eyes on the fifteen-year-old daughter of a gentlemanly fellow prisoner, a debtor called Sutton, who had fallen on hard times.

Jenny, who lived with her mother in lodgings in Lant Street, was a pretty, lively blonde, and when Bowes first saw her was holding up a pigeon to peck split peas from her full, tempting lips. She was irresistible to a man who, as Foot puts it, 'like a roaring lion, sought night and day whom he could devour'.[3] He waylaid her, flattered her, and easily got her into his bed. Foot, who he asked to treat her for a summer cold, found her agreeable, and ended up admiring her – as well he might, for she was, he says, always cheerful and very faithful, staying with Bowes until his death and bearing him several children. He took a room for her near his own and was extremely possessive, never introducing her to his friends or acquaintances, and even when Foot attended her for illness Bowes remained in the room and locked the door on her when they left. Any other prisoner who made eyes at Jenny was a target for Bowes's maliciousness or his rather odd sense of humour. When 'an amorous gentleman' who occupied a room across the way was detected watching the girl rather too assiduously, Bowes dressed himself in some of her clothing and flirted heavily with the poor gull, then when he had been encouraged to think that perhaps an assignation was possible, threw off the female skirt and demonstrated himself very obviously a man.

Bowes was still receiving the income from his wife's estates and was indeed eager to remind everyone that he held the purse-strings: during October 1787 he paid for no fewer than four insertions in the press of an advertisement pointing out that 'no debts incurred by Lady Strathmore, or by Mary Morgan her servant, or any other servant or person on her account, since her ladyship's elopement from her friends, relations or children, or any part thereof, will ever [be] paid or otherwise discharged by me, or by any other person whatsoever'. He also made it known that 'Lady Strathmore NEVER CAN OR WILL possess any power over, or any right to receive the rents of [her] estate during THE TERM OF MY LIFE' and that he would not 'give her an allowance or alimony unless she quits the society of artful, interested attornies and menial servants'.[4]

Bowes nursed, now, an unreasonable anger against James Farrer, of whom he was rather afraid – he complained that once, in court, the lawyer glared at him so malevolently through his glasses that he almost fainted. He had plenty of time to nurture his animosity, and composed an extraordinary attack on the attorney which appeared in *The Times* on 28 January 1788. It is a startling example of how far the newspapers and their correspondents would go in the matter of libel, confident that – as remains the case over two hundred years later – the expense of bringing a case would deter all but the wealthiest from reacting otherwise than in silent fury.

The libel was in the form of a letter addressed to Farrer, which starts off by referring to the entirely imaginary 'midnight orgies' he had enjoyed with Mary Morgan, and goes on to accuse him of knowing perfectly well that all the evidence of the husband's cruelty to the wife was fabricated, and to hint strongly that Farrer's motives were entirely financial. Bowes continues – at the length of three full columns of the paper – to scatter the wildest allegations about Farrer and the Countess: she had been 'the worst of wives' to Lord Strathmore, who had been 'the best of husbands'; she had sought means to destroy all her children while they were still embryos; she had attempted to persuade Bowes's servants to assassinate him; she had been entirely under the thumb of Mary Morgan, who 'dictated the whole of her conduct with all impervious impertinence of upstart tyranny'; Farrer had known all this, perjured himself as had his client, and interfered with witnesses at the late trial. Moreover, he had 'thrown the Strathmore estates into confusion'. The only thing Farrer could do was ignore the whole thing, though of course, as always, there were plenty of people who would believe whatever wild assertions Bowes cared to throw about.

It was ten months after Bowes's trial and imprisonment that the Lord Chancellor heard the Countess's plea to uphold the deed she had executed immediately before her marriage, and Bowes's counterclaim that it was fraudulent and should be set aside so that he could continue to control his wife's income from her father's estate. It was argued on Bowes's part that he had married knowing nothing about the deed, and that it was highly improper that anything should interfere with a husband's right to receive the income from any estates owned by his wife. The wife should and could do nothing to deprive him of that right. Bowes, determined not only to have what was his but to deprive his wife of any alimony, had also instructed his lawyers to argue that the Countess had been guilty of fraud, and had therefore forfeited any right to be supported by him.

The Lord Chancellor decided that the rights of the case hinged on the question whether the Deed of Revocation made on 1 May 1777 had or had not been obtained under duress. This should be decided, in his view, by a jury, and indeed it was set before a jury on 19 May 1788 in the Court of Common Pleas, with the Chief Justice, Lord Loughborough, presiding, and with Mr Serjeant Adair leading four counsel for the plaintiff (the Countess's trustee, Mr Stephens), and Mr Partridge leading three (including Mr Chambre) for the defendant, Bowes.

Mr Sergeant Adair, the Recorder of London and a popular, industrious and much-respected counsel, opened with a scathing attack on Bowes, who having married for money, had spent his first wife's fortune, become a bankrupt and subsequently wed the Countess, who 'raised him from indigence and obscurity to affluence and fashion'.[5] Then, 'when her spirit was broken with continual and unexpected ill-usage, when she had no free will of her own' he had extorted a deed vesting all her estates in him – which meant that while he had previously existed on a half-pay lieutenancy, her rentals now brought him £15,000 a year.

Adair summarised the 'ill-usage' – the violence, persecution, restrictions of her liberty, the fact that she was 'drove from her own table, or often forced to sit at it in company with [Bowes's] prostitutes' – and then called his witnesses. A number of servants, including George Walker, gave evidence about black eyes and torn clothing, about Bowes's instructions to them not to answer the Countess's bell when she rang, not to allow her to receive any post directed to her, and so on. Bowes's counsel attempted to intervene with the argument that such evidence did not prove that Mary Eleanor was 'under duress', that the fact that Bowes may once or twice have struck her did not mean that she feared him so greatly that she was forced to sign the deed; but the arguments were dismissed by the judges.

Bowes's leading counsel, Mr Partridge, then did his best, opening for the defence, to blacken the Countess's reputation, with snide comments about her relationship with Walker (whom she knew '*well*', he said with heavy emphasis), and of course with references to Gray, 'the first lover she had chosen, and whose addresses she had received till the very day she married Mr Bowes'.[6] The judge however ruled that her relationship with Gray had nothing to do with the case, and grew more and more impatient with this line of defence.

The chief witness for Bowes was Mrs Stephens, who said she well recalled the signing of the deed of revocation. She had asked the Countess at the time whether she had indeed signed over all her estates to her husband. Had she kept nothing back for herself? 'Nothing,' the Countess had replied; 'I am sure Mr Bowes will never use me ill.' She was, Mrs Stephens said, 'intemperate in her drinking of wine' . . . 'very improper in eating, drinking and clothing, and was too familiar with her servants, and particularly with George Walker.' Her ladyship had been 'very improperly connected' with Mr Gray and had never complained of her husband's behaviour to her. She, the witness, had never seen the Countess with a black eye or any other physical damage, and was convinced that there was 'no improper influence' used in persuading her to sign the deed of revocation.

But the judge was not impressed, and Thomas Mahon's evidence that Bowes had been seen coming out of her bedroom at five in the morning did nothing to convince the court that Mrs Stephens was a witness with a spotless character.[7] Neither did Lord Loughborough think much of the Revd Stephens's claim that Bowes had always treated his wife 'perfectly properly'. He also questioned the clergyman closely about the £1,000 he had received on the day after the wedding, and was not impressed by Stephens's admission that Bowes was paying his expenses while he was in London attending the trial.

Much was said about the duel, which the Judge clearly thought, and said, was a fraud (in his view indeed such a fraud as would, if cash had been involved, have laid Bowes open to prosecution). His direction to the jury was plain enough. He clearly disbelieved Bowes's witnesses, and for the most part believed those who had appeared for the Countess. So did the jurymen. They did not trouble themselves to leave the box, and 'found the deed of revocation to have been executed under duress'.

The case then went back again to the Court of Chancery, where the deed of revocation was set aside, and Mr Justice Buller delivered the final verdict. It had not been proved, he said, that the Countess had deceived Mr Bowes – a deed could not be considered void simply because the husband had not been told about it. Moreover, Bowes had demanded that the original deed should be set aside, but had not suggested that he was ready to offer any support for the wife whose means he aimed to remove. If a husband came to court wishing to acquire his wife's fortune, he really must offer and make a settlement.

It was clear that the judge did not feel that Bowes was an altogether admirable person. The court had heard evidence about 'a carefully staged duel', and since it had not been contradicted it was presumably to be believed. A man who could organise such a deception was not worthy of much consideration, in the court's view. Moreover, a man who married a very wealthy wife without securing a marriage treaty should not complain if he had to take her as he found her.

Bowes's cross bill was dismissed with costs, and he was ordered to pay the Countess's costs as well. The Deed of Revocation which she had signed on 1 May 1777 was ordered to be handed over to her, and she could cancel it. The deed she had signed on the day before her marriage had been established in law, and should stand. Bowes was ordered to return to his wife all and any of her possessions which he had confiscated, including the silver, jewellery and plate, and George Stephens, the only trustee still living, was appointed to administer her estates.

Bowes, of course, appealed. His lawyer produced yet again the argument that husband and wife were one – effectively that upon marriage, a wife ceased to exist in her own right. The man became liable for any improper or illegal behaviour on her part, liable for all her debts, and even for any criminal behaviour committed by her in his presence, because he was supposed to be in command of her. As compensation for this heavy responsibility, the law awarded him all her property, and it was preposterous to say that the wife could deprive her husband of what the law had awarded him.

The argument about the wife's subordination to her husband was an important and highly emotive one, moreover one with which most male readers of the press, which still avidly reported the progress of the case, greatly sympathised. A husband was the head of his family, and if the law were to ordain that a wife could make herself independent of him, the structure of family life would be undermined, if not fatally damaged. A husband would find himself powerless in his own home, incapable of educating his children, incapable of governing his wife. What Bowes's advocate was saying struck a solemn note with married men – and indeed women – which further injured the Countess's reputation; such radical views were out of tune with the time, and made her the butt of ill-humoured jokes and snide raillery for almost the rest of her life.

The Countess's advocates relied on legal argument rather than hyperbole. The original settlement, they pointed out, had been made to safeguard the well-being of her children, and while she was certainly wealthier than Bowes, at the time of his marriage he had by no means been a poor man, and could well have afforded to offer a settlement. He had known that she was an emotional woman and had mounted a carefully calculated campaign to win her hand, a campaign of which the feigned duel had been an important part.

In his summing up the Lord Chanceller said that he had not a moment's doubt about the rights and wrongs of the case. There had been in his view no fraud on the Countess's part, and the deed she had executed had been good (though he did allow himself the comment that he would not reflect on the morality of the transaction). The Countess had decided she wished to marry, but did not wish to part with her fortune. That was a view to which she had a perfect right. The settlement she made immediately before her marriage had been the result of a lucid interval, and Bowes had no argument against it. He found for the Countess, with costs.

As a result of the Lord Chancellor's judgement, a Master in Chancery went into the matter of the rents and profits Bowes had continued to receive from his wife since the suit had been brought, eventually concluding that he owed the Countess the sum of £10,295 11s 1d. In desperation, Bowes appealed to the House of Lords – which had the result only that they found him in contempt of the Court of Chancery for not immediately handing over to Mary Eleanor her plate and jewellery, and not so far paying the costs awarded her.

But he was not about to give up entirely; after all, stuck in his rooms in prison, he had nothing much to do except continue to consider his appeals. The last course open to him was an appeal to the High Court of Delegates. The final appeal in matrimonial cases had originally been to Rome, but this right was abolished by Henry VIII, who instead set up a body not of permanent judges, but of three puisne judges (judges of a superior court, but inferior in rank to a chief justice), one from each court of common law, sitting with three or more civilians. It was to this High Court of Delegates that Bowes now appealed.

SEVENTEEN

Divorce

*I fancy any man that had a wife and knew she was criminal with
the Footman would behave with some degree of severity.*

Dr James Battie

On 13 February 1789 the Lords Commissioners of the High Court
of Delegates sat in Sergeant's Inn Hall to hear Lady Strathmore's
case for divorce.

Once again, the Countess was absent from the proceedings and her
interest restricted to the taking of relevant cuttings from the
newspapers, which continued to report every aspect of the case,
understandably in view of the sensational evidence placed before the
court. She seems to have resigned herself to be the centre of continued
scandal, for though much of what was now said of her past behaviour
was repetition, the press was always happy to recapitulate it. Removed
now, by her own wish, from the society she had once courted and
enjoyed, she lived quietly at Blackheath and waited upon events.

She was represented in court by the lawyer and scholar Dr Thomas
Bever – it was one of his last notable cases before his death in 1791. He
was more interested in scholarship than in actual practice – he was said to
be 'a better scholar than writer, and a better writer than pleader'[1] – and
his attention to detail was such that he never actually finished any of his
fine projects, such as his 'History of the Legal Polity of the Roman State'
and his 'Discourse on the Study of Jurisprudence and the Civil Law'.

'My Lords,' he said, 'the case now before your Lordships is not upon
the common wranglings and disputes between John and Betty – that
kind of beating can do no worse, perhaps, than break a head without
wounding a heart, and does not consist in anything more than broken
heads and bloody noses which are the common consequences of the
marriage state and which are very easily and very happily made up by a
little matrimonial consolation at night – that is not the cruelty we
complain of.'[2]

If this seemed to suggest that cruelty to a Countess was considerably
more culpable than cruelty to any ordinary Betty, the suggestion was

carefully underlined when Bever went on to point out that Bowes's conduct was more atrocious than common, 'in accordance to the Education, the Fortune, the Rank and the Condition of the Person' of his victim. In the case before them, their Lordships would be appalled by the way in which the husband had entirely destroyed his wife's peace and happiness, the manner in which he had attacked and terrified her, depriving her of that contentment which 'by every law, both human and divine, she is certainly entitled to'.

The whole now familiar story of Bowes's treatment of his wife was recapitulated – the judges must surely have been well acquainted with it from previous reports; and the husband's counsel, Dr James Battie, did his best to defend his client. If Bever was pompous, Battie was incoherent: the Countess's conduct

> was such it would make every species of rigour not going absolutely to acts of cruelty but, however, every species of coercion and restraint not only justifiable in Mr Bowes but, in my opinion, absolutely necessary, I mean it justifies him if I can show, and I flatter myself that I can, from the answers given to several of the interrogatories, that her conduct was such as to raise strong suspicions in Mr Bowes to justify great rigour and severity – I mean to say this is a great excuse for a husband who behaves with some degree of rigour and severity to a wife under such circumstances . . . I fancy any man that had a wife and knew she was criminal with the Footman would behave with some degree of severity.

The footman in question was, of course, Mary Eleanor's confidant George Walker, who had eventually been dismissed by the Countess, probably at Bowes's behest. Mr Stephens (now demoted from his position as a private chaplain to that of curate of a poor Northumberland parish) said he was certain that misconduct had taken place between his former friend and patron and her footman 'on innumerable occasions'. He had seen the lady 'use many unbecoming familiarities' with Walker before her marriage to Mr Bowes, and she had continued those familiarities afterwards, though 'with more Reserve'. He had no doubt that there had been 'a criminal intercourse' between her and her footman; she was, he attested, 'violent and sudden in her attachments' and 'without regard to the principles of religion, decency, or morality'.

Then a new allegation was made, of crim. con. or 'criminal connection' between the Countess and one of the gardeners at Gibside. This was provided in the misspelt and rambling statement given by one Joseph Hill, who had originally been employed by the Earl of Strathmore and had, he said, been taken on by Bowes as groom and gamekeeper after the Countess's marriage to Bowes.

Some time towards the end of March 1784, he alleged, he had been strolling on the terrace walk at Gibside with his fellow servant Charles Chapman, and 'perceiving their Mistress . . . to come out of the Green House (where she left a Woman behind her, but whether a Gentlewoman or a Servant he knows not) and to go into the Garden House and to be followed by Robert Thompson, who then lived in the family in the Capacity of Gardiner, and whom they saw go into the Garden House after the said Mary Eleanor Bowes commonly called Countess of Strathmore had entered into it, they therefore, and in consequence of Suspicions they entertained of the said Robert Thompson, from having several times seen him talking to his said Mistress with his Hat on, and from having heard him declare at the public House that he had made his Fortune by coming to Gibside, determined to go and see what was going forward in the said Garden House. . . .'

The two curious servants 'made what Haste they could to the said Garden house and on their arrival at the Back part . . . perceived a Blue Apron, appearing to be such a One as the Gardiner usually wore, hanging up against the Window at said Back part, and which window it intirely covered, except at one Corner where an open space of two or three Inches was left.' Hill and Chapman 'crept on their Hands and Knees till they came close to the said Window; they then raised themselves up gently and the Deponant looking thro' the space left at a Corner aforesaid perceived the aforesaid Robert Thompson lying upon the body of the said Mary Eleanor Bowes upon a Bench in the said Garden House and which Bench was about six feet long and three feet broad and was placed against the Wall, and the Dept. having seen this, pulled the said Charles Chapman by the Coat as a Signal for him to look in which he immediately did and, as he then informed the Dept. saw the said Mary Eleanor Bowes and Robert Thompson in the same Situation as the Dept. had saw them himself, and they thereupon crept away again and hid themselves in some Bushes but the Dept. says that he verily believes that the said Mary Eleanor Bowes and Robert Thompson at the time aforesaid were in the act of adultery.'

The accusation must surely have sounded more curious to the court than the allegations of misconduct with George Walker; cases of ladies being over-familiar with their footmen were not unknown – but the Countess and the gardener? However, the allegation did not detain the judges long, for Dr Bever produced the sworn statement of another witness, Francis Bennett, a gamekeeper at Gibside who had worked for sixteen years with Hill and Chapman – or Cummins (as he said, there was no knowing what the man was likely to call himself next). Hill was more an ostler than a groom, Bennett said, his job looking after the horses which worked at Marley Hill colliery neither demanded much knowledge or appreciation of horse-flesh nor any special talent in grooming them. Chapman was merely a 'banksman', employed in removing coals from the mouth of the pit at Norbanks colliery.

Bennett pointed out in his written evidence that it was extremely unlikely that either man would ever have been anywhere near Gibside itself, for 'pitmen and other persons of the like Rank and Degree by orders of Andrew Robinson Bowes were not permitted or allowed to walk on or be in any of the Walks, Gardens or such like places belonging to or situate near the Mansion House of Gibside or within Sight thereof, and more especially so when any Part of the Family was there'.

Bowes had instructed his servants to keep 'Pitmen, Banksmen and other Workmen employed in and about the Collieries and other mean Persons from entering or walking in any of the Walks or other such Places'. Not only had Hill sent a number of such impertinent intruders packing, but he had often seen Bowes himself 'go after such people'. He didn't for a moment believe that either Hill or Chapman would dare come near the terrace, or 'long walk', as it was called, more especially as he, Hill, had often heard Bowes express his dislike and mistrust for both men, calling Chapman 'one of the damndest villains in the Country'; indeed, not only their employer but many of his neighbours who knew the pair believed them to be 'base and infamous persons who would depose falsely and untruly for Gain and Reward'.

Hill also said that he knew Robert Thompson well. During the time when he was supposed to be making love to the Countess, he was 'in a bad and declining State of Health, and so ill at times that he could hardly stand upright and walked almost double and was greatly troubled by a Shortness of Breath or difficulty of breathing which often rendered him incapable of labour'. He was a menial whose wages never exceeded 9s or 9s 4d a week, on which he kept himself and his two daughters. He 'always appeared in a dirty, ragged and wretched Condition, and very lousy, this Deponent having frequently seen him pick the Lice from off his Body and his Cloaths and throw them on the ground'.

It was clear that Thompson would not have made a prepossessing or vigorous lover, and the court made its opinion equally clear – that Hill's evidence was a pack of nonsense. Similarly, the court rejected the allegation that Walker had been Mary Eleanor's lover, though it was learned that she had given him a lock of her hair, and had promised to give him a farm (indeed, he and his wife later purchased a farm in Northumberland, and there is no telling how he managed to raise enough capital to buy it since a footman's wage was at most only £8 a year). More attention was paid to the tributes of those witnesses who described her as meek, mild and obedient, while Bowes had been cruel, sadistic and adulterous.

In response to the various charges brought against him of his numerous adulterous alliances – and Dr Bever mentioned in particular Dorothy Stevenson, Elizabeth Waite and Mrs Houghton – Bowes replied that Stevenson had been debauched by the Revd Reynett, his chaplain, that Waite was a common prostitute, and that Mrs Houghton's child had been sired by her husband.

There could never have been much doubt about the Commissioners' verdict, and indeed on 2 March 1789 they pronounced that Andrew Robinson Bowes 'being unmindful of his conjugal vows, and not having the fear of God before his eyes, did, on the several days and times mentioned in the pleadings of this case, commit the several acts of cruelty therein mentioned, and did also on the days therein set forth commit the heinous crime of adultery. The Court therefore order and decree, that the said Andrew Robinson Bowes and Lady Starthmore be divorced, and live separately from each other.'[3]

The divorce case had been followed almost as eagerly as the trial for abduction, and the press published the result – that 'Lady Strathmore was at length restored to the large possessions of her family, and divorced from a marriage contracted in an evil hour, and which was a source of a series of bitter calamity to herself'.[4]

Prosecuting her case had cost the Countess almost £2,000; though Bowes was liable for costs, he never paid a penny.

EIGHTEEN

Cats, Dogs and Daughters

Death would have been comparatively an Elysium.

Jessé Foot, *Lives*

Bowes's trial for abduction over, and the Countess's divorce granted, the two protagonists settled down to live out the rest of their respective lives.

Never yet downcast for a moment even in the King's Bench prison, Bowes was now utterly disconsolate. Jessé Foot describes how 'for the first time, perhaps, in his whole life, he began to sink into the most complete state of despondency. Every faculty seemed to have deserted him, but his instinct for deception. He pretended lameness and took to his bed, saw scarcely anyone, and kept himself in a constant state of intoxication.'[1] His biographer attempted to remonstrate with him, but had little effect. Foot was even more depressed when, faced with enormous legal costs, Bowes could no longer afford to live in the Marshal's 'state rooms', and had to move into smaller, dirtier, darker quarters, 'mauled, stripped, disgraced, and blasted . . . and in a state which to some, death would have been comparatively an Elysium'.

He soon found some relief, however, in his old game of making his former wife's life as miserable as possible. He unexpectedly received a letter from Mary Farrer, the wife of Captain Henry Farrer, asking if she could call on him in the King's Bench. What she had to say interested him greatly, and between them they decided to publish to the world the alleged history of Farrer's relationship with the Countess, and to blacken his reputation further with a few stories of his other amorous adventures.[2] They arranged for the publication of the *Appeal of an Injured Wife Against a Cruel Husband, written by Mrs Farrer, dedicated to Lady Strathmore*. This useful document enabled him to embarrass not only Mary Eleanor and Captain Farrer, but Farrer's brother James, who had been so active in the Countess's defence. The *Letter* gives all the details of Captain Farrer's life before meeting her, and leaves no doubt either about his affair with his former mistress Mrs Parks, or (if we believe the author) with Mary Eleanor. Reading Mrs

Farrer's account it is impossible not to hear Bowes's voice dictating some of the paragraphs – they have just his sarcastic tone. Having told the story of Captain Farrer and Mrs Parks, Mrs Farrer goes on:

> I am now to apologise to Lady Strathmore. Her Ladyship may feel offended that I should for so long have made her a secondary character in this melancholy memoir. Her Ladyship may be hurt that I should have neglected allowing her that precedence which her rank calls for, and her conduct merits, in the detail of my husband's profligate connections. Her Ladyship may feel her pride piqued that, being the principal cause of my miseries, she has not been brought forward with early and particular attention . . . I will now, however, introduce a few anecdotes, perhaps flattering to her Ladyship's vanity as a woman of intrigue, though they would disgrace a woman who pretended to what her Ladyship seems to disregard – honour and reputation.[3]

Mrs Farrer takes a sideways swipe at the faithful Mary Morgan (a 'companion described to me by the Captain as a person of fashion; but I now find she is Lady Strathmore's convenient friend, preferred from the kitchen, where she officiated as cook, to private confidence and a seat in the carriage'), before going on to accuse her husband – not, we may think, altogether without reason – of looking forward to 'the plunder of those treasures which would come into [the Countess's] possession, the moment she succeeded in her attempt of being divorced from her husband'. But it was Mary Eleanor who is the main object of her attack, or of Bowes's invective.

'When women deviate from the path of virtue and launch into the indiscriminate indulgence of vice,' she writes, '"every rank fool goes down", but as Lady Strathmore's attachments were not the result of love or the offspring of sentiment, as the sex and not the particular individual was the object of her passion, she might have confined that passion to single men. . . .'[4]

She ends by 'forbidding the unhallowed banns' which might announce the marriage of her husband and Lady Strathmore – for who could doubt but that he would marry her, even if it meant committing bigamy? 'I know there is a legal punishment for such transgressions; but what satisfaction would it be to me to prosecute this profligate husband, should he dare violate the Laws of God and Man, by committing the perjury and falsehood of a second marriage . . . ?' There is Bowes's voice again, surely, though it was Mary Farrer who swore before John Burnell, Mayor of London, that the contents of her *Letter* were 'strictly true in every part'.

There is a personal note at the end: a copy of an instrument signed on 1 November 1787 between Henry Farrer and 'one Mary Goldsmith' – his wife – stipulating that having decided to part, they would never make any financial or other claim upon each other, and that on receipt of £100 she would promise never to disturb or molest him and never to come within 100 miles of London. The couple had been tolerating each other since Farrer's adventure with the Countess had ended; now their marriage was finally over.

The *Letter*, as far as one can judge, had little effect on the public. After all the scandal that had been noised abroad during the various trials, there was little that could further blacken the Countess's name – and of course it *was* blackened; her behaviour had been no worse than that of many a society woman, but the fact that she had been so completely exposed left its mark on the public's apprehension, as did her unfashionable view that as a wife she was not completely the property even of a brutal and adulterous husband.

Perhaps disappointed at the lack of response to his latest ploy, Bowes next decided to assist the destitute Mrs Farrar in a more practical manner. He organised a benefit performance of *Tamerlaine*, a tragedy by Nicolas Rowe first produced in 1701 and a play in which the eponymous hero was modelled on King William III. The announcement in *The Times* read:[5]

Theatre-Royal, Haymarket.
By permission of The Lord Chamberlain
For the benefit of Mrs Farrer
On Monday the 22nd of December
Will be performed,
A Favourite Tragedy, called,
TAMERLANE THE GREAT;
Or, the FALL of
BAJAZET, EMPEROR of the TURKS
Tamerlane, Mr SIMPSON . . .
And Arpasia, Mrs FARRER

The paper added a note that 'Mrs *Farrer*, who a short time ago published a pamphlet dedicated to Lady *Strathmore*, will perform the part of *Arpasia*, and there are flattering expectations that from her person, voice and expressive countance she may prove a successful candidate for the winter theatres'. Lest the public should fear some scandalous interpretation, the programme for the evening announced that 'the utmost care and attention will be taken to render the performance respectable and to merit their appreciation and support'. No notice of the production has survived. Apart from keeping Mrs Farrer in the public eye, and therefore keeping the scandal alive, it is difficult to see what Bowes hoped to gain from this incident. Could it be that he was making a genuine attempt to assist Mrs Farrer in her penury? It does not seem in character. The episode may perhaps have raised his spirits a little, if only by giving him something to occupy his mind.

No one could expect Mary Eleanor's spirits to be particularly high. No doubt she had been enormously relieved at the outcome of her suit for divorce, but felt that she had been utterly disgraced; whether or not the many readers believed the various accounts of Bowes's accusations against her – that she drank, and had accepted a gardener and a footman among her lovers – it can have been no pleasure to read about them in the gossip schedules and pamphlets of the time, and she could not deny her connection with Gray or the illegitimate child conceived before the Earl's death. Her one consolation was that some members of Lord Strathmore's family had renewed their acquaintance with her, and if not sympathetic showed signs at least of tolerating her and even from time to time actually acknowledging her. More importantly, her eldest son, John Strathmore, travelled from Caen, where he was learning French, and stayed with her in the house in which she was now living in Fludyer Street, on the borders of Lewisham and Hither Green; his visit laid the foundations of a friendly relationship after years during which the two of them had scarcely communicated, and the Countess had nursed a completely unreasonable dislike for him. The 10th Earl of Strathmore became at last the apple of the Countess's eye, and worthily so.

Lady Anna lived with her mother, but under conditions which she must have found extremely trying, for Mary Eleanor kept her almost a prisoner, only allowing her to leave the house when heavily chaperoned. Her fear seems to have been that her daughter would fall in love as unsuitably as she herself had. The result, as most people would predict, was that she did so. A young man called Jessup, a lawyer, lived in a house across the narrow street from her and her mother, and had managed to communicate with Lady Anna. One night, she pushed a ladder out of her bedroom window; he caught it, laid it on his window-sill, and guided her across (one of the Countess's acquaintances remarked admiringly that 'Leander was a Fool to her').[6] The couple was married, but Lady Anna's husband died young leaving her with two daughters. Her relationship with her mother irreparably damaged, she was supported by her brother until her death.

The Countess now had only her family to occupy her, and her dogs (dogs having displaced cats in her affections). In 1790 she finally revoked the Ante-Nuptial Agreement which had been the cause of all Bowes's manipulations, for John had come of age, and was to receive all the income from her estate, apart from some sums set aside to support her two youngest children, Mary Bowes (her daughter by Gray) and William Johnstone Bowes, who at last were placed in her custody. Mary, at twelve years old, was delighted:

I cannot express the joy it was to me to be informed . . . of my turn of Fortune in being now, I hope, under your Protection. When I parted from you, I was much too young to know the loss of a mother . . . I long very much to see you and hope there is nothing more now wanted to complete my happiness. I am sure you will be very glad to see my dear little brother William, indeed he is a very fine Boy. Although I have been almost five years absent from you I have not forgot any place where I spent my infancy and believe I could find my way over one half of Paul's Walden and Gibside houses . . . .[7]

George, the second son, turned twenty-one in 1792, and the Countess gave him St Paul's Waldenbury. In that same year, John Byng, Viscount Torrington, on one of his many journeys around England, rode through Durham and on the way from Barnard Castle to Durham 'quitted the high road and took down some fields to Streatlam Castle, a house of the late Mr Bowes, a place in neglect and wild disorder: there is a rookery on one side and a stream (of great capacity) in front, with a miserable kind of park! The house appears to be of the worst kind'.[8]

The Countess now quit both London and St Paul's for Purbrook Park, a house on the Portsmouth Road some 7 miles from the coast. William, her son by Bowes, joined the navy, and his mother took a proud interest in his career. Two of her daughters, Mary Bowes and Lady Maria, lived with her, sharing the house with more dogs than any reasonable person might expect to find in one establishment. Each had its own bed in its own basket, near which was a plate on which a servant set a specially cooked hot dinner each day, refreshing the water in the individual bowl by its side.

The faithful Mrs Morgan remained with the Countess until she died in 1796, when Mary Eleanor attended her funeral at Christchurch, and set up a monument in her memory, bearing an inscription she composed herself:

DEDICATED to the most rare of all connections, a perfect and disinterested friend, by the COUNTESS OF STRATHMORE, who, conscious of the treasure, valued its possession and mourned its loss. To her heroic qualities, her cool, deliberate courage, and her matchless persevering friendship, the tears of blood shed by one who despises weakness, the records of law and justice and perhaps even the historic page will bear witness to an astonished and admiring posterity.

So little information has survived about the remaining four years of the Countess's life that we can only assume that it was placid and reasonably contented. There was a flurry of excitement in 1799, when young William, serving on the frigate *Proserpine*, was stranded by shipwreck on pack-ice in the estuary of the River Elbe. Several of his shipmates, attempting to walk over the ice to safety, froze to death, but William and a few friends climbed back on to the wrecked ship, which was washed from its position by the tides and drifted to the island of Baltrum, where they were rescued. His mother carefully collected all the press cuttings of the event and pasted them into her scrapbooks. It was the last agitation of her life.

She died in the following year, on 28 April 1800, and dressed in her wedding dress was buried in Westminster Abbey.[9] She lies in the south transept, on the margin of Poets' Corner – she would have been pleased at that – next to Mr Thomas Parr, who had died in 1635 at the age, it is said, of 152, beneath a black marble slab on which could once have been read the inscription

IN MEMORY
OF RIGHT HONOURABLE
MARY ELEANOR BOWES
COUNTESS OF STRATHMORE
ONLY CHILD OF
GEORGE BOWES ESQ
OF STREATLAM CASTLE
AND OF GIBSIDE
IN THE COUNTY OF DURHAM
WHO DIED 28th APRIL 1800
AGED 51 YEARS

Today, all that can be deciphered, and that with difficulty, is her surname, Bowes.

NINETEEN

'A Villain to the Backbone!!'

Cowardly, insidious, hypocritical, tyrannic, mean, violent, selfish,
deceitful, jealous, revengeful, inhuman and savage.

Jessé Foot, *Lives*

By the time he heard of his former wife's death, Bowes had been in prison for over ten years. Mary Eleanor had not found it difficult to relax into anonymous contentment. Bowes had no talent for contentment. He was not the kind of man to accept his situation and make the best of it. Nor had imprisonment improved his temper – in 1790 he had been involved in a fracas with a fellow prisoner which resulted in his being fined 6s 8d for gaming (he had been accurately accused of cheating by the man with whom he was gambling). Later the same year he broke several of another prisoner's teeth for standing in front of a fire of which he himself wanted to take advantage. When in 1791 there was a riot in the prison, he took the side of the prison authorities, and as a result was made chairman of the prisoners' association. He somewhat placated his fellows by presenting them with a clock – not, one would have thought, a particularly happy choice of gift, considering the slowness with which time passed in prison.

He still continually attempted to get money out of the Countess, but was reduced now to swearing occasional affidavits witnessed by magistrates, such as that in which on 30 January 1790 he again appealed for justice. When he had married Lady Strathmore, he pointed out, 'he was possessed of the sum of seven thousand five hundred pounds in money [cash] or money well secured and of a clear yearly income of near four hundred pounds arising from lands and houses'.[1] But 'the said Lady Strathmore's expensive mode of life' and expensive litigations in which she had involved him had resulted in very heavy debts and confinement in the King's Bench prison. During the past three years he had 'with very great difficulty maintained cloathed and educated and still has to maintain cloath and educate two of the children of the said Lady Strathmore, one of the age of twelve years and the other of the age of seven years and he hath never received any assistance from the said Lady

Strathmore'. The Countess had now had all her property returned to her while the unfortunate prisoner was entirely destitute, and if the courts did not force her to assist him, he and the children would be 'reduced to very great distress if not absolute want'.

The idea that he had been doing anything to maintain the Countess's daughters or his only legitimate son was ludicrous, and in any case, now that he had exhausted the patience of every possible court, what use was he to make of his affidavits? But he persevered: sooner or later his luck would change, he would secure his rights. And there was a good sign, and some relief, at about the time of Mary Eleanor's death.

In 1797 Peacock, once a friend, attempted to force him into bankruptcy, but on a legal nicety the petition was dismissed. Heartened by this, the following year Bowes petitioned the Lord Chancellor, claiming the right to one-third of the income from two farms in County Durham which had been bought by George Bowes. His claim rested on a legal cavil to do with the date of the signing of George Bowes's will and a codicil to it, and on the production of a lease signed by the Countess in 1781, assigning her rights in the income from the farms to a solicitor, to be administered on behalf of Bowes, her then husband. The arguments were complex and arcane, the sole witness to her signature could remember nothing about the affair, and Mary Eleanor claimed that in any case she had been so frightened of Bowes at that time that she signed anything put before her without looking at it.

However, for once the court decided in Bowes's favour, the Countess's appeal to the House of Lords failed, and he was able to enjoy the income he had claimed, which encouraged him later to leave the prison and live more comfortably, though still 'within the rules'.[2] So he set up house in the London Road, St George's Fields,[3] with Jenny Sutton, their children and a large number of cats and dogs, most of them almost starving.

He still had plenty of life in him – indeed, sufficient life to provoke a considerable amount of domestic strife, for he took a second house not far from his own and rather more attractive, with a pretty garden attached, and installed another (pregnant) mistress, a neat and modest young woman according to Jessé Foot, a seamstress whom Bowes had met when she visited a clergyman who found himself in the King's Bench prison. Bowes sent his eldest daughter to share her rooms and care for the young woman. But the seamstress had domestic ambitions, and when Jenny was away from home for a while, moved into Bowes's house – or attempted to do so, for his daughters took violently against her, ran off to tell their mother about the situation, and Bowes was forced to send his pregnant friend back to her own house, fearful that if the matter became public it might affect his status as a prisoner. Indeed, the last possibility concerned him so much that he offered the seamstress £250 a year to swear that the father of her child was another prisoner in the King's Bench. Not unnaturally, she accepted the offer, and so swore; upon which Bowes discarded her, and never paid her a penny or set eyes on their child.

All this time, he lived on his half-pay as an army lieutenant, and on what he could persuade his lawyers to lend him on the promise of property which he was never to succeed in possessing. He was extremely persuasive, as Foot tell us. He would pretend to be losing his faculties, to be going deaf, and would plead 'his immediate wants, his tattered appearance, and state of his children, which he so contrived that they may be seen without shoes or stockings. . . . In this practice, perhaps, there never was a more perfect adept; as I do not know an instance in which he did not succeed to a certain degree. This was the game he played for the last ten years of his life, and always more or less coming off a winner.'[4] Bowes usually managed to prevent lawyers coming to examine him by sending a message that he was so ill that an interview would probably terminate his life.

Foot managed to see him fairly regularly, but the deception was kept up. 'He affected not to know me; I was to speak very softly; the barber was sent for; he was to describe to me the fit he had had; while the barber was describing the fit, he fell into one before us both. The farce being over, he began to mend, and to expose his intention, which was to get me to inform his attorney of the extreme dangerous state of his health.'[5] Foot was almost deceived, but then there was a fracas in the yard outside Bowes's room, where two cocks had been set fighting by one of his children; Bowes leaped out of bed and bawled at his son with such violence that it was clear there was nothing wrong with his health. Foot left without a word.

Gradually, everyone who dealt with him recognised his tricks, and his income from loans began to dry up. He was forced to begin selling his collection of watches, his rings, gold snuff-boxes, the silver plate he had hoarded, and the rich clothing which he had had made for him in London and Paris in his heyday. He may have hoped that the Countess's death would enable him to claim something from her estate; but on the contrary, as executor of his mother's will Lord Strathmore took him to the Court of Common Pleas and succeeded in proving to the court's satisfaction that his mother's signature on the deed allowing Bowes part of the income from the three farms in County Durham had been obtained under duress, and thus relieved him of the portion of the income he had until recently been able to enjoy.

Deprived of this, Bowes now made an attempt to extort some money from his own family. One of his sisters journeyed from Ireland with her daughter to visit him. Foot liked her very much, and was appalled at Bowes's attitude to her: he put on a tremendous act, pretending shortness of breath and loss of appetite and vomiting blood (he later confessed to Foot that he had acquired some calves blood, gargled with it just before the doctor came into the room, and then spat it into a basin). He described the faithful Jenny Sutton as a depraved termagant and thief, who had dominated him for years, neglected their children and acted most cruelly to him. He drew up a will in which he ostentatiously left his sister all his money and the whole of the Countess's estate.

So impressed was his sister by his plight that she sent an account to her husband in Ireland, telling him of the will and pleading with him to send money for the relief of her brother, money which would be repaid with interest at Bowes's death, when she would inherit the Strathmore estates. Her husband returned a message that he 'thought it was indecent, and not becoming a relation, to take advantage in any bargain of a DYING man, not even in the shape and under the pretence of affection, and therefor he declined it altogether, hoping that his dear brother-in-law might long live to enjoy that, and all his other estates'.[6]

Bowes was disappointed, but recovered his health remarkably quickly. The will he had signed in favour of his sister was never seen again. A secretary came in occasionally to write letters for him, among them one to a creditor announcing that he had shot himself, and that the secretary had seen him dead and weltering in blood. He also dictated letters addressed to himself – a forged letter from Lord Strathmore, for instance, offering him a home. He had now worked his way through four attorneys, all of whom had tired of his continual deceptions. A fourth, a young, inexperienced and wealthy man, was putty in his hands, and supported him for some time, providing, among other things, a good cellar of wine, which Bowes drank alone, declining to offer visitors so much as half a glass. Foot, who visited him regularly, noticed that he now drank spirits as well as wine; he had dismissed all his servants, and one or other of his daughters was to be found on hands and knees scrubbing the floor. Jenny still attended him, but he rarely threw her a word, and allowed her only one sparse meal a day. She only stayed with him because of their children. He continued to insult her by making up to other women, though he was now in such poor physical condition and so ill-looking that he was unsuccessful except with the most obvious fortune-seekers, who deserted him as soon as they realised he had no fortune to seek.

Gradually, his physical condition deteriorated until he was scarcely in control of his faculties. He would walk – or rather totter – to the nearest public house, where he would sit over a newspaper with a drink; he almost always carried with him a dog-eared copy of the Countess's *Confessions*, which he would leaf through, and show proudly to any stranger whose interest he could engage.

Jessé Foot, for some years now his only physician, was so used to his feigned illnesses that at first he ignored the signs that Bowes was fatally ill. On 10 January 1810 the latter's younger son came to Foot's house to summon him. When he reached Bowes's house, Jenny Sutton let him in – she had never previously been allowed to open the front door to anyone. As she took him to Bowes's bedroom, she tearfully complained that he had made a new will, and had cheerfully told her that while he was leaving something to all their children, he was leaving nothing to her.

When he examined Bowes, Foot concluded that he had only days to live, and frankly told him so. Bowes confessed that he had made his will and that indeed the faithful Jenny was to receive nothing. He claimed that he had made the Marshal of the King's Bench one of his executors, and Foot went to him to try to persuade him to see Bowes and to arrange a codicil leaving Jenny some reward for her years of service. But the Marshal denied he had ever been asked to act as an executor, and said he could do nothing. Next morning Foot tried to find the second executor, Bowes's current attorney, a Mr Meredith. But he was out of town.

In the meantime another of Bowes's sisters had arrived in London, and she and Foot together with a sympathetic clergyman attempted to persuade the dying man to fulfil his obligation to Jenny. Eventually, Bowes was persuaded to leave her an annuity of £100. Bowes died within the week, on 16 January 1810. The cortège consisted of two coaches, the first carrying his three sons, and the second Jessé Foot and a second doctor. He was buried in a vault in St George's Church, The Borough, adjacent to Marshalsea debtors' prison.

No one mourned him, except perhaps his sisters, and even they understood by now what sort of man he had been, and what sort of life he had lived. Jessé Foot, who knew him as well as anyone, did not spare him, labelling him 'a villain to the backbone!!' and believing him incapable of making friends, and indeed not knowing what friendship was. As a womaniser, he 'considered all females as natural game, and hunted them down as so many *feræ naturæ*'.

'To sum up his character in a few words,' Foot writes, 'he was cowardly, insidious, hypocritical, tyrannic, mean, violent, selfish, deceitful, jealous, revengeful, inhuman and savage, without a single countervailing quality.' It is difficult to disagree – the only 'countervailing quality' must have been a degree of charm, for without it Bowes would have been unlikely to capture the Countess, to have captivated at least some of his neighbours and acquaintances, and persuaded the long-suffering William Davies to put up with him for so long and to exert himself so considerably on his behalf. The use he made of some of his servants was balanced by the scorn with which he regarded them – and the same can be said of his attitude to his numerous mistresses.

The history of the Countess and the half-pay lieutenant is not an edifying one. It certainly provided the readers of the burgeoning popular press with a great deal of entertainment and pleasure. There was not much public sympathy for Stoney Bowes – he was not a figure for whom it was possible for even the most chauvinist of men to have much regard. But sadly, the Countess suffered more than she deserved, not only from Bowes's treatment but from public obloquy. The latter was undeserved, and the result of the common view of the time: that a woman's place was in the home, while her husband's was in the counting-house dealing with the deployment of her property. These days, in similar circumstances, she would be regarded almost as a heroine, her adultery (considering the coldness and lack of sympathy of her first husband) regarded as at worst a venial sin, and her determination not to give way to Bowes's violent attempts to get his hands on her property prompting admiration rather than contempt.

Mary Eleanor Bowes had no claims to extraordinary intelligence, but thanks to her father's tutelage her mind was developed to a degree unusual for women of her time. She would never have made an impact as a writer; that is clear from her surviving play, and indeed from her *Confessions*, which even considering the pressure and circumstances of its production is not an inspiring book. But had she been allowed to pursue her passion for horticulture she might have created fine gardens, and perhaps have been in the forefront of the late eighteenth-century interest in the subject.

Jessé Foot was hard on her. 'Her judgement was weak, her prudence almost none, and her prejudice unbounded',[7] he wrote, and he bracketed her with Bowes: 'Neither of them received one single check from any compunctious visitings of nature; neither of them had disciplined their minds by the strict observance of any rule of right;

both of them appeared as if they had been taken from a land not yet in a state of civilization, and dropped by accident where they have been found.'[8] Her first biographer was no doubt thinking of her admittedly loose interpretation of her marriage vows, and in the context of his time it would have been difficult for him to take a more charitable view. We may feel free to differ from him, and to consider that a woman of normal sexual appetites, whose husband regarded the fathering of children as the only sufficient reason to enter his wife's bed, might be forgiven for finding consolation elsewhere.

Nor does the fact that she invariably fell for the wrong man – the libidinous and sympathetic but bland, weak Gray; the villainous Bowes; the ambitious Farrer – make her 'silly', the view clearly taken by her later biographer, Ralph Arnold, whose attitude in the 1950s was not so far removed from the chauvinism of the eighteenth century as might have been hoped. If not an exceptional woman, the Countess possessed quite extraordinary strength of mind and body – the sang-froid with which she met the terrifying ordeal of her abduction would have been admirable in any age, and was particularly so in a period when most women would tremulously have signed their rights and fortune over to Bowes with scarcely a moment's hesitation.

Coda

Stoney Bowes's only legitimate son, William Bowes, does not seem to have been specially dear to his mother, although towards the end of her life she took an interest in his naval career. He died without issue in 1817. His half-sister Mary also died unmarried. Lady Anna, as we have heard, became Mrs Jessup and had two daughters; the family was largely supported by her eldest brother, and Anna lived until her death in a cottage in the park at Gibside.

Mary Eleanor's eldest son, the 10th Earl, John Lyon-Bowes, from whom she was estranged until he was a young man, was quite as handsome as his father, but no one could have accused him of being temperamentally cool. On the contrary, if not precisely a womaniser he certainly enjoyed female company, and when he came of age and was able to escape from his overbearing and often physically violent guardian, Thomas Lyon, he might have been expected to come seriously to grief. As it was, the worst thing the 10th Earl did was to fall in love with a married woman, the wife of the 2nd Earl of Tyrconnel and more notably a former mistress of Frederick, Duke of York. John saw her acting in an amateur performance of Nicholas Rowe's *The Fair Penitent*, staged in a private house not far from Gibside, and within weeks became her lover, apparently with his friend Lord Tyrconnel playing the part of a complaisant husband.

Alas, the lady developed tuberculosis and died at Gibside, with her lover at her side. The inconsolable Strathmore almost bankrupted himself in paying for her magnificent funeral: 'Her face was painted like the most brilliant life. He dressed her head himself! And then, having decked her out in all her jewels, and covered her with Brussels lace from head to foot, he sent her up to London, causing her to lie in state at every town upon the road, and finally to be buried in Westminster Abbey!'[1]

The Earl then fell in love with his mistress's daughter, but the opposition of her father and his own doubts about the propriety of the affair prevented him from marrying her. He concentrated on commuting between Gibside and Streatlam, modifying and rebuilding the former and establishing a fine thoroughbred stud at the latter. In

1809 he fell in love again. The inveterate gossip Augustus Hare takes up the story:

> John, Earl of Strathmore was a very agreeable and popular man, but by no means a moral character. Living near his castle at Streatlam was a beautiful girl named Mary Milner, daughter of a market-gardener at Staindrop. With this girl he went through a false ceremony of marriage, after which, in all innocence, she lived with him as his wife. Their only boy, John Bowes, was sent to Eton as Lord Glamis. On his death-bed Lord Strathmore confessed to Mary Milner that their marriage was false and that she was not really his wife. She said, 'I understand that you mean to marry me now, but that will not do; there must be no more secret marriages'; and, ill as he was, she had everyone within reach summoned to attend the ceremony, and she had him carried to church and was married to him before all the world.[2]

The strange story was true: the Earl was carried from his death-bed to his wedding at St George's, Hanover Square, and died the following day. While John Bowes, his son by Mary Milner, was still at school, the Hon. Thomas Bowes, Mary Eleanor's third and now only surviving son announced himself as Lord Strathmore, claimed the title, and instructed his lawyer – James Farrer, who had remained a close friend of the family – to petition the King to that effect. He had been left the income from his father's English estates (about £720,000 in modern terms), but if he was successful in his claim he would also receive the income from the entailed Scottish estates (an additional £864,000).

The dispute about the succession went to the Committee of Privileges in the spring of 1821. The case against John Bowes rested on the argument that the 10th Earl had been too ill to consummate his death-bed marriage, and that as one of his 'essential duties' as a husband had not been performed, his had not been a true marriage. John's lawyers argued that the marriage had been valid because the Earl's mental faculties had not been impaired, and that he himself had recognised John as his son and heir. But the committee found for Thomas, on the grounds that John's main residence had been in England, and that while in Scotland a child could be legitimised by his parents' subsequent marriage, English law did not have that effect. John remained a bastard despite his parents' marriage, and therefore Thomas was the true Earl of Strathmore. John had been the 11th Earl for only three months. His mother, however, was recognised as properly the Countess of

Strathmore, married John's former tutor, and lived contentedly at Gibside until her death in 1860.

John, who as his father's favourite had inherited at least half his estate, remained a rich man, and had an eventful life. He entered Parliament as soon as he was twenty-one, but was more interested in breeding horses and in the theatre – he married a French actress, Mlle Joséphine Delorme, and eventually left Streatlam and settled in Paris, where he owned and managed the Théâtre de Variétés. A knowledgeable collector of pictures and antiques, from a distance he keenly supervised the completion of the long-drawn-out plans for the rebuilding of Streatlam. He became a shrewd businessman and much enriched the family through his management of his collieries and of a ship-building company he and a colleague started at Jarrow (and incidentally by winning £20,000 by backing his own horse, Mündig, to win the 1832 Derby – his horses won the race three times). It was John who became a friend of Thackeray whom he met while the latter was still at university, and told the novelist the story of the first Countess.[3]

Bowes sold his Paris theatre in 1868, and in the following year Mrs Bowes laid the foundation stone of the Bowes Museum at Barnard Castle, which was completed by Bowes after his wife's death and dedicated to her memory – the idea of a museum had originally been hers. He married a second time, but died at Streatlam (after securing a divorce) in 1885.

The Strathmore title descended through the 12th Earl, Thomas, Lord Glamis, then through the thirteenth and fourteenth holders of the title. The latter succeeded to the title in 1904. In 1900 his daughter Elizabeth was born, perhaps at St Paul's Waldenbury (or in London, or at Glamis – extraordinarily, the family itself was unsure). In 1923 she married the Duke of York, the second son of King George V, and became his consort when in 1936, on the abdication of his elder brother Edward VIII, he succeeded to the British throne as George VI. As Queen, and especially during the Second World War, Elizabeth showed much of the feisty spirit of her ancestress Mary Eleanor, whose great-great-great-great-granddaughter is the present Queen Elizabeth II.

APPENDIX I

The Siege of Jerusalem

A verse-play in five acts, *The Siege of Jerusalem* was published at Lady Strathmore's own expense in 1769; presumably it was written during the previous one or two years. Apart from the fact that she seems to have hoped that she had a real talent for writing, the play's text clearly reflects her disillusionment with marriage and her regret that she had allowed herself to make an alliance with a man who, however handsome and well-born he might be, was someone with whom it was impossible to form any real, close relationship. She had found herself in the position of just the sort of woman her Bluestocking friends despised: a woman whose every action was subject to her husband's commands, and whose only purpose in life was to produce children. The fact that her husband was rarely at her side only highlighted the tedium of her existence – clearly she meant little more to him than one of his brood mares.

The plot of her play need not detain us long. She drew heavily upon Tasso and his best-known work, *Gerusalemme Liberata*, an extremely, almost neurotically melancholy poem to which her father may well have introduced her as a child. Its main protagonist is Tancred, the heroic Norman crusader who accompanied his uncle Bohemond I on the 1097 crusade against the forces of Saladin, the chivalrous sultan of Egypt who had successfully invaded the Holy Land and recaptured Jerusalem from the crusaders, and who later ruled as regent in Antioch. In Mary Eleanor's play he loves Clorinda, the heroic female warrior of Saladin's forces. But at the centre of the piece is Erminia, the sister of Saladin's ally Argantes, Prince of Syria. She loves Tancred, but is offered by her brother to Saladin. Clorinda, who discovers that she is of royal blood and was born a Christian though raised as a Muslim, is killed by Tancred while dressed in male armour, courageously attempting to set fire to one of the Christians' siege towers. Meanwhile Erminia has escaped and taken refuge at a monk's cell. Tancred discovers her, and is slain by her brother, Argantes. Erminia ends her life in a nunnery.

The plot is clumsy and clumsily handled. The Countess clearly had no dramatic flair, and her command of syntax, punctuation and prosody is shaky. But her identification with her characters' situations – particularly that of Erminia – is heartfelt. Time and again she returns to the problem of the woman forced to disregard love in favour of duty. Learning in the first act that she is to be offered by her brother as a bride for Saladin, Erminia sadly reflects that 'A virgin princess matches not for love / Her ev'ry thought devoted to the state'.[1] Later, she revisits the theme:

> In real happiness no pomp is seen,
> But gloomy grandeurs e'en attend a queen,
> While the poor peasant in his humble cot
> Lives to the world, forgetting and forgot;
> With meek content he spends his guiltless days,
> Peace in his paths and pleasure in his ways.
> No kingdom can a sacrifice command —
> He reigns sole master of his heart and hand.
> He's free to choose the partner of his bed
> And love alone directs him where to wed.
> Far other springs our regal actions move
> Who ne'er must taste the dear-bought joys of love.

If she identified herself and her position with Erminia and her quandary, the Countess went a little too far. She had not been forced into a marriage with Strathmore; initially impressed by his looks, she had recognised her mistake almost as soon as she accepted him. It may certainly be true that it would have been embarrassing to back out of the contract before the wedding – and perhaps even legally difficult, after it had been signed; but it could have been done. However, she clearly felt as trapped as her heroine, and it is that feeling of entrapment which she portrays in the character of Erminia, who later in the play once again complains that women should not be forced into marriage by a sense of obligation:

> . . . surely our more tender sex
> Should be exempted from this barbarous duty,
> Nor pay, with every comfort, every joy of life,
> The forfeit of [men's] untam'd ambition.

Throughout the action of the play Erminia is unable to forget that circumstances have deprived her of the opportunity to enjoy life with a man she actually loves:

Would we had been some neighbouring shepherd's babes
Together bred in equal humble state:
We then had frequent met at rural sports,
In sweeter converse oft beguil'd the day
'Til love insensibly had crept into our hearts
And our glad parents had with rustic joy
Join'd willing hands, and heard our nuptial vows.

The unhappiness of Mary Eleanor's marriage is easy to read between the lines – as in other parts of the play there is a longing for real love which she equated with her feelings for young Campbell Scott, dead of the smallpox, the only man whom she felt she could have accepted as both lover and husband, and whom she remembered with all the regretful passion with which we recall a lost opportunity:

I thought, great love, that I had shook thee off . . .
But like a practis'd spy, the subtle god
Did lurk about, whilse seemingly he fled,
That when he unexpectedly returned
And found the sentinels were fast asleep,
Who should defend the citadel of my heart?
To the besiegers he might yield the town
And with a force unlook'd-for and resistless
Break down the ramparts, and with fury rush
On every foe, and bear down all before him.

We also sense a real emotion behind the lines in which she writes of Erminia's failure to forget Tancred:

The too short moments spent with Tancred fled
On downy wings, but left a sting behind
Which I attempted not to pluck, or if I did
'Twas with a hand so fearful that the gentle touch
Did only force it deeper in. 'Twas like
The tooth of timorous doe, who tries
To draw the dart her hunter hath infixed;
But wanting strength, doth more enlarge the wound,
Making it wider gape, and bleed the more.

In the eighteenth century female playwrights enjoyed successes at Drury Lane and Covent Garden – Hannah More (1745–1833) and

Sophia Lee (1750–1824) among them – but the Countess's script would have had a negligible chance of success. Not too many years later Byron, on the management committee of Drury Lane, was complaining of 'the trash among the four hundred fallow dramas lying on the shelves' of the theatre, and claiming that he 'never thought so highly of good writers as lately – since I have had an opportunity of comparing them with the bad'.[2] Mary Eleanor's play would doubtless have ended up among the rejects. It was as well, perhaps, that she did not think of submitting *The Siege of Jerusalem* to professional scrutiny. She was to have a trying enough time of it, without courting that kind of rejection.

Thackeray and the Stoney Bowes Story

Thackeray published his novel *Barry Lyndon* in 1844, when he was thirty-three, as a serial in *Fraser's Magazine*. Its first title was *The Luck of Barry Lyndon*; it was subsequently republished in book form in 1752 (after the appearance of *Vanity Fair*, *Pendennis* and *Esmond*) as *The Memoirs of Barry Lyndon, Esquire, by Himself*, and later became simply *The Memoirs of Barry Lyndon, Esquire*. It tells the story of a ne'er-do-well Irishman, as written by himself when an old man confined in the Fleet Prison. The characters of Redmond Barry and the Countess of Lyndon are by no means portraits of Andrew Robinson Stoney and the Countess of Strathmore – he had after all died a year before the writer was born, and she twelve years earlier – but there is no doubt that the author drew on those two notorious personalities and the events of their lives.

The story of the Countess's abduction and the court cases which followed was too notorious and entertaining to be easily forgotten, and people were still alive in the 1840s who could clearly recall it and its protagonists. It was when he was staying with the Countess's grandson, his friend John Bowes, at Streatlam Castle that Thackeray 'found materials (rather a character) for a story'. Thackeray met Bowes in Paris,[1] and got to know him well. It was certainly he who told the writer the whole tale of his grandmother's seduction, marriage and abduction. It seems very likely that he also showed Thackeray Jessé Foot's memoir, which had come out in 1810. Thackeray took the character rather than the simple narrative, and embroidered upon it. Like Bowes, his hero was an impoverished Irishman from the upper middle class who married an heiress and in the end was outmanoeuvred by her, but the events in the novel do not mirror those in the lives of the real characters.

Redmond Barry, like Stoney Bowes, was a gambler whose luck varied from good (chapter 10 of the novel) to excellent (chapter 16) then to poor (chapter 18) and finally to catastrophic. Like Bowes, Barry serves in a Regiment of Foot, but unlike him remains a simple soldier, with an eventful career during the Seven Years' War, taking part (without heroism) in the battle of Minden. He participates in some brutal actions, without compunction bayoneting a young French officer and robbing the body; but he is less ostentatiously cruel to women than Bowes, viewing them far more romantically.

Barry, telling his own story, naturally sees himself as its hero – one of the shocking things about the novel when it was first published was that there was no condemnation of his disreputable behaviour, for there is no one in the novel to condemn it. He sees himself for what he is, and when for instance he indulges in the almost random cruelty of war – he refers to 'some of us' burning the cottage of a harmless old woman whom they had earlier befriended – he does not distinguish between himself and the rest of the ruthless mob of soldiery.

There are clear parallels between the character of Lady Lyndon, the 'heroine' of the novel, and Lady Strathmore. Sir Charles Lyndon, her first husband, describes her as 'the noblest and greatest heiress in England . . . enormously rich, but somehow I have never been so poor as since I married her. I thought to better myself, and she has made me miserable and killed me.'[2] 'I am dying, a worn-out cripple at the age of fifty. Marriage has added forty years to my life,' he complains, in much the strain of Lord Strathmore's last letter to his wife.[3]

Thackeray makes Lady Lyndon a god-daughter of Mary Wortley Montagu, and herself just such a blue-stocking as Mary Eleanor Bowes aspired to be: she 'wrote poems in English and Italian, which still may be read by the curious in the pages of the magazines of the day. She entertained a correspondence with several of the European *savants*, upon history, science and ancient languages, and especially theology . . . Every adventurer who had a discovery in chemistry, a new antique bust, or a plan for discovering the philosopher's stone, was sure to find a patroness in her.'[4] Given that Mary Eleanor's enthusiasm was rather for botany than the antique, the sketch fits reasonably well.

Barry's courtship of Lady Lyndon is not so far from Bowes' courtship of Lady Strathmore: 'I resolved to become acquainted with Lady Lyndon. . . . Why should I not win her, and, with her, the means of making in the world that figure which my genius and inclination desired? I felt I was equal in blood and breeding to any Lyndon in Christendom, and determined to bend this haughty lady. When I determine, I look upon the thing as done.' Lady Lyndon, like Lady Strathmore, was a prize; the similarity extended too to her personality and appearance:

Truth compels me to say, that there was nothing divine about her at all. She was very well, but no more. Her shape was fine, her hair dark, her eyes good, and exceedingly active; she loved singing, but performed it as so great a lady should, very much out of tune. She had a smattering of half a dozen modern languages, and as I have said before, many more sciences than I even knew the name of . . . She had as much love of admiration, as strong, uneasy a vanity, and as little heart as any woman I knew.[5]

After his marriage, as Stoney had done, Barry takes his wife's name. Barry Lyndon's treatment of his wife was coarse enough, but Thackeray drew the line at making him quite as cruel as Stoney Bowes. Lyndon is annoyed when his wife objects to his smoking: she is 'a haughty woman, and I hate pride, and I promise you that in both instances I overcame this vice in her. On the third day of our journey' (a journey to the bride's family seat, as it were Streatlam), 'I had her to light my pipe-match with her own hands, and made her deliver it to me with tears in her eyes.'[6] Later, when drunk, 'perhaps I *did* use my lady rather roughly, fling a glass or two at her, and call her by a few names that were not complimentary. I may have threatened her life (which it was obviously my interest not to take), and have frightened her, in a word, considerably.'[7]

He speaks of '*persuading*' her (Thackeray's italics) to sign papers which would allow him to use her income to pay his gambling debts; he is proud of subjugating her: 'she had a temper, yet I had a better one. A temper, psha! A wild cat has a temper, but a keeper can get the better of it, and I know very few women in the world whom I could not master.'

Many readers of *Fraser's Magazine*, and certainly the older ones, would have had no doubt of the identity of the models for Lyndon and Lady Lyndon. The editor of the magazine even printed a note to underline the resemblance, though without actually naming names:

From these curious confessions, it would appear that Mr Lyndon maltreated his lady in every possible way; that he denied her society, bullied her into signing away her property, spent it in gambling and taverns, was openly unfaithful to her; and, when she complained, threatened to remove her children from her. Nor, indeed, is he the only husband who has done the like . . .[8]

There are other parallels between Bowes's life and the plot of *Barry Lyndon*: Bowes cut down all the timber on the Countess's estate, but found that no one would buy it at the price he demanded; Barry had much the same experience. The fictional hero's taste for practical jokes was very like that of Bowes, and the tricks the former played on his son's tutor were played by Bowes on his chaplains. We should not approach the novel with any idea that it will tell us anything useful about the real characters; but it certainly reflects the interest which many people of the next generation took in the relationship between Bowes and the Countess of Strathmore.

Genealogical Table

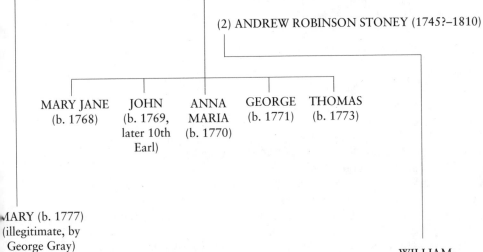

GEORGE BOWES m. (1724) MARY GILBERT

MARY ELEANOR BOWES (1749–1800) m. (1) JOHN, 9th Earl of STRATHMORE (1737–76)

(2) ANDREW ROBINSON STONEY (1745?–1810)

| MARY JANE (b. 1768) | JOHN (b. 1769, later 10th Earl) | ANNA MARIA (b. 1770) | GEORGE (b. 1771) | THOMAS (b. 1773) |

MARY (b. 1777) (illegitimate, by George Gray)

WILLIAM JOHNSTONE (b. 1782)

Notes

Preface

1. The Countess of Strathmore, *The Confessions of the Countess of Strathmore, written by herself, carefully copied from the original, lodged in Doctors Commons* (London, 1793), pp. 51–2.
2. Quoted in Kirstin Olsen, *Daily Life in 18th Century England* (Westport, Conn., Greenwood Press, 1999), p. 34.
3. Quoted in Roy Porter, *English Society in the Eighteenth Century* (New York, Penguin Books, 1982), p. 293.
4. Ralph Arnold, *The Unhappy Countess* (London, Constable, 1957).

Chapter One

1. In 2006 the value of the 1740 pound stood at £72.
2. Cal. State Papers, for. 1569–71, p. 199.
3. William Cecil, Lord Burghley, to the Queen in a letter of 1559, quoted in A.F. Scott, *Every One a Witness* (London, White Lion Publishers, 1975), p. 272. No provenance given.
4. F.L. Nussbaum, *Economic Institutions of Modern Europe* (New York, Simon & Schuster, 1937), p. 252.
5. Anon., quoted in Oliver Garnett, *Gibside* (London, National Trust, 1999), p. 22. No provenance given.
6. The Countess of Strathmore, *The Confessions of the Countess of Strathmore, written by herself, carefully copied from the original, lodged in Doctors Commons* (London, 1793), p. 49.
7. He is said to have introduced the sport to County Durham.
8. The term has now become obscure: in the eighteenth century the Whigs were not really a political party, but an alliance of country aristocrats and businessmen held together by trading interests.
9. Garnett, *Gibside*, p. 22.
10. Her late Majesty, Queen Elizabeth the Queen Mother, whose maiden name was Bowes-Lyon, may have been born in this house.
11. Quoted in Susan Lasdun, *The English Park* (New York, Vendome Press, 1992), p. 84. No provenance given.
12. Strathmore, *Confessions*, p. 48.
13. Jonathan Swift, 'Of the education of ladies', in *The Prose Works of Jonathan Swift*, ed. Temple Scott, Vol. 2 (London, Bell & Sons, 1907), p. 64.

14. B.B. James, *Women of England* (Philadelphia, PA, Fosset, 1908), p. 335.

15. Sarah Fyfe Egerton, 'The Emulation' (1703), ll. 19–20; quoted in Roger Lonsdale (ed.), *New Oxford Book of Eighteenth-century Verse* (Oxford, Oxford University Press, 1987), p. 37.

16. Strathmore, *Confessions*, pp. 49–51.

17. Ibid., p. 50.

18. Ibid., p. 48.

19. Ibid., p. 50.

20. Richard Brinsley Sheridan, *The Rivals*, 1775, Act I, sc. ii.

21. Jessé Foot, *Lives of Andrew Robinson Bowes and the Countess of Strathmore*, p. 11.

22. The Green House was turned into a conservatory in 1855 by the Countess's grandson. It is now roofless, though the National Trust plans renovation.

23. Strathmore, *Confessions*, p. 51.

24. A.D. White, *Warfare of Science with Theology in Christendom* (New York, 1929), Vol. 2, p. 55.

25. Strathmore, *Confessions*, p. 94.

26. Old Moore's almanac still came out every year, despite the fact that Francis Moore himself had died a century earlier, and its author promised, besides looking into the future, to cure 'the Dropsie, and most other Distempers incident to the Body of Mankind' – and offered 'Medicine for the *Epilipsia* or *Falling-Sickness*'.

27. In 1764 she moved to 4 Grosvenor Square, a highly fashionable address; it is not known whether it was rented or purchased, but if the latter the price would certainly have been as much as £8,000, not much less than the annual rent of the whole of Covent Garden Market.

28. Strathmore, *Confessions*, p. 60.

29. Ibid., p. 55.

30. Ibid., p. 55.

31. Ibid., p. 56.

32. Ibid., p. 57.

Chapter Two

1. Priscilla Wakefield, *Reflections on the Present Conditions of the Female Sex, with suggestions for its improvement* (London, Joseph Johnson, 1978), p. 97.

2. The Countess of Strathmore, *The Confessions of the Countess of Strathmore, written by herself, carefully copied from the original, lodged in Doctors Commons* (London, 1793), pp. 56–7.

3. Ibid., p. 27.

4. Ibid., p. 54.

5. Ibid., p. 56.

6. Mrs Delany, *Autobiography*, ed. Lady Llanover (London, n.p., 1788), 3 vols, 1861, 2nd series, 3 vols, 1862; p. 134.

7. Morrison MS, Comm. 9th rep., Pt 2, p. 480a, quoted in *Dictionary of National Biography*; entry under Montagu.

8. They wore blue stockings, it was said, in imitation of a French guest, Madame de Polignac; hence the name 'Bluestockings'.
9. Horace Walpole, *Horace Walpole's England*, ed. Alfred Bishop Mason (Boston, Houghton Mifflin, 1930), p. 6.
10. Strathmore, *Confessions*, pp. 61–2.
11. Foot, *Lives*, p. 49.
12. James Boswell, *The Life of Samuel Johnson, LL.D.* (London, 1791; London, Everyman edn, J.M. Dent, 1949), Vol. 1, p. 264.
13. Roy Porter, *English Society in the Eighteenth Century* (London, Penguin Books, 1990), quoted at p. 22.
14. Strathmore, *Confessions*, pp. 63–4.
15. Capt. Rees Howell Gronow, *Memoirs*, Vol. 2 (London, self-published, 1864), p. 93.
16. Barley-water.
17. Strathmore, *Confessions*, p. 65.
18. Ibid., pp. 65–6.
19. Though as a matter of fact, a bride's best friend often accompanied her on her honeymoon.
20. Strathmore, *Confessions*, pp. 53–4.
21. Ibid., p. 26.
22. *London Chronicle*, 6–8 August 1771, p. 131a.
23. According to Jessé Foot in his biography of Mary Eleanor.
24. See Appendix I.

Chapter Three

1. Foot, *Lives*, p. 13.
2. Her passion seems to have been common knowledge – the caricaturist James Gillray drew an unsympathetic cartoon of her suckling two kittens.
3. Carl Chinn, *Better Betting* (New York, Harvester Wheatsheaf, 1991), p. 32.
4. Horace Walpole, *Horace Walpole's England*, ed. Alfred Bishop Mason (Boston, Houghton Mifflin, 1930), pp. 106, 212.
5. Roy Porter, *English Society in the Eighteenth Century* (New York, Penguin Books, 1990), p. 24.
6. Foot, *Lives*, p. 27.
7. From the *Letters* of the Hon. Mrs Osborne, quoted in James Laver, *Costume and Fashion* (London, Thames & Hudson, 1969), p. 140. No provenance given.
8. Quoted in Norah Waugh, *Corsets and Crinolines* (New York, Theatre Arts Books, 1970), p. 61. No provenance given.
9. He later became a friend and patron of Robert Burns.
10. The Countess of Strathmore, *The Confessions of the Countess of Strathmore, written by herself, carefully copied from the original, lodged in Doctors Commons* (London, 1793), p. 75.
11. Ibid., p. 70.
12. Throughout her book she insists that flirtation was as far as any of her attachments went; but one must remember that this was written at the

demand of her second husband, and it is unlikely that she would have
been completely frank.

13. Strathmore, *Confessions*, p. 9.
14. Ibid., p. 12.
15. '*Aller se faire pendre*', she wrote.
16. Strathmore, *Confessions*, pp. 67–8.
17. Foot, *Lives*, p. 16.
18. Strathmore, *Confessions*, pp. 14–15.
19. See the 'charade' presented by the Revd Mr Elton to Emma Woodhouse in
    Chapter 9 of Jane Austen's *Emma*.
20. Strathmore, *Confessions*, p. 22.
21. Ibid., pp. 78–9.
22. *Low-Life*, London, 1764.

Chapter Four

1. The Countess of Strathmore, *The Confessions of the Countess of
   Strathmore, written by herself, carefully copied from the original, lodged
   in Doctors Commons* (London, 1793), p. 88.
2. Jonathan Swift, 1745, in *Prose Works of Jonathan Swift*, ed. H. Davis
   (Oxford, Oxford University Press, 1959), pp. 52–3.
3. Norman E. Himes, *Medical History of Contraception* (London, n.p.,
   1936), pp. 188–200; quoted in Reay Tannahill, *Sex in History* (London,
   Hamish Hamilton, 1980), p. 336.
4. Strathmore, *Confessions*, p. 23.
5. Foot, *Lives*, p. 16. The letter was originally thought to be lost, but a copy
   turned up in the middle of the twentieth century – we must presume, an
   accurate copy.
6. MS letter in the Bowes Museum; quoted in Ralph Arnold, *The Unhappy
   Countess* (London, Constable, 1957), pp. 40ff.
7. Strathmore, *Confessions*, p. 7.
8. Ibid., p. 83.
9. Ibid., p. 33.
10. Perhaps Walker, the footman, helped in the elopement; this might explain
    Eliza's strange gift to him of a lock of her hair.

Chapter Five

1. Almost £1.5 million in present currency.
2. Foot, *Lives*, p. 3.
3. Ralph Arnold, *The Unhappy Countess* (London, Constable, 1957),
   p. 49.
4. The 30th Regiment of Foot ultimately became, in 1970, the Queen's
   Lancashire Regiment – one of those at the centre of the scandal in 2003
   over faked photographs of the alleged abuse of Iraqi prisoners.
5. See Appendix I.
6. Foot, *Lives*, p. 6.
7. See plate section, pictures 1 and 15.

8. *Paddy's Progress, or, the exploits of an Irishman in England*, ll. 9–12, was published anonymously in 1788 as 'a full and particular Account of the Rise and Fall of Captain S****y, a true and faithful Narrative of his various Schemes, Tricks, Plots and Contrivances; the cruel and barbarous Treatment of his Lady, Domesticks, and other Dependants; together with a Display of the different Stratagems and Deceptions he made Use of, in Order to divert, elude, and retard the various Sentences in the Law from being given against him'. Inside the front cover of a copy in the British Library is a manuscript note: 'The following poetical production, was written by Martin Brown, a shopkeeper, at Sunniside, in the parish of Wickham and county of Durham, where Residence so near to Gibside and his Intimacy with Bowes's Servants, led him to a pretty general knowledge of the circumstances detailed in it. . . . It was very generally circulated, but having in a few years become very scarce, Brown was led to reprint it, which was done in 1807, by Marshall, Gateshead, with some additions from the former edition . . .'. Quotations here are from the 1808 edition. While in most cases one would be shy of taking as fact any statements in a set of anonymous verses, Brown (whose name was printed as author in the later edition) certainly knew Stoney Bowes well, and it is probably safe to say that both the facts and opinions of the versifier are dependable.
9. Anon., *Paddy's Progress*, p. 3, ll. 17–22.
10. Most likely Pearl Court, off Temple Lane, in Farringdon. There is no Pear Street listed in the directories of the time.
11. Foot, *Lives*, pp. 38–40.
12. William Makepeace Thackeray, *Barry Lyndon* (Oxford, Oxford University Press, reissued 1999), p. 185.
13. Relatives – a dig at Strathmore's family.
14. Angelica was one of the Countess's many cats, recently deceased.
15. A living cat.
16. In Homer's *Odyssey* a god who has the power of assuming different shapes in order to escape answering questions.
17. Foot, *Lives*, pp. 23–4.
18. Thackeray, *Barry Lyndon*, p. 184.
19. Jane Austen, *Pride and Prejudice*, Vol. 3, Chapter 1.
20. She writes, 'I married you, which together with *my previous connection with you*, I reckon among my crimes.' Strathmore, *Confessions*, p. 7.
21. Foot, *Lives*, pp. 24–6.

Chapter Six

1. *Morning Post*, 3 January 1777.
2. *Morning Post*, 7 January 1777.
3. By Ralph Arnold in his 1957 biography.
4. Foot, *Lives*, p. 36.
5. Report in the *Gazetteer*, 24 January 1777.
6. It was this incident which introduced him to Stoney and subsequently Lady Strathmore, and interested him in the whole story.

7. Writing some years after the event, Foot refers to Stoney as 'Bowes' throughout his narrative.

8. Foot, *Lives*, pp. 37–8.

9. The *Trial between Stephens, Trustee to E Bowes . . . and Andrew Robinson Stoney Bowes . . . in the Court of Common Pleas*.

10. *Gazetteer*, 24 January 1777.

11. *Trial between Stephens and Bowes*, p. 5.

12. Proceedings in the Court of Chancery, 19 June 1788.

13. Anon., *Paddy's Progress*, p. 4, ll. 3–4.

Chapter Seven

1. Foot, *Lives*, pp. 47–9.

2. *Trial between Stephens and Bowes*, p. 28.

3. Trust document, quoted in Ralph Arnold, *The Unhappy Countess* (London, Constable, 1957), p. 73.

4. By Jessé Foot; and Ralph Arnold seems to concur.

5. The Countess of Strathmore, *The Confessions of the Countess of Strathmore, written by herself, carefully copied from the original, lodged in Doctors Commons* (London, 1793), pp. 29–30.

6. Whether she had second thoughts and retracted her orders, or whether Walker himself had a shrewd idea that the deed was worth preserving, he did not destroy it, but hid it among his own possessions. It was to appear when it was needed, some years later.

7. Foot, *Lives*, pp. 89–90.

8. *Trial between Stephens and Bowes*, p. 9.

9. MSS, Public Record Office, DEL 2/012.

10. The general view was often right. Sir Robert Walpole himself used an Admiralty vessel to smuggle wine into the country (Roy Porter, *English Society in the Eighteenth Century* (London, Penguin Books, 1982), p. 100).

11. *Newcastle Courant*, 2 March 1777, p. 3, col. 1.

12. Ralph Arnold in *The Unhappy Countess* (p. 78) quotes a Mr Montagu of Denton Hall, a supporter of Sir John Trevelyan, but gives no reference.

13. W.M. Thackeray, *The Memoirs of Barry Lyndon, Esq.* (Oxford, Oxford University Press, World's Classics, 1984), p. 276.

14. *Trial between Stephens and Bowes*, p. 30.

15. Strathmore, *Confessions*, pp. 12–13.

16. Foot, *Lives*, p. 51.

17. Ibid., pp. 54–8.

Chapter Eight

1. Foot, *Lives*, p. 51.

2. Male midwives were common in the eighteenth century – in country areas because female midwives had had the reputation of being witches. But although feminist historians have claimed otherwise, there is some evidence that women simply preferred to be attended by men, and

it is perfectly possible that the Countess may have been delivered by
male midwives at her previous *accouchements*, and have stated a
preference.

3. *Paddy's Progress*, ll. 61–76.
4. Foot, *Lives*, p. 60.
5. Ibid., p. 63.
6. The Countess of Strathmore, *The Confessions of the Countess of
   Strathmore, written by herself, carefully copied from the original, lodged
   in Doctors Commons* (London, 1793), p. 9.
7. Foot, *Lives*, pp. 10–11.
8. Strathmore, *Confessions*, p. 99.
9. Ibid., pp. 46–7.
10. These details, and those below of Bowes's violence towards his wife, are
    from the account of Bowes's trial for adultery and cruelty, published by
    Randall of Shoe Lane, Fleet Street, in 1789. The account included the
    testimony of many of Bowes's servants, with details of their seduction, and
    Mr Randall promised a sequel which would 'abound in amorous scenes,
    which will be illustrated with Capital Engravings'. This, however, never
    appeared. Court reporting had begun in about 1670 with summaries of
    criminal trials, and within a century collections of reports of sensational
    trials were frequently published. Some were respectable and accurate, for
    the use of lawyers; but many focused on the detailed descriptions of
    adultery provided by witnesses, often servants. The more prurient often
    simply invented details when the reported ones were insufficiently
    lubricious.
11. Foot, *Lives*, p. 84.
12. Used to great effect by Amanda Vickery in her book *The Gentleman's
    Daughter* (New Haven, Conn., Yale University Press, 1995).
13. Ibid., p. 216.
14. Foot, *Lives*, pp. 93–5.
15. The man was probably William Davies.
16. Foot, *Lives*, pp. 89–90.

Chapter Nine

1. Revd William Cole, *A Journal of My Journey to Paris in the Year 1775*, ed.
   F.G. Stokes (London, Constable, 1931), p. 6.
2. Coach blinds were closed by being drawn up, rather than down.
3. *The Trial of Andrew Robinson Bowes, Esq., for Adultery and Cruelty, first
   heard in the Arches Court of Doctors Commons*, p. 7.
4. Tobias Smollett, *Travels in France and Italy* (London, Fielden, 1764), letter
   of 19 October 1763.
5. *Trial for Adultery*, p. 9.
6. Foot, *Lives*, p. 97.
7. Ibid., pp. 102–3.
8. Ibid., pp. 108–9.
9. No evidence tells us what the family was doing in Buxton, but Bowes
   seems to have taken a house there for a short period.

10. Foot, *Lives*, pp. 111–12.
11. *Trial for Adultery*, p. 14.

Chapter Ten

1. Foot, *Lives*, p. 120.
2. *The Times*, 3 October 1751.
3. For instance in M. Dorothy George's standard *Catalogue of Political and Personal Satires Preserved in the Department of Prints and Drawings in the British Museum*.

Chapter Eleven

1. The Countess not only sent the letter to Lord Mansfield, but subsequently had it published in the *Universal Register* of 20 November 1786.
2. The information about Farrer comes mainly from a document which Bowes helped Mary Farrer to publish in 1788. Entitled *The Appeal of an Injured Wife against a Cruel Husband*, it tells a melancholy tale of violence and degradation, revealing Farrer as a character not unlike Bowes himself. The latter clearly had an interest in publishing this short autobiography – he wanted to revenge himself on Farrer for the efforts the man made to protect the Countess from her husband. But the document itself rings true, and was attested before the Mayor of London and witnesses. There is no reason to suppose that Mary Farrer was not telling her story as she believed it to be true.
3. We have no way of knowing whether he also transported her six children; presumably so – she would scarcely have left them in India. The captain's quarters on the *True Briton* must have been crowded.
4. It is fair to say that we have only Mrs Farrer's word for the existence of these letters, which were never seen by anyone else.

Chapter Twelve

1. Apart from the groom, Charles Chapman was certainly a real person and we shall hear more of him.
2. Brown, a Newcastle doctor, knew the Countess and had attended her at Gibside.
3. Anon., *Paddy's Progress*, ll. 173–87, 195–206.
4. Ibid., ll. 258–62.
5. Bowes got Orme at a bargain: a good postboy could earn as much as £5 a week, plus tips.
6. The evidence of Peter Orme, reported at p. 23 of *The Trial of Andrew Robinson Bowes, Esq., Edward Lucas, Francis Peacock, Mark Prevot, John Cummins, otherwise called Charles Chapman, William Pigg, John Bickley, Henry Bourne, and Thomas Bowes, Attorney at Law, on Wednesday, the 30th day of May, 1787, in His Majesty's Court of King's-bench, Westminster, before the Hon. Mr Justice Buller, and a special jury,*

for a Conspiracy against the Right Hon. Mary Eleanor Bowes, commonly called Countess of Strathmore, to which are added the Speeches of Mr Erskine, Mr Chambre, and Mr Fielding, in Mitigation of Punishment on Behalf of the Conspirators; and of Mr Mingay, Mr Law, and Mr Garrow, in Support of the Prosecution, previous to the Judgement of the Court, on Tuesday the 26th Day of June, which is also included. Taken in short hand by E. Hodgson, short-hand-writer to the Session at the Old Bailey. London: printed for G.G.J. and J. Robinson, No. 25 Pater-noster-Row. M.DCC.LXXXVII. This document subsequently referred to as *The Trial*.

7. Ibid., p. 2.
8. At the trial, the prosecuting attorney, Mr Mingay, remarked that Dr Hobson must be 'one of the most astonishing surgeons in the world' for his attendance to have resulted in Bowes being one day too sick to see anyone, then to have travelled 200 miles overnight.
9. *The Trial*, p. 4.
10. Ibid., p. 5.
11. Peter Pringle, *Hue and Cry* (New York, William Morrow, n.d.), p. 126.
12. A mixture of hot beer and gin, sometimes known as 'dog's nose'.
13. A handbill put out at the Sign of the Naked Boy and Three Crowns in the Strand, in the John Johnson collection in the Bodleian Library; quoted in Liza Picard, *Dr Johnson's London* (London, Weidenfeld & Nicolson, 2000) at p. 243.
14. *The Trial*, p. 19.
15. This was not an unusual stratagem: at least two other unfortunate women at about this time were declared by their husbands to be mad, and were confined in madhouses; see the *Gentleman's Magazine* for August 1749.
16. *The Trial*, p. 22.

Chapter Thirteen

1. *The Trial*, p. 5.
2. Ibid., p. 17.
3. Foot, *Lives*, p. 130.
4. Bedlam: the Bethlehem Hospital for the insane.
5. Foot, *Lives*, p. 130.
6. *The Trial*, p. 12.
7. Ibid., p. 7.
8. *Morning Post*, 20 November 1786.
9. *The Trial*, p. 31.
10. Foot, *Lives*, p. 131.
11. *The Trial*, p. 17.

Chapter Fourteen

1. Horace Walpole, *Horace Walpole's England, as his letters picture it*, ed. Alfred Bishop Mason (Boston, Houghton Mifflin, 1930), p. 143.
2. Foot, *Lives*, pp. 137–8.

3. Ibid., pp. 132–3, 138.
4. Published on 2 December by E. Jackson, of Marybone (*sic*) Street, Golden Square.
5. Letter of 24 November 1786; quoted in Ralph Arnold, *The Unhappy Countess* (London, Constable, 1957), pp. 131–2. He gives no provenance.
6. See Peter Ackroyd, *London: the Biography* (London, Chatto & Windus, 2000), p. 691.
7. Anon., quoted in ibid., at p. 692.
8. See Richard Byrne, *Prisons and Punishments of London* (London, Harrap, 1989), p. 109.
9. Foot, *Lives*, p. 139.
10. Ipecacuanha – the root of a South American plant used as an emetic or purgative.
11. Foot, *Lives*, p. 150.
12. One hopes that her peace was not disturbed by the nearby yowls of an infant born that month in that same street, who in thirty years would be the most famous Englishman in Europe, Lord Byron.
13. *Universal Register*, 1 June 1787.
14. *Universal Register*, 6 June 1787.
15. By Arnold in his *The Unhappy Countess* (pp. 124–5).
16. *Universal Register*, 15 December 1786.

Chapter Fifteen

1. Hodgson used the Mason system of shorthand, as set out by William Mason (1672?–1709) in his book *La Plume Volante* (1707). Thomas Gurney, who was official shorthand writer to the Central Criminal Court in the 1740s, used Mason shorthand, and so for many years did other court shorthand writers.
2. Published on 27 November 1782.
3. An act passed during the reign of King Edward I declared that writs summoning juries to Westminster should appoint a time and place for hearing the causes in consultation with the county courts – these were known as writs of nisi prius (Latin: 'unless before'). The jury would hear the case at Westminster unless the justices had assembled a court in the county to deal with the case beforehand. Mr Justice Buller wrote a famous commentary on this.
4. *The Trial*, p. 1. All quotations in this chapter are from the full account of the trial, previously noted. I add page numbers only where the quotation is substantial.
5. Ibid., p. 7.
6. No women, of course, could serve.
7. *The Trial*, p. 32.
8. Ibid., p. 35.
9. Ibid., pp. 38–42.
10. *Universal Register*, 23 January 1787.
11. Quotations from the hearing for sentence also come from *The Trial*, pp. 43–63.

Chapter Sixteen

1. *London Packet*, 28 December 1786.
2. Foot, *Lives*, p. 142.
3. Ibid., p. 151.
4. *Universal Register*, 2, 6, 16 and 20 October 1787.
5. *A full and accurate report of the Trial between Stephens, trustee to E. Bowes, commonly called the Countess of Strathmore, and Andrew Robinson Stoney Bowes, her second husband . . . printed for George Kearsley in Fleet Street* (n.d.), p. 2.
6. Ibid., p. 21.
7. See p. 65, above.

Chapter Seventeen

1. Obituary, *The Times*, 10 November 1791.
2. All quotations are from the three large MS volumes which record the divorce case of Bowes v. Strathmore, National Archive ref. DEL 2/012.
3. Ibid., divorce decree.
4. *Gentleman's Magazine*, 4 March 1789.

Chapter Eighteen

1. Foot, *Lives*, p. 147.
2. As related in Chapter 11.
3. Mary Farrer, *Appeal of an Injured Wife* (London, C. Stalker, Stationer's Court, Ludgate Hill, 1788), p. 16.
4. Ibid., p. 20.
5. *The Times*, 17 December 1788.
6. Ralph Arnold, *The Unhappy Countess* (London, Constable, 1957), p. 147.
7. Letter in Bowes Museum, quoted in ibid., pp. 148–9.
8. Streatlam was inherited by John Bowes, the illegitimate son of the 10th Earl, who rescued the house and completed it in the 1860s. It was abandoned during the first half of the twentieth century, and during the Second World War was used for battle training. It is now a ruin.
9. This was not unusual, and often resulted in grave-robbery which, however, was unlikely to take place within Westminster Abbey.

Chapter Nineteen

1. National Archives, DEL 2/012, part 2.
2. See p. 122.
3. St George's Fields was famous for its violets, and was a popular place for strolling on a Sunday afternoon. The No Popery rioters had met there in 1780. It has now vanished, but it was near St George's Circus, where six streets meet.
4. Foot, *Lives*, pp. 161–2.
5. Ibid., pp. 162–3.

6. Ibid., p. 168.
7. Ibid., p,11.
8. Ibid., p. 2.

Coda

1. Augustus Hare, *The Story of My Life*, 6 vols (London, Murray, 1872–6), Vol. 1, p. 207.
2. Ibid., p. 209.
3. See Appendix II.

Appendix I

1. All quotations are from *The Siege of Jerusalem*, privately published in London in 1774 by the Countess of Strathmore. The punctuation has been corrected.
2. Byron, *Selected Letters and Journals*, ed. Leslie A. Marchand (London, John Murray, 1982), p. 115.

Appendix II

1. Where he owned and managed a theatre.
2. William Makepeace Thackeray, *Barry Lyndon* (1744; Oxford, Oxford University Press in Oxford World's Classics, 1999), pp. 182–3.
3. See p. 37.
4. Thackeray, *Barry Lyndon*, p. 184.
5. Ibid., p. 188.
6. Ibid., p. 235.
7. Ibid., p. 268.
8. Ibid., footnote, p. 245.

Bibliography

The chief source of information about Andrew Robinson Bowes and of some perhaps questionable views on the character of the Countess of Strathmore is a book published in 1810, the year of Bowes's death, by the surgeon, Jessé Foot. Foot was born in 1744 in Wiltshire, was educated in medicine and became a member of the Surgeon's Company. In his early twenties he went to the West Indies and practised on the island of Nevis; then to St Petersburg, where he made a considerable amount of money as a fashionable English doctor. Back in England he became house-surgeon at the Middlesex Hospital before setting up in practice in Salisbury Street, off the Strand, and then in Dean Street, Soho.

He attended Bowes and the Countess professionally for thirty-three years. He did not like Bowes and saw into his character and motives perfectly clearly; but he almost treats him more kindly than he treats the Countess, for while he does not condone Bowes's treatment of her, he is always critical of and ungenerous towards her. This was partly because he disapproved of her liaisons: his text clearly shows him to have been somewhat puritanical, and though living in an age when both novelists and journalists were bold in their publication of sexual innuendo, he went out of his way to criticise the Countess's *Confessions* for undue frankness. At some points – notably his account of her seduction and later abduction – other sources such as the accounts of Bowes's trial make it easy to correct Foot's view of Mary Eleanor. At others, we can only suggest that prejudice led him astray.

Primary Sources

Anon., *A full and accurate report of the Trial between Stephens, trustee to E. Bowes, commonly called the Countess of Strathmore, and Andrew Robinson Stoney Bowes, her second husband; in the Court of Common Pleas before the Right Honourable Lord Loughborough on Monday, May 19th, 1788: on an issue directed out of the High Court of Chancery, taken in short hand. Printed for George Kearsley in Fleet Street. Price 2s. Entered at Stationers-Hall. (n.d.)*

Anon., *A Full, True, and Particular Account of the Trial of Andrew Robinson Bowes, (husband to the Countess of Strathmore), Lucas, nick-named Four Eyes, and others, in the Court of King's Bench, on Thursday last, for an Assault on the said Lady Strathmore, by forcibly carrying her into the Country, with the Evidence of the different Witnesses on the Occasion. They were all found Guilty. Printed and sold in London. (n.d.)*

Anon., *The Trial of Andrew Robinson Bowes, Esq., Edward Lucas, Francis Peacock, Mark Prevot, John Cummins, otherwise called Charles Chapman,*

William Pigg, John Bickley, Henry Bourn, and Thomas Bowes, Attorney at Law, on Wednesday, the 30ᵗʰ day of May, 1787, in His Majesty's Court of King's-bench, Westminster, before the Hon. Mr Justice Buller, and a special jury, for a Conspiracy against the Right Hon. Mary Eleanor Bowes, commonly called Countess of Strathmore, to which are added the Speeches of Mr Erskine, Mr Chambre, and Mr Fielding, in Mitigation of Punishment on Behalf of the Conspirators; and of Mr Mingay, Mr Law, and Mr Garrow, in Support of the Prosecution, previous to the Judgement of the Court, on Tuesday the 26ᵗʰ Day of June, which is also included. Taken in short hand by E. Hodgson, short-hand-writer to the Session at the Old Bailey. London: printed for G.G.J. and J. Robinson, No. 25 Pater-noster-Row. M.DCC.LXXXVII [1787]

Anon., *The Trial of Andrew Robinson Bowes, Esq. for Adultery and Cruelty; First heard in the Arches Court of Doctors' Commons; and, in consequence of an Appeal, determined in a Court of Delegates on the 2ⁿᵈ of this instant; when the Right Honourable the Countess of Strathmore obtained a divorce. Printed for R. Randall, No. 1 Shoe-lane, Fleetstreet, MDCCLXXXIX [1789]*

Farrer, Mary, *The Appeal of an Injured Wife against a Cruel Husband written by Mrs Farrer, London, printed for the authoress and sold by C. Stalker, Stationers Court, Ludgate-hill, MDCCLXXXVIII [1788]*

Foot, Jessé, *The Lives of Andrew Robinson Bowes, Esq., and the Countess of Strathmore, written from thirty-three years professional attendance, from Letters and other well authenticated documents* (London, Becket & Porter, Sherwood, Neely and Jones, 1810)

Strathmore, the Countess of, *The Confessions of the Countess of Strathmore, written by herself, carefully copied from the original, lodged in Doctors Commons* (London, printed for W. Locke, 1793)

Secondary Sources

Ackroyd, Peter, *London: the Biography* (London, Chatto & Windus, 2000)

Arnold, Ralph, *The Unhappy Countess* (London, Constable, 1957)

Austen, Jane, *Pride and Prejudice, Sense and Sensibility*, Oxford Illustrated Jane Austen, ed. R.W. Chapman, 1988

Boswell, James, *The Life of Samuel Johnson, LL.D.* (London, 1791; Everyman edn, London, J.M. Dent, 1949)

Braudel, Fernand, *Civilisation and Capitalism, 15th–18th Century*, Vol. 1: *The Structures of Everyday Life: The Limits of the Possible* (London, Collins, 1981); Vol 2: *The Wheels of Commerce* (London, Collins, 1982)

Buck, Anne, *Dress in Eighteenth-Century England 1500–1900* (New York, Holmes & Meier, 1986)

Byng, John (Viscount Torrington), *Rides Round Britain*, ed. Donald Adamson, (London, Folio Society, 1996)

Byron, George Gordon, Lord, *Selected Letters and Journals*, ed. Leslie A. Marchand (London, John Murray, 1982)

Chinn, Carl, *Better Betting* (New York, Harvester Wheatsheaf, 1991)

Cole, Revd William, *A Journal of My Journey to Paris in the Year 1775*, ed. F.G. Stokes (London, Constable, 1931)

de Marly, Diana, *Fashion for Men* (London, Batsford, 1989)

Durant, Will and Durant, Ariel, *The Story of Civilisation*, Vol. 9: *The Age of Voltaire* (New York, Simon & Schuster, 1965)

Ferguson, Moira (ed.), *First Feminists* (Bloomington, Indiana University Press, 1985)

Garnett, Oliver, *Gibside* (London, National Trust, 1999)

Girouard, Mark, *Life in the English Country House* (New Haven, Conn., Yale University Press, 1978)

Gronow, Captain Rees Howell, *Memoirs*, ed. Christopher Hibbert (London, Kyle Cathie, 1991)

Hill, Bridget, *Servants: English Domestics in the Eighteenth Century* (Oxford, Clarendon Press, 1996)

Himes, Norman E., *Medical History of Contraception* (London, n.p., 1936)

Hufton, Olwen, *The Prospect Before Her: A History of Women in Western Europe 1500–1800* (New York, Knopf, 1996)

Hussey, Christopher, *English Gardens and Landscapes, 1700–1750* (London, Country Life, 1967)

James, B.B., *Women of England* (Philadelphia, PA, Fosset, 1908)

Lasdun, Susan, *The English Park* (New York, Vendome Press, 1992)

Laver, James, *Costume and Fashion* (Thames & Hudson, London, 1969)

Lonsdale, Roger (ed.), *New Oxford Book of Eighteenth-century Verse* (Oxford, Oxford University Press, 1987)

Mayhew, Henry and Binny, John, *The Criminal Prisons of London* (London, 1862; repub. London, Frank Cass, 1971)

More, Hannah, *Selected Writings of Hannah More*, ed. Robert Hale (London, Pickering, 1996)

Nussbaum, F.L., *Economic Institutions of Modern Europe* (New York, Simon & Schuster, 1937)

Olsen, Kirstin, *Chronology of Women's History* (Westport, Conn., Greenwood Press, 1994)

Picard, Liza, *Dr Johnson's London* (London, Weidenfeld & Nicolson, 2001)

Plumb, J.H., *England in the Eighteenth Century* (London, Penguin Books, 1990)

Porter, Roy, *English Society in the Eighteenth Century* (London, Penguin Books, 1982)

Pringle, Peter, *Hue and Cry* (New York, William Morrow, n.d.)

Salmond, Anne, *The Trial of the Cannibal Dog* (London, Allen Lane, 2003)

Scott, A.F., *Every One a Witness* (London, White Lion Publishers, 1975), p. 272.

Stone, Lawrence, *Road to Divorce: A History of the Making and Breaking of Marriage in England* (Oxford, Oxford University Press, 1995)

Swift, Jonathan, 'Of the Education of Ladies', in *The Prose Works of Jonathan Swift*, ed. Temple Scott, Vol. 11 (London, Bell & Sons, 1907)

Tannahill, Reay, *Sex in History* (London, Hamish Hamilton, 1980)

Thackeray, William Makepeace, *Barry Lyndon* (Oxford, Oxford University Press, Oxford World Classics; reissued 1999)

Vickery, Amanda, *The Gentleman's Daughter* (New Haven, Conn., Yale University Press, 1998)

Wakefield, Priscilla, *Reflections on the Present Conditions of the Female Sex, with suggestions for its improvement* (London, Joseph Johnson, 1978)

Walpole, Horace, *Horace Walpole's England, as his letters picture it*, ed. Alfred Bishop Mason (Boston, Houghton Mifflin, 1930)

Waterson, Merlin, *The Servants' Hall* (New York, Pantheon Books, 1980)

Waugh, Norah, *Corsets and Crinolines* (New York, Theatre Arts Books, 1970)

White, A.D., *Warfare of Science with Theology in Christendom* (New York, 1929)

White, T.H., *The Age of Scandal* (London, Jonathan Cape, 1950)

Journals

The files of *The Gentleman's Magazine, London Packet, Morning Post, Newcastle Courant, Newcastle Chronicle or General Weekly Advertiser, The Times, Universal Register*

Index